Praise for *Heaven and Hell*

"This elegant history explores the evolution of the concept of the afterlife in Western thought. . . . Well-trod subjects are presented with engaging clarity, and more contentious theories are laid out carefully."

—*The New Yorker*

"The reader is struck by his nimbleness in drawing the thread of this rich-layered narrative, sprinkling larger thematic arcs with anecdotes that honor the non-lineal and multivalent nature of eschatological thought."

— *The Boston Globe*

"Bart D. Ehrman's *Heaven and Hell* is an inadvertently prescient read."

—*Smithsonian* magazine

"*Heaven and Hell* is a tour de force: erudite, provocative, and often fun."

—Washington Independent Review of Books

"Ehrman's eloquent understanding of how death is viewed through many spiritual traditions is scintillating, fresh, and will appeal to scholars and lay readers alike."

—*Publishers Weekly* (starred review)

"Expect delightful, informative examinations of ancient ideas about heaven and hell; ideas that have evolved as human needs and desires have also evolved."

—*Library Journal* (starred review)

Also by Bart D. Ehrman

HEAVEN AND HELL

A History of the Afterlife

Bart D. Ehrman

SIMON & SCHUSTER PAPERBACKS

New York   London   Toronto   Sydney   New Delhi

Simon & Schuster Paperbacks
An Imprint of Simon & Schuster, Inc.
1230 Avenue of the Americas
New York, NY 10020

Copyright © 2020 by Bart D. Ehrman

All rights reserved, including the right to reproduce this book or portions thereof
in any form whatsoever. For information, address Simon & Schuster Subsidiary
Rights Department, 1230 Avenue of the Americas, New York, NY 10020.

First Simon & Schuster trade paperback edition March 2021

SIMON & SCHUSTER PAPERBACKS and colophon are
registered trademarks of Simon & Schuster, Inc.

For information about special discounts for bulk purchases, please contact Simon &
Schuster Special Sales at 1-866-506-1949 or business@simonandschuster.com.

The Simon & Schuster Speakers Bureau can bring authors to your live event. For
more information or to book an event, contact the Simon & Schuster Speakers
Bureau at 1-866-248-3049 or visit our website at www.simonspeakers.com.

Interior design by Alexis Minieri

Manufactured in the United States of America

7   9   10   8

The Library of Congress has cataloged the hardcover edition as follows:

Names: Ehrman, Bart D., author.
Title: Heaven and hell : a history of the afterlife / Bart D. Ehrman.
Description: New York : Simon & Schuster, 2020. | Series: First Simon & Schuster hardcover
edition | Includes bibliographical references and index.
Identifiers: LCCN 2019012958 (print) | ISBN 9781501136733 (hardcover : alk. paper) | ISBN
9781501136757 (ebook)
Subjects: LCSH: Future life—Christianity—History of doctrines—Early church, ca.
30–600. | Heaven—Christianity—History of doctrines—Early church, ca. 30–600. | Hell—
Christianity—History of doctrines—Early church, ca. 30–600.
Classification: LCC BT903 .E37 2020 (print) | LCC BT903 (ebook) | DDC 236/.2—dc23
LC record available at https://lccn.loc.gov/2019012958
LC ebook record available at https://lccn.loc.gov/2019980078

ISBN 978-1-5011-3673-3
ISBN 978-1-5011-3674-0 (pbk)
ISBN 978-1-5011-3675-7 (ebook)

For Aiya, Sierra, and Elliot, grandkids extraordinaire

Contents

CONTENTS

Acknowledgments

Writing this book has been a fulfilling and happy experience, and I now have the privilege of acknowledging my debts. First, I am grateful for the expertise of numerous scholars who have trod these paths before me—not only in the burgeoning literature on the afterlife from Gilgamesh to Augustine (my beginning and ending points) but also in translations of the ancient texts. I have taken quotations of the Hebrew Bible and the Apocrypha from the New Revised Standard Version. Translations of the New Testament are my own. Translations of all other ancient texts are acknowledged in the endnotes.

The book discusses views of the afterlife in the ancient Near East, Greece and Rome, the Hebrew Bible, Second Temple Judaism, the New Testament, and Early Christianity. I asked experts in each of these areas to read all or parts of my manuscript. They all generously complied and made helpful and even face-saving comments. Any mistakes or bad judgments that remain are my fault, sometimes in refusing to accept their sage advice.

And so thanks go to the following: Meghan Henning, scholar of the

New Testament and early Christianity at the University of Dayton, who has herself written an important scholarly account of how the Christian view of hell was used for educational purposes in the early church; my brother Radd Ehrman, a longtime professor of classics at Kent State, who years ago convinced me that the *Iliad* and the *Odyssey* were not written by Homer but by someone else named Homer, and who has invariably proved generous and helpful when it comes to complicated bits of Latin syntax; my colleague in Ancient Near East/the Hebrew Bible at UNC, Joseph Lam, always willing and eager to provide keen assistance with the mystifying texts of Near Eastern antiquity; my other colleague in Hebrew Bible at UNC, David Lambert, a remarkably perspicacious reader whose views invariably challenge what I've long thought; my longtime colleague in early Christianity at UNC and onetime collaborator, Zlatko Pleše, whose enormous expertise from classical philology to ancient philosophy has always been a source of both marvel and assistance; my brand-new colleague in New Testament and early Christianity at UNC, Hugo Mendez, an unusually thorough and nuanced reader of texts who is unfailingly generous in his help; and my old friend and colleague from Duke, Joel Marcus, one of the finest exegetes on the planet, who for over thirty years has been more than willing to read my work and (alas) tell me what he really thinks about it.

Another group of readers are not from within the academic guild. These are members of the Bart Ehrman Blog who volunteered to read my manuscript and give their opinions on it, not as experts but as lay readers with intelligent insights. For some background, a word about my blog, an ongoing venture for seven years now. I write five posts each week, covering just about everything connected with the literature of the New Testament and the history of early Christianity, from Jesus to Constantine. Joining the blog requires a small fee, which I in turn donate to charities helping those in need. This past summer I gave members of the blog an opportunity to read my manuscript, and the following generous souls took me up on it, making numerous helpful suggestions for improvement: Will Ballard, David Ballinger, Alan Bishop, Paul Ellis, Rob Gilbert, Steve Otteson, Bobby Ross, and Steve Sutter. To all of them I owe many thanks.

Special gratitude goes to Megan Hogan, associate editor at Simon & Schuster, who has handled most of the nitty-gritty. She is talented, efficient, prompt, and patient with an occasionally wayward author.

I am especially fortunate to have such a superb editor in Priscilla Painton. This is the second book Priscilla and I have done together and both experiences have been beyond exemplary. She is discerning, clearsighted, judicious, and editorially savvy. Luckily for me, she also has an extraordinary sense of style.

I continue to be deeply indebted to my erstwhile editor, current literary agent, and longtime friend, Roger Freet, who not only represents me but also actively participates in imagining, framing, and evaluating my writing. He has that rare ability to know what "works" in a book, on both the macro and micro levels; he is creative, enthusiastic, and proactive. And he occasionally lets me do what I want. What could be better?

Finally, I want to express my love, admiration, and thanks to my much-adored wife and life partner, Sarah Beckwith, scholar of medieval and early-modern English at Duke, expert on Shakespeare, and a profound reader of texts, who is inordinately perceptive, imaginative, and intellectually deep, and who, among other things, assumed the mantle of matrimonial duty by reading the manuscript and making considerable useful comments on it.

I am dedicating the book to my three grandchildren, all of whom are far more intelligent, interesting, and good-looking than any other being on the planet: Aiya, Sierra, and the newcomer, Elliot.

Preface

When I thought about God as a child, I thought about the afterlife. I obviously had no clear understanding of death. But I did believe that after I died I would go to heaven or hell. And I was bound and determined to make it one and not the other.

Looking back, the afterlife later helped motivate me to become more deeply involved in my Episcopal church, participating in worship, saying prayers, singing hymns, confessing my sins, learning the creeds, becoming an altar boy. Naturally I worshiped God and tried to live the way I thought he wanted because I thought it was the right and good thing to do, but also, at least in part, it was because I knew full well what would happen to me if I didn't.

I am also sure that hope for heaven and fear of hell played a large role when later, as a mid-teenager, I had an even deeper spiritual experience. Some of my high school friends were committed Christian kids who believed it was necessary to make an active and specific commitment to God by "asking Jesus into my heart." They convinced me, and as a fifteen-year-old I became a born-again Christian.

From that point on, I had no doubt: I was going to heaven. I was equally convinced that those who had not made this commitment—namely, most of the billions of other people in the world—were going to hell. I tried not to think I was being arrogant. It was not as if I had done something better than anyone else and deserved to go to heaven. I had simply accepted a gift. And what about those who hadn't even heard about the gift, or who had never been urged to consider it seriously? I felt sorry for them. They were lost, and so it was my obligation to convert them. Believing this made me a Christian on a mission. It is not at all unlikely that I was more than a little obnoxious about it.

These views were confirmed for me in my late teens, first at the Moody Bible Institute, the fundamentalist Bible college I attended after high school, and then at Wheaton, the evangelical Christian liberal arts college where I finished my undergraduate degree. After graduating I chose to pursue the study of the New Testament more seriously, and went for various reasons to the decidedly non-fundamentalist Princeton Theological Seminary. It was there I started having doubts about my faith. In part, the doubts were caused by my studies, as I began to realize that the Truth I had believed since high school was actually rather complicated and even problematic. My scholarship led me to realize that the Bible was a very human book, with human mistakes and biases and culturally conditioned views in it. And realizing that made me begin to wonder if the beliefs in God and Christ I had held and urged on others were themselves partially biased, culturally conditioned, or even mistaken.

These doubts disturbed me not only because I wanted very much to know the Truth but also because I was afraid of the possible eternal consequences of getting it wrong. What if I started doubting or even denying that the Bible was the inspired word of God? Or that Christ was the unique Son of God? Or even that God existed? What if I ended up no longer believing and then realized too late that my unfaithful change of heart had all been a huge blunder? Wouldn't my eternal soul be in very serious trouble?

There was a particular moment when these worries hit me with special poignancy. It involved a late-night sauna.

In order to pay for my graduate school, I worked a part-time job at the Hamilton Tennis Club outside of Princeton. Most days of the week I was on the late shift. Members of the club with busy lives would schedule their tennis matches deep into the night, and I worked the desk taking reservations and sweeping the courts afterward. One of the benefits of the job was that I could take advantage of the facilities, including the sauna when the place was shut up.

The evening in question I had been sweeping the courts and thinking about everything I had been hearing—and resisting—in my biblical studies and theology courses at Princeton Seminary, pondering just how different my professors' perspectives were from what I had been taught to believe as a conservative evangelical Christian in my high school and college years. These new views were very liberal from my former point of view. I was hearing, and starting to think, that the Bible was not a consistent revelation whose very words came from God; that the traditional Christian doctrines I had always held as obviously true (e.g., the Trinity) were not handed down from heaven but were formulations made by very fallible human beings; and that there were lots of other views out there—even Christian views—that did not jibe with what I had long believed. I was doing my best to figure it all out. Whatever I decided to believe and think, I wanted it to be right. I was willing to change my views if necessary, but I didn't want to leave a faith I loved, especially if it turned out that I had been right in the first place and had simply begun to backslide down the slippery slope that leads to perdition.

After sweeping the courts, I decided to have a sauna, and so I cranked up the heat as high as it would go, stripped down, and went in for a good after-work sweat. As I sat on the upper wooden bench all alone late at night, perspiring profusely, I returned to my doubts and the questions I had about my faith and the fears I had for the possible outcomes of pursuing them—fears not just for my life, but even more for my afterlife. Then I started realizing: Wow. It sure is *hot* in here! Oh, man, is it hot in here! It is *really, really* hot in here! And then, naturally, the thought struck me. Do I really want to be trapped in a massively overheated sauna for all eternity? And what if the sauna is many, many times hotter than this? Do I want to be in fire forever? Is it worth it? For me, at that moment, that meant: Do I really want to change my beliefs and risk eternal torment?

I don't need to discuss my long transition here. Suffice it to say that I eventually did begin to change, and over a number of years I moved into a liberal form of Christianity that cherished questions and thinking more than belief based simply on what others told me. Finally I left the faith altogether. As a friend of mine, a Methodist minister, sometimes jokes, I went from being born again to being dead again.

And yet I continue to be fascinated by the question of the afterlife—not so much because I fear it anymore but because it plays such a crucial role in the thinking and literature of the earliest Christians, which is my particular field of academic interest. Knowing where ideas of the afterlife came from, how they developed, and how they changed can tell us, historically, a lot about how Christianity came to be what it is today: the most historically significant and culturally influential religion in the world.

But these ideas are even more important for nonacademic reasons. Traditional Christian beliefs in the afterlife continue to be widely held in our society. A recent Pew Research Poll showed that 72 percent of all Americans agree that there is a literal heaven where people go when they die; 58 percent believe in an actual, literal hell.[1] These numbers are, of course, down seriously from previous periods, but they are still impressive. And for the historian, it is important to realize that in the Christian West prior to the modern period—think, for example, the Middle Ages or, for that matter, the 1950s—virtually *everyone* believed that when they died their soul would go to one place or the other (or to Purgatory in painful preparation for ultimate glory).

One of the surprising theses of this book is that these views do not go back to the earliest stages of Christianity. They cannot be found in the Old Testament and they are not what Jesus himself taught. Then where did they come from?

A related thesis is that neither ancient Christianity nor the Judaism it was built on—let alone the other religions in their immediate context—had a single, solitary view of the afterlife. Both religions—and all the religions at the time—were remarkably diverse in their views. These various views competed with one another. Even within the New Testament, different key figures promoted divergent understandings. The apostle Paul had different views of the afterlife from Jesus, whose views were not the same as those found in the Gospel of Luke or the Gospel of John or the book of Revelation. Moreover, none of these views coincides exactly with those of Christian leaders of the second, third, and fourth centuries whose ideas became the basis for the understandings of many Christians today. So how did all these views originate?

I have called this book *Heaven and Hell: A History of the Afterlife*. When I've told people the title, they have often been puzzled or even slightly offended. But let me be clear: I am not saying that a literal heaven and hell have experienced historical changes. I'm saying that the *ideas* of heaven and hell were invented and have been altered over the years.

And I think that can be proved. There was a time in human history when no one on the planet believed that there would be a judgment day at the end of time. At another time, people did believe it. It eventually became a standard Christian teaching and is accepted as orthodox truth by many millions of people today. Between the time no one believed it and many people did, someone came up with the idea. That is, it was invented. So too with every idea of the afterlife. That doesn't make the ideas wrong. It just means they were ideas that once did not exist and then later did. That, of course, is true of all ideas, views, theories, perspectives, rules, laws, formulae, proofs—everything thought up by human agents.

Some of them are right, some are wrong, and some are not susceptible to the categories of right and wrong. But whether right, wrong, or neither, all of them came into someone's mind at some point in time. A physicist came up with the theory of gravity, a mathematician with the formula for determining the area of a rectangle, a political thinker with the idea of democracy, and on and on and on. We evaluate these formulations and their claims to the truth independently of the fact that for most of human history no one subscribed to them.

So too with understandings of the afterlife. In this book I will not be urging you either to believe or disbelieve in the existence of heaven and hell. I am interested, instead, in seeing where these ideas came from within the dominant culture of the West, Christianity, especially as it emerged out of the pagan religions of its world and out of Judaism in particular. I want to see how views of the afterlife came about and how they were then modified, transformed, believed, doubted, and disbelieved over time.

Through the course of this book we will see that there was indeed a time when literally no one thought that at death their soul would go to heaven or hell. In the oldest forms of Western culture, as far back as we have written records, people believed everyone experienced the same fate after death, an uninteresting, feeble, and rather boring eternity in a place often called Hades. This is the view clearly set forth in Homer's *Odyssey*. But eventually people came to think this could not be right, largely because it was not fair. If there are gods with anything like our moral code who oversee the world, there must be justice, both in this life and the next. That must mean that faithful, well-meaning, and virtuous people in the world will be rewarded for how they live, and the wicked will be punished. This is the view that developed next, as we will see in the writings of Plato.

A similar transformation happened in the ancient religion of Israel.

Our oldest sources of the Hebrew Bible do not talk about "life after death" but simply the state of death, as all people, righteous and wicked, reside in their grave or in a mysterious entity called Sheol. The focus for these texts, therefore, is on life in the present, in particular the life of the nation Israel, chosen and called by God to be his people. He would make the nation great in exchange for its worship and devotion. But that long-held view came to be challenged by the realities of history as tiny Israel experienced one disaster and calamity after another: economic, political, social, and military. When parts of the nation came to be destroyed, some survivors wrestled seriously with how to understand the disaster in light of God's justice. How could God allow his own chosen people to be wiped out by a foreign, pagan power?

Starting in the sixth century BCE, Hebrew prophets began to proclaim that the nation that had been destroyed would be restored to life by God. In a sense, it would be "raised from the dead." This was a national resurrection—not of the people who lived in the nation but a restoration of the nation Israel itself—to become, once more, a sovereign state.

Toward the very end of the Old Testament period, some Jewish thinkers came to believe this future "resurrection" would apply not to the fortunes of the nation but to individuals. If God was just, surely he could not allow the suffering of the righteous to go unrequited. There would be a future day of judgment, when God would literally bring his people, each of them, back to life. This would be a resurrection of the dead: those who had sided with God would be returned to their bodies to live forevermore.

Jesus of Nazareth inherited this view and forcefully proclaimed it. Those who did God's will would be rewarded at the end, raised from the dead to live forever in a glorious kingdom here on earth. Those opposed to God would be punished by being annihilated out of existence. For Jesus this was to happen very soon. Evil had taken control of this world and was wreaking havoc in it, especially among the people of God. But God would soon intervene to overthrow these forces of evil and establish his kingdom here on earth.

After Jesus's death, his disciples carried on his message, even as they transformed it in light of the new circumstances they came to face. Among other things, the expected end never did come, which led to a reevaluation of Jesus's original message. Some of his followers came to think that God's vindication of his followers would not be delayed until the end of human history. It would happen to each person at the point of death. Believers in Christ would be taken into the presence of Christ in heaven as they awaited the return to their bodies at the future resurrection. Those opposed to God, however, would be punished. Eventually Christians came to think this punishment would not entail annihilation (Jesus's view) but torment, and not just for a short day or two but forever. God is eternal; his creation is eternal; humans are eternal; and eternity will show forth God's glorious judgments: paradise for the saints and pain for the sinners. Heaven and hell were born.

In short, the ideas of the afterlife that so many billions of people in our world have inherited emerged over a long period of time as people struggled with how this world can be fair and how God or the gods can be just. Death itself cannot be the end of the story. Surely all people will receive what they deserve. But this is not what people always thought. It was a view that Jews and Christians came up with over a long period of time as they tried to explain the injustice of this world and the ultimate triumph of good over evil.

A study of the evolution of these beliefs can lead to important and salutary ends. On the academic and intellectual level, it will tell us a lot about the historical development of Christianity, the most important religious movement in the history of our civilization. On a more personal level—in fact, in the most personal terms possible—a fuller understanding of where the ideas of heaven and hell came from can provide assurance and comfort because, contrary to what I once thought, even if we do have something to hope for after we have passed from the realm of temporary consciousness, we have absolutely nothing to fear. I believe this assurance, on a practical level, can free us to appreciate and enjoy our existence in the here and now, living lives full of meaning and purpose in the brief moment given us in this world of mortals.

CHAPTER ONE

Guided Tours of Heaven and Hell

I n the winter season of 1886–87 a French archaeological team digging in Akhmim, Egypt, about eighty miles north of Luxor, made one of the most remarkable manuscript discoveries of modern times. The site was a cemetery; the archaeologists were digging in a portion dating to the eighth century CE. In one of the tombs, taken to be that of a Christian monk, they discovered a sixty-six page book, written in Greek and containing a small anthology of texts. One of them was a portion of a Jewish apocryphon known today as 1 Enoch. Another was a previously unknown Gospel that provided an alternative version of Jesus's trial, death, and resurrection, allegedly written by his closest disciple, Peter. A third was also a book claiming to be by Peter, which in some respects was the most intriguing of all. This was an account, written in the first person, of a guided tour of the afterlife, a detailed description of the torments of sinners in hell, and, in far less detail, the blessings of saints in heaven. It is the earliest Christian forerunner of Dante's *Divine Comedy* and the most authoritative such account ever to appear—allegedly authenticated by one of Jesus's own apostles.

Except no one today thinks Peter actually wrote the book. It was produced by a later Christian who simply wanted his readers to *think* he was Peter. And why not? What better way to convince them that his descriptions of heaven and hell were bona fide?

Before the text was discovered, scholars had known that some such *Apocalypse of Peter* once existed in the second Christian century. It is mentioned by church fathers from the period. In fact, in some circles, down to the fourth century, Christian authors considered the book a legitimate part of the New Testament, with church leaders arguing whether it, rather than the Apocalypse of John (the book of Revelation), should be included in the canon. Eventually it lost this battle and then disappeared from sight, until serendipitously uncovered by our French archaeologists.[1]

Some years after its discovery, a longer and more detailed version appeared in an ancient Ethiopic translation. Careful analysis has shown that this Ethiopic text provides a more accurate version of the original writing.

The Realms of the Damned and Blessed

The account begins with Jesus seated on the Mount of Olives, speaking to his disciples, who want to know what will happen at the end of the world, a discussion familiar to readers of the New Testament (Matthew 24; Mark 13).[2] Jesus responds by telling them that false Christs will appear before the end of time, and there will be unimaginable cosmic disasters: cataracts of fire will be let loose, the whole earth will burn, the stars will melt, the heavens will pass away, and the entire creation will dissolve. Only then will Christ come from heaven with his righteous ones and angels. At that point the dead will be raised and all people will face judgment: punishments for sinners and rewards for the righteous, for all eternity.

The account proceeds to describe in graphic and stunning detail the torments awaiting the damned, who are being punished for their most characteristic sin while living, often following the famous "lex talionis" ("the law of retaliation"), in which the punishment is modeled directly on the transgression (an eye for an eye, a tooth for a tooth). And so those who "blasphemed the way of righteousness"—that is, those who maligned both the ways of God and the saints who tried to practice them—are hanged over "unquenchable fire" by their tongues, the body part most culpable in their sin. Women who plaited their hair, not just to make themselves beautiful but also to seduce men into fornication, are hanged by their necks and hair over the eternal flames. The men they seduced are hanged by their genitals. In their case they make a perpetual lament: "We did not know we should come to everlasting punishments" (ch. 7). Indeed.

Somewhat less expectantly, women who procured abortions are cast into an extremely deep pit up to their necks in excrement and foul substances. Opposite them are their aborted children, who send forth flashes of lightning, piercing the eyes of their mothers who "for fornication's sake have caused their destruction" (ch. 8). So too, men and women who committed infanticide (i.e., by exposing unwanted children to the elements) are tormented forever while their murdered children look on from a place of delight. The mothers experience a particularly graphic torment: milk flows perpetually from their breasts and congeals; out of the milk come beasts that devour the parents' flesh (ch. 8).

There are also strictly religious crimes and punishment: Those who persecuted Christians are cast into an area of darkness with half their bodies aflame and worms devouring their entrails (ch. 9). Those who slandered God's righteousness are placed in eternal darkness, where they have red hot irons continuously thrust into their eyes (ch. 9).

Some of the crimes may not seem worthy of eternal torment to us moderns, but the author is merciless. Those who lent money at interest spend eternity in a pit with filth up to their knees; those who disobeyed their parents are hanged and ceaselessly pecked by flesh-devouring birds; girls who lost their virginity before marriage have their bodies torn to shreds; slaves who disobeyed their masters are forced to gnaw their tongues endlessly.

Altogether there are twenty-one sins and punishments. None of the punishments is reformatory: they are not meant to teach sinners a lesson so they will do better next time. On the contrary, they are all retributive and vindictive. And they will never, ever end.[3]

It is surprising that such a detailed and graphic description of eternal torment would be accompanied by only a brief and vague description of the blessings of the saints, but such is the case. Possibly eternal joy is not as satisfying to describe as everlasting torture. All we are told is that the elect and righteous come to the glorious Elysian fields, where they are adorned with flowers and rejoice with Christ, given an eternal kingdom where they enjoy good things forever.

We do learn, however, that these righteous—the objects of opposition and persecution in life—have considerable satisfaction in their reversal of fortunes in the life to come, a bit of eternal Schadenfreude, as "they shall see their desires on those who hated them, when [God] punished them and the torment of every one shall be forever according to his works" (ch. 13). Seeing your enemies horribly tortured for eternity is apparently considered one of the greatest joys possible. This may not exactly be consistent with Jesus's instruction to "love your enemies," but texts like this regularly suggest that whatever the earthly Jesus may have advised his followers, God himself has other plans. Once a person dies in sin, that is the end: there are no more chances to repent. What awaits is some well-deserved torment for all eternity.

It is not difficult to understand the function of a text such as the *Apocalypse of Peter*. The author is not interested in providing an objective statement about what actually happens in heaven and hell. He has a set purpose in mind. He wants people to behave in certain ways and he is using his graphic descriptions of eternal torment as a way of convincing them. He is not so much scaring the hell out of people as scaring people out of hell.[4] And even though his descriptions of paradise are remarkably vague, they contribute to the same end. Which do you, as a reader, want? Do you want to spend eternity hanging by your genitals over eternal flame, standing in a deep pit up to your knees in excrement, having your flesh perpetually shredded into pieces by ravenous birds? Or do you want to luxuriate in a lovely garden with the pleasant smells and cool breezes of eternity wafting over you in the presence of those you love and admire? You get to choose.

Other early Christian texts similarly take up this question with yet other visionary journeys to the worlds beyond. Some of them focus not on the eternal torture of sinners but the fantastic paradise awaiting the saints. Of these, none is more poignant than the dream of a young Roman matron who was on the path to be martyred as a Christian. Her name was Vibia Perpetua and her dream-vision is recorded in a book that claims to contain her own diary.[5]

The Heavenly Vision of Perpetua

The book, called the *Passion of Perpetua*, was written in Latin and is one of the most moving pieces of early Christian literature, an allegedly firsthand account of time in prison experienced by a Christian awaiting trial and execution. Scholars remain divided on whether the diary is genuine or, more likely, a later literary ploy claiming to be from Perpetua's own hand.[6] Whether authentic or not, the account is filled with verisimilitude and provides a unique glance into the hopes, expectations, and, literally, dreams of Christians in a world of animosity, hatred, and persecution.

Perpetua was a twenty-two-year-old recent convert to Christianity—so recent that she was still, at the time of her arrest, receiving basic instruction in her faith prior to baptism. She had also recently given birth, and in the account her child accompanies her to prison, along with a handful of other "catechumens" (converts being instructed in the rudiments of the faith) arrested as Christians in a town in North Africa in 203 CE. In the "diary" Perpetua narrates her encounters with her pagan father, who, to no avail, repeatedly urges her to recant her faith for the sake of her child and family. She provides details of her time in the dark, dank prison. And, most important for our purposes, she narrates several dream-visions that involve life beyond the soon-to-be experienced grave. Her first vision of going to heaven is of particular interest.[7]

One of Perpetua's two brothers asks her to see if God will reveal to her whether she is actually to be martyred or if, by chance, she will be set free. She prays her request, and in response God provides a detailed vision, striking in its metaphorical images.

Perpetua sees a tall ladder leading up to heaven, so narrow that only one person can climb it at a time. In other words, each person who wants to reach heaven must do so on the basis of her own will and decisions. Groupthink will not get you there. This is no ordinary ladder, however. It is enormously high (as one might expect) and has attached to its sides "all sorts of metal weapons . . . swords, spears, hooks, daggers, and spikes," so that, as Perpetua says, "if anyone tried to climb up carelessly or without paying attention, he would be mangled and his flesh would adhere to the weapons." No one should think the trip to heaven is safe and easy. The path is narrow, frightening, and fraught with danger. One misstep and you will be cut to shreds.

But that is not all. At the foot of the ladder lies an enormous dragon set to terrify and attack anyone who makes an attempt to climb. For readers versed in the Christian tradition, this fierce dragon is no mere beast. In the New Testament, the large serpent-dragon who attacks God's chosen ones is the devil himself (see Revelation 12:3, 9; 20:2). For Perpetua, the devil is determined to prevent anyone from taking the dangerous path of martyrdom that would lead to heavenly bliss.

Perpetua then sees that one of her Christian companions has already ascended the ladder, a man named Saturus who, in real life, had been providing the converts with their instruction. He too had been arrested, and by reaching heaven he has blazed the way for others. He looks down from the heavenly height and urges Perpetua to come up as well, warning her: "Do not let the dragon bite you." Perpetua assures him that the dragon "will not harm me in the name of Christ Jesus"—then boldly moves to the first rung of the ladder by stepping on the serpent's head. The devil holds no terror for her, since she has faith in her savior.

And so she ascends the ladder, avoiding all the threatening metal weapons: the trials and tribulations of this life that might lead one to slip from the faith, the persistent urgings of relatives to recant, the attractions of life that might lull one into apostasy. When she reaches the top, she sees "an immense garden." In it is a "grey-haired man . . . in shepherd's garb," milking sheep. Perpetua does not identify who this is, but the Christian reader has no difficulty recognizing the "Good Shepherd" as Christ himself. He is "grey-haired" because, as other Christians have said, he is the one who has existed before time, who chose to come into the world to save sinners, "the first and the last, the alpha and the omega" (Revelation 1:8; 22:13).

Around the shepherd are thousands of people clad in white: others of the saved who had already made the heavenly ascent. Christ greets Perpetua and tells her he is glad she has come. He gives her milk in her cupped hands, and she drinks it while all those around her say "Amen." This seems like a eucharistic meal, but why milk? One might think it is because that is what sheep naturally produce, but there is more to it than that. Milk is the nourishment given to a newborn. Perpetua is now about to be born into eternal life.

She wakes up and tells her brother the news: they will not be released from prison but are to suffer and die, and so find their eternal reward. They will be martyred.

And so it happens. The end of the narrative, allegedly written by a different author in the third person, describes how Perpetua and her fellow Christians refuse to recant and are thrown to the wild beasts in the arena, viciously mauled to their gory deaths.

The Afterlife of Martyrs

The tale of Perpetua is beautiful and moving. At the same time, it has an unintended dark side. Here is a well-educated, cultured, thoughtful young mother who is willing to throw away her life—despite the needs of her child and the love of her family—for the sake of her religious commitment. Those still today who stand within her faith community may see this as a noble and admirable act. But what of those outside? Do we really agree that people who subject themselves to violent and bloody deaths will gain the glories of heaven? What do we think of other people in our own world who are so fervently religious, in one religion or another, that they choose to undergo voluntary martyrdom so they can be rewarded afterward?

What we might think of such people today—in a world where the news is full of them—is much like what ancient non-Christians thought of the voluntary suicides of the Christians. There are no pagan authors from the time who mention Perpetua herself, but there are some who were familiar with followers of Christ like her. The Roman emperor Marcus Aurelius (121–80 CE) maligned Christians who insisted on dying out of obstinacy (*Meditations* 11.3). And the Latin satirist Lucian of Samosata (120–after 180 CE) spoke of Christians as "wretched people" who "have convinced themselves that they will be immortal and live forever, which leads the majority of them to despise death and willingly give themselves up to it."[8]

Even if determined religious martyrdoms may seem senseless, reckless, and even damnable to outsiders, one can see how faith in a glorious afterlife—and the belief that suffering will more quickly take you there—might lead some to take the exit sooner rather than later, especially if the rewards will be greater when considerable blood is shed. And apart from the question of what martyrs themselves were actually thinking, it is important to consider the function of the literary *descriptions* of such acts. As already suggested, Christian visions of the afterlife, both heaven and hell, were meant to provide guidance for how one should live in the here and now: avoiding sin, in the case of the *Apocalypse of Peter*, and remaining true to one's religious commitments, in the case of Perpetua.

There are more visions of the afterlife for us to examine. What is striking is that then, as now, some of them come not in dreams but in what are described by their authors as near-death experiences. Of these, none is more intriguing than those set forth in a book written in the late second Christian century, a legendary account of the missionary activities of Jesus's own twin brother, Judas Thomas.

The *Acts of Thomas*

To modern readers it may seem peculiar indeed to think that Jesus had a twin brother, but stories of the Son of God's mortal sibling circulated in parts of the second-century church. We are never told how, exactly, the two could be brothers, let alone twins. Possibly ancient Christians thought that, just as the pagan demigod Hercules was reputed to have a mortal brother, Iphicles (his divinely impregnated mother had been made pregnant as well by her mortal husband), so too did their own divinity, Jesus.

In any event there were numerous stories in circulation about his brother Judas, also called Thomas—a name that actually means twin. The best preserved of these stories gives an extended account of Thomas's missionary activities. Even today many people think of Thomas as the first to bring the gospel to India. That tradition goes back to the second-century account known as the *Acts of Thomas*.[9]

The narrative begins after Jesus has been raised from the dead. The twelve disciples are divinely appointed to spread the gospel throughout the known world, and decide how to divide up the territory for their missionary endeavors by drawing lots. The lot for India falls to Judas Thomas, but as it turns out, India is the last place on earth he wants to go. He refuses. But he is resisting God's will, and so, to provide suitable encouragement, Jesus himself appears in a vision telling Thomas he needs to go. He still refuses. So Jesus pulls a rather clever divine trick on him.

There is a foreign merchant named Abban who has come to Jerusalem all the way from India (for some unexplained reason) to find a carpenter for his master, a king named Gundaphorus. As Abban is making inquiries in the marketplace, Jesus appears to him and tells him he has a carpenter-slave he can sell. He then writes out a bill of sale: "I Jesus, son of carpenter Joseph, declare that I have sold my slave, Judas by name, to you Abban, a merchant of Gundaphorus, King of the Indians."

Jesus tracks down his brother, Judas Thomas, and brings him to Abban, who points to Jesus and asks, "Is this your master?" What can Thomas say? He has to admit it: Jesus is indeed his lord and master. Abban then shows him the bill of sale and Thomas realizes he has been duped and sold into slavery. Against all his wishes, he embarks with Abban back to India, where he will be used to ply his trade.

Thomas experiences a number of adventures both en route and once he is firmly on Indian soil. Two of them involve near-death experiences, one of hell and the other of heaven. Like near-death-experience narratives so popular in our own day, these are not simply disinterested accounts of the realities of the other world. They are meant to convince people what to think and how to live in the here and now.

Avoiding the Torments of Hell: The Near-death Experience of a Murdered Woman

One of the most bizarre accounts of the *Acts of Thomas* involves an episode of sex, mad jealousy, murder, and resurrection. The story begins with a young Christian man who has come to a worship service in Thomas's church in India, where he tries to take communion. But he is thwarted by a divine miracle: as the man brings the Eucharistic bread to his mouth, his hands wither. The parishioners who see this happen report to Thomas, who asks the man what sin he has recently committed.

Underlying the man's tale is a major ideological point made repeatedly by this entire long narrative: to be a truly committed Christian means abstaining from the pleasures of the flesh. And that means not having sex. The man explains to Thomas that he had recently converted to Christianity, opting, when he did so, to go all in for the new faith and live a life of chastity. This was not welcome news to the woman he loved, who refused to make that kind of commitment herself. So the man flew into a fit of rage, imagining that she would become sexually involved with someone else, and murdered her with a sword. This had just happened before he arrived to take communion.

Thomas responds by lamenting deeply the lust and sexual immorality of the world (the root of all evil, apparently) and instructs the man to wash his hands in a basin of sacred water. The man does so, and his hands are restored. Thomas then asks to be shown the woman's corpse, and they go off to the inn where the murder had been committed. When they find the body, the apostle prays that God will raise her from the dead. He instructs her former lover to take her by the hand, and she comes back to life. But rather than exulting in her new lease on life, she looks on them with terror, exclaiming that when she was dead she had been taken to a horrible place of immense suffering. She desperately does not want to go again. She then tells her tale.

After she died, an exceedingly hateful man in filthy clothes came and took her to a place filled with deep chasms and an unbearable stench. He forced her to look into each chasm, all of which contained souls of the dead being subject to hellish torments. In the first were souls hung on wheels of fire that were running and ramming each other. These people, she was told, had "perverted the intercourse of man and wife." We're not told what exactly they had done. Committed adultery? Engaged in illicit sexual practices within the confines of marriage? Something else? Whatever it was, it involved sex and it brought eternal torment.

Another chasm was filled with souls wallowing in mud and worms. These were women who had left their husbands to commit adultery. Yet another contained people hanging by various body parts: women who had gone into public without head coverings, possibly to show off their beauty, were hanging by their hair; thieves who reveled in their wealth and didn't give to the poor were hanging by their hands; those who walked in the ways of wickedness were hanging by their feet.

After seeing the various chasms, she was shown a vast, dark cavern filled with a vile stench. This was a holding pen for souls: some were there after being tortured in one chasm or another, others were those who had perished in their anguish, and yet others were waiting for tortures to come. Some of the demonic torturers who guarded the cavern asked the woman's guide to give her soul over to them to torture, but he refused. He had received strict instructions not to hand her over yet.

She then was met by someone who looked like Thomas himself (presumably Jesus, his twin) who told her guide: "Take her, for she is one of the sheep that have gone astray." At that moment the woman regained consciousness, not awakening from a dream but arriving back from the reality of hell itself. When she sees Thomas, she begs him to save her from "those places of punishment which I have seen" (ch. 58).

Thomas tells those who have come to observe her resuscitation that they need to repent or they themselves will end up in that place of torment: "You have heard what this woman has recounted. And these are not the only punishments, but there are others worse than these." Worse than these? How could they be worse than these? Apparently they are. You don't want to go there.

And neither did Thomas's hearers. He tells them how to escape. They need to turn to God, believe in Christ for forgiveness, and cleanse themselves "from all your bodily desires that remain on earth." They are no longer to steal, commit adultery, covet, lie, get drunk, slander, or execute vengeance. As one would expect in a Christian text such as this, Thomas's brief sermon, backed with irrefutable visions of fire and brimstone, has its desired effect: "The whole people therefore believed and presented obedient souls to the living God and Christ Jesus."

Clearly this tale of hell had, for the author of the vision, a didactic purpose: a brief life of chastity and purity is the only prophylactic for fiery punishments awaiting those who cannot control themselves. Still, the ethical function of the near-death experience does not mean that the hearers of this tale took it all to be metaphor. On the contrary, early Christians appear to have believed the literal truth of such grisly descriptions of what is to come. Many Christians today still do. The point may be to behave now, but it is a point rooted in the belief that there will be torment later for those who misbehave.

However, the lessons of such narratives were not always negative. As we have seen with Perpetua, there was also the upside of a different kind of life, one of obedience. Such benefits can be seen in the second near-death experience related in the *Acts of Thomas*. This is a vision not of hell but of heaven, and the lesson relates not to chastity but to charity. Just as Jesus gave all he had to save the world, those with resources should also give all they have for those in need. That is how they will find treasures in heaven.

The Near-death Experience of a Royal Brother

Earlier in the narrative, when he first arrives in India, Thomas is taken to meet his new master, King Gundaphorus. Gundaphorus is delighted and asks the apostle-slave if he can use his carpentry skills to build a new royal palace. Thomas agrees and accompanies him to the distant site. After surveying the property Thomas draws up plans, shows them to the king, and is given a large amount of money to begin construction.

The king returns home, leaving Thomas to his work. But instead of buying the materials he needs, Thomas gives all the funds to the poor. After some time Gundaphorus, unaware of what is happening, sends a messenger to see how the building is going. Thomas tells him that the palace itself is finished, but he needs more money for the roof. The king sends another installment.

Soon afterward Gundaphorus comes to inspect his new regal residence, only to learn there is nothing for him to see. The king calls his Jewish carpenter to account and asks where the palace is. Thomas's reply may seem hopelessly idealistic: he has used the money to build an even better palace, not one on earth but in the heavens, not to be seen until the king departs this life. To that end, all the money has gone to those in need.

The pagan Gundaphorus is not in a charitable mood. He orders Thomas arrested and imprisoned, vowing to have him flogged and burned to death for his scandalous waste of funds. But, as fate would have it, that night the king's dear brother, a man named Gad, falls mortally ill and dies. The angels take the soul of Gad up to heaven and there offer him a number of residences to choose from for his eternal habitation. But he is particularly impressed by one not on offer, an especially enormous and beautiful palace. He tells his angelic guides that he would rather spend his happily-ever-after in just one of the lower rooms of this amazing abode than in any of the mansions otherwise available. But they tell him he cannot live there. It is a palace that belongs to his brother Gundaphorus.

Gad pleads with the angels to allow him to return to life to ask his brother for it; he's certain that fraternal love will secure the place for himself. The angels allow him to go and he returns from the dead, to the joy and surprise of his brother. Gad tells the king all about his near-death experience and pleads with him to sell him the massive palace in the sky, built for him by the Christian Thomas. Once Gundaphorus realizes what has actually happened, he refuses, telling Gad to have Thomas make him his own palace for an eternal dwelling.

Naturally enough for a Christian text, Gundaphorus releases the apostle from prison and begs his forgiveness, asking for help to be made worthy of the house that has been built for him out of Christian almsgiving. He converts to the Christian faith and decides no longer to live for himself and his own pleasures but for God, devoting his vast resources to the good of others.

Once again, the point of the story is clear. It is a narrative exposition of the words of Jesus: "Sell your possessions and give to charity; make for yourselves purses that do not grow old, a treasure that does not fail, in heaven, where no thief comes near and no moth corrupts. For where your treasure is, there also will be your heart" (Luke 12:33–34). Sometimes it takes a near-death experience to show people how to live on this side of eternity.

Visions of Heaven in the Early Christian Tradition

Here then are four visions of the afterlife, each unique but all tending toward the same end of guiding people's lives in the here and now by confronting them with what awaits them in the hereafter. Eternal glory or torment hangs in the balance. Christian readers at the time would not have taken these tales to be pure fictions but would have accepted that they were rooted in the realities of the world to come.

None of these visions can be found in the Bible, because they do not, in fact, represent the earliest Christian views of the afterlife. The ideas of a glorious hereafter for some souls and torment for others, to come at the point of death, cannot be found either in the Old Testament or in the teachings of the historical Jesus. To put it succinctly: the founder of Christianity did not believe that the soul of a person who died would go to heaven or hell.

But this became the standard Christian view over time, and it will be helpful to see where it ultimately came from, when it started to be adopted, and why it seemed so attractive. These are important questions, because belief in a literal heaven and hell continues to be held by most Christians in the world today—that is by millions, even billions of people. To see where this belief originated, we will need to begin our explorations many years before Christianity—before even the most ancient writings of the oldest parts of the Bible.

CHAPTER TWO

The Fear of Death

As usual, Shakespeare put it best. In *Measure for Measure*, Claudio, facing his execution, bemoans:

> 'tis too horrible.
> The weariest and most loathed worldly life
> That age, ache, penury, and imprisonment
> Can lay on nature is a paradise
> To what we fear of death. (Act 3, Scene 1, lines
>   143–47)

Now, four centuries later, we have not conquered this fear of death, and still, as then, it comes in different guises. Many people fear the process of dying, struck by dread or even terror when thinking about becoming old, lonely, decrepit, miserable, in pain, and a huge burden on family and others. But Shakespeare is not reflecting on the progress toward dying but on being dead—the fear of no longer living. But what's to fear?

Throughout history, for many people it has been the fear of torment: that when we die the justice of the Almighty will wreak vengeance on our poor souls—and possibly on new physical embodiments of our souls, created for the purpose—as we are punished for sins, disbelief, and ingratitude for the divine mercies available to us while still drawing breath. Others do not think it likely God will order demonic torments for us mere mortals, but they still fear the unknown. We are moving blindly into death, not knowing what it will be like or what to expect, terrified of "the undiscovered country /from whose bourn / No traveler returns . . ." (*Hamlet*, Act 3, Scene 1, lines 87–88).

Many others believe that at death our life is extinguished and we cease to exist in every way. The idea of nonexistence itself—of not waking up, of a personal identity permanently lost, world without end—inspires not relief but horror. How can we even imagine it? At all times of our lives, since we have been able to think, we have existed. How can we think of not existing?

And so it is no surprise that death is often lamented in the great literature of the world, including the Bible. As the psalmist says, praising God for saving him for the time being from death, imaged as the realm of Sheol:

> *I will give thanks to you, O Lord my God, with my*
> *   whole heart. . . .*
> *For great is your steadfast love toward me;*
> *you have delivered my soul from the depths of Sheol.*
> *   (Psalm 86:12–13)*

Or, again:

> *O Lord, my God, I cried to you for help,*
> *and you have healed me.*

O Lord, you brought up my soul from Sheol,
restored me to life from among those gone down to
the Pit. (Psalm 30:2–3)

In no small part the Bible's authors praise God for saving them from untimely death because they realize all too clearly that life is short and death certain. And so the psalmist laments that people "like smoke . . . vanish away" (Psalm 37:20); elsewhere we hear that "our days on earth are like a shadow" (1 Chronicles 29:15); or, as the New Testament book of James says, "[we] are a mist that appears for a while, and after which it disappears" (James 4:14) That is our life. Short and temporary like smoke, a shadow, or the morning mist. Once gone it will never return. And we don't have long to wait.

The obsession with death and fear of what comes next extends beyond even the most ancient biblical records to the beginning of recorded history. It can be found in the ancient Mesopotamian epic known as Gilgamesh.

The Fear of Death in the Gilgamesh

The epic of Gilgamesh is the longest literary composition in Akkadian (Old Babylonian) and one of the the oldest narratives in our literary canon. The epic was unknown for many centuries until unearthed on clay tablets in the mid-nineteenth century, discovered in archaeological excavations of Nineveh, the ancient capital of Assyria. The tablets, composed in cuneiform script and dating from the seventh century BCE, created an international sensation, in no small measure because, once deciphered, they were recognized as preserving a "flood narrative" from centuries before the biblical accounts of Noah. This older Babylonian myth may well have been the source for the ancient Israelite version.

Other discoveries eventually turned up that contained portions of the Gilgamesh story. Now we have multiple versions from different periods of antiquity. The oldest are Sumerian tales that date all the way back to 2100 BCE. (The oldest strands of the book of Genesis were probably produced more than a full millennium later.)

In antiquity, the eponymous protagonist of these stories, Gilgamesh, was considered a historical character, a king of Uruk, a city of Sumer. The epic in its various forms involves mythical accounts of this original superhero, a Mesopotamian Hercules, an amazingly powerful but unruly he-man who was two parts divine and only one part human.

The tales portray this wild beast of a man as a fierce bully to other men and a sexual threat to women. In order to bring him under control, one of the goddesses creates a mortal equal to him, named Enkidu, who begins as his adversary but after confronting him in hand-to-hand combat becomes his most beloved friend and partner in rampaging mischief. In one of their adventures, the gods send a sacred beast, the "bull of heaven," to wreak havoc in retribution for Gilgamesh's ungodly and outlandish behavior, but the two supermen kill it. The gods are incensed at this violation of their divine prerogative and decide that one of the two supermen must die. Enkidu mourns because he knows it will be he, and in expressing his grief he provides us with the earliest record in human history of the terror of death. He has a dream of being overwhelmed by a powerful man and recounts the nightmarish outcome in poignant terms:

> He seized me, drove me down to the dark house,
> > dwelling of Erkalla's god,
> To the house which those who enter cannot leave,
> On the road where travelling is one way only,
> To the house where those who stay are deprived of
> > light,
> Where dust is their food, and clay their bread.

They are clothed like birds, with feathers,
And they see no light, and they dwell in darkness.
(Gilgamesh, *Tablet VII, v*)[1]

Even the most powerful superhumans alive are powerless in the face of death. We all will eat dust and dwell forever in darkness. Not a happy prospect. And then Enkidu experiences it. He dies.

Gilgamesh bitterly mourns his lost companion and roams the countryside, disconsolate. Most of his grief, however, is not for his friend but for himself: he too will eventually be confronted by death, and he hates the prospect:

Shall I die too? Am I not like Enkidu?
Grief has entered my innermost being,
I am afraid of Death, and so I roam open country
(Gilgamesh, *Tablet IX, i*)

He decides he needs to find a path to immortality, and for that he needs advice. There is only one man in all of history who has escaped death to live life everlasting, a man named Ut-napishtim. Gilgamesh ventures on a journey to find him, to learn the secret of immortal existence.

Ut-napishtim is the Mesopotamian version of Noah, and, as already intimated, the tale of his involvement in the worldwide flood bears striking similarities to the later account of Genesis 6–9. The gods decide to destroy the human race with water, and Ut-napishtim is instructed to build an enormous boat, an acre in size, with seven levels. Once it is completed, he is to bring aboard his wife and specimens of all living creatures. The floods come and only those in the boat survive the onslaught. When the rains stop, Ut-napishtim sends out birds to find dry land. When the flood has subsided adequately, he emerges from the boat and the creatures come forth to repopulate the earth (*Gilgamesh*, Tablet XI).

As a reward for his upright actions, the gods reward Ut-napishtim by making him like themselves: immortal. He is still a human, but he will never die. Gilgamesh knows of his existence, and he wants to find him to learn the secret of life everlasting. But of course Ut-napishtim is not easily found: he is in a secret place of immortality. Gilgamesh sets out on a virtually impossible mission, a long and arduous journey, passing through lengthy realms of impenetrable darkness before arriving at the land he is seeking, a place of light.

In that realm he first comes upon a mysterious woman identified simply as an "alewife." It is not clear who she is or what she is doing there, but Gilgamesh is pleased to find a human of any sort and spills out to her the dreadful reason for his mission:

> I am afraid of Death, and so I roam open country . . .
> How, O how could I stay silent, how, O how could I
>   keep quiet ?
> My friend whom I love has turned to clay: Enkidu
>   my friend whom I love has turned to clay.
> Am I not like him? Must I lie down too,
> Never to rise, ever again? (Gilgamesh, Tablet X, iii)

The alewife tells him how to find Ut-napishtim, and so he continues his journey, finally arriving to meet the one immortal human ever to have lived. At first Ut-napishtim is not encouraging about Gilgamesh's hopes for immortality:

> Since [the gods] made you like your father and
>   mother
> [Death is inevitable . . .] at some time, both for
>   Gilgamesh and for a fool . . . (Gilgamesh,
>   Tablet X, v)

Ut-napishtim goes on to provide a moving exposition on the nature of Death.

> *Nobody sees Death,*
> *Nobody sees the face of Death,*
> *Nobody hears the voice of Death.*
> *Savage Death just cuts mankind down.*
> *Sometimes we build a house, sometimes we make a*
>   *nest,*
> *But then brothers divide it upon inheritance.*
>   (Gilgamesh, *Tablet X, vi*)

It is a gloomy prospect. We do our best to accomplish things in life, but then we die without warning and our life is over, leaving everything we have done and produced in the possession of others. We have no more existence or meaning.

Ut-napishtim goes on to speak about the role played by a group of gods, known as the Anunnaki, and one god in particular, named Mammitum, in assigning a time for people to die:

> *The Anunnaki, the great gods, assembled;*
> *Mammitum, who creates fate, decreed destinies with*
>   *them.*
> *They appointed death and life.*
> *They did not mark out days for death,*
> *But they did so for life.* (Gilgamesh, *Tablet X, vi*)

Ut-napishtim is speaking truth to terror: there is a limit to the days of life but no limit to the days of death.

Gilgamesh asks Ut-napishtim why he is different, why he alone has been granted immortality, and it is that point that the immortal one tells his story of the flood. But even more important, he tells Gilgamesh that there is indeed a chance for him too to escape death, but through a different route. At the bottom of the sea is a certain thorny plant that can restore him to his youth as an "antidote to the fear of death."[2] Utnapishtim tells his intrepid seeker how to find it.

And so Gilgamesh goes on another quest. With the boatman Urshanabi as a guide, he sails to the designated spot, ties stones to his feet, sinks to the bottom of the sea, and retrieves the plant of life, exclaiming:

> Ur-shanabi, this plant is a plant to cure a crisis!
> With it a man may win the breath of life . . .
> Its name shall be: "An old man grows into a young
>   man."
> I too shall eat it and turn into the young man that I
>   once was. (Gilgamesh, Tablet XI, vi)

Anyone familiar with tales about plants that can bring eternal life—think, the Garden of Eden (Genesis 2–3)—should be braced for what is to come next. Gilgamesh's plans are tragically foiled. On his return home he comes to a calm pool of water and decides to have a dip to cool off. While he is in the water, a "snake [smells] the fragrance of the plant" that had been left in the boat, and it slithers to the spot and absconds with the plant. "As it [takes] it away, it shed[s] its scaly skin" (Gilgamesh, Tablet X, vi).

More familiar resonances: immortality is lost because of the nefarious working of a sly serpent. As one can imagine, Gilgamesh is deeply distraught and weeps, having lost his one chance at immortality. His fear will be realized. Like all mortals, he has to die.

So, of course, will we. We may seek immortality—in our day and age, not by finding the plant of immortality per se, but certainly by finding the right diet, exercise regimen, vitamin and mineral supplements, and other protocols to prolong our lives. But we too, like Gilgamesh, are mortal, and our time is short. The question is whether we stand in terror before the inevitable or have resources to deal with what is certainly to be.

There is another version of the Gilgamesh story that similarly highlights the inevitability of a miserable end to all flesh. This comes from a fragmentary Akkadian tablet containing a different tale involving Gilgamesh and Enkidu. Gilgamesh has made two wooden objects for himself out of a sacred tree, but they have mysteriously disappeared into the earth and gone to the underworld. He sends Enkidu to find them, and that is where the story picks up.

Gilgamesh gives Enkidu instructions about how to retrieve what was lost without himself being trapped in the underworld. But Enkidu ignores his instructions and is ensnared, lost to the world above. He has, in effect, died in his effort. But the god Ea orders the king of the underworld to send the ghost of Enkidu up to meet with Gilgamesh:

> *You must open up a hole in the Earth now,*
> *So that the spirit [of Enkidu can come out of the*
>   *Earth like a gust of wind].*
> *[And return . . .] to his brother [Gilgamesh].*
>   *(Gilgamesh, Tablet XII, iii)*

He does so, and Enkidu gives his friend an account of what it is like to reside in the realm of the dead. It is a gloomy prospect indeed.

> *And the spirit of Enkidu came out of the earth like a*
>   *gust of wind.*
> *They hugged, and kissed . . .*
> *They discussed, they agonized.*
> *"Tell me, my friend, tell me my friend,*
> *Tell me Earth's conditions that you found!"*

"I can't tell you my friend, I can't tell you!
If I tell you Earth's conditions that I found,
You must sit (and) weep! . . .
[Your wife?] whom you touched, and your heart was
    glad,
Vermin eat [like?] an old [garment].
[Your son? whom] you touched, and your heart was
    glad,
Sits in a crevice full of dust.
'Woe,' she said, and groveled in the dust.
'Woe' he said, and groveled in the dust." (Gilgamesh,
    Tablet XII, iv)

The message is clear: if you knew what the afterlife was really like, you would weep. No wonder people have stood in terror in the face of death for as long as we have human records.

An Alternative to Fear: Death in the Words of Socrates

But do we really need to fear? Over the centuries, even in antiquity, philosophers and other thinkers reflected deeply on the problem, and eventually there arose a counterview, an alternative to standing in terror before the face of death. Nowhere is this other view expressed in more cogent and compelling terms than on the lips of the great Greek philosopher Socrates, speaking many centuries after the original readers of Gilgamesh had long been laid to rest.

We do not have any writings from Socrates himself. All we know of him comes from the works of his contemporaries, in particular Plato (circa 428–circa 348 BCE), whose *Dialogues* almost invariably feature Socrates as the main character through whom, ventriloquist-style, Plato himself speaks. Some of the words put on Socrates's lips by his greatest pupil, however, almost certainly reflect the thoughts of the teacher, and none of them expresses the Socratic view of death more clearly than those he spoke at his own trial when he was brought up on capital charges for crimes against the state. The account of his trial comes in one of Plato's most famous writings, the *Apology*. The Greek word for "apology" (*apologia*) does not mean "saying you're sorry." It means "making a defense." The *Apology* of Socrates was the speech he made in his own defense in 399 BCE before a jury of Athenian men, the majority of whom, in the end, rejected his case and ordered his execution.

Several charges had been leveled against Socrates. Some of them, at least as Plato portrays them, merely involved intellectual mischief making, considered offensive to the public interest. (Socrates made "the weaker argument defeat the stronger.") But others carried dire consequences, especially the claims that he had "corrupted" the youth of Athens by altering how they thought about their lives and civic responsibilities and, even more serious, that he had introduced into the city new deities, urging his fellow citizens to worship gods not sanctioned by the state.

This was a very serious charge in antiquity, when no one made a clean distinction between realms we today would designate as the "religious" and the "political." There were not even ancient Greek words that neatly distinguished the two, in part because it was widely understood that the gods were intimately involved with affairs of state and that the state should therefore be deeply concerned with promoting the proper worship of the gods. It was the gods, after all, who brought success to the state and prosperity to its citizens. In times of crisis—such as those facing Athens in the late fifth and early fourth centuries during the Peloponnesian War and its aftermath—failure to worship the gods properly could have disastrous consequences. And so the state would not and could not sanction dangerous religious views.

It is not clear that Socrates actually did promote the worship of non-sanctioned gods. But he certainly was perceived by those in power as a social nuisance, a cancer on the body politic, and a promoter of beliefs other than those that had proved salutary in making Athens the state power that it was.

In his self-defense, as recorded in the *Apology*, Socrates claims that his primary purpose in his life as a public figure has always been to do what he knew was right, regardless of the consequences. It is far better, he insists, to suffer for doing what is right than to prosper while doing what is wrong. So too in the face of death: if his actions should lead to his execution, that is not his concern. He can only control his own actions, not those of others who choose to punish him for them. And so, no matter what, he will continue doing what he has always done by following the direction given to him by his god.[3]

Most important, he does not believe God will punish him for doing what is right. If others do so, he will not cower in fear, even if it means his execution. It is in the context of this defense that Socrates explicates his understanding of what death is, why he is not afraid of it, and why no one else should be either.

With wit and some humor, Socrates argues that people dread death as if they know it is a great evil. But how do they know that? In fact, death might be the greatest blessing; maybe it's even better than life. Yet people do everything they can to avoid it, especially when it involves premature death by execution by the state—as if they think they will never die if they aren't executed!

Socrates's deliberations in this context reflect a constant theme of his recorded words: many people who think they are wise in fact know almost nothing. Many of Plato's dialogues are designed to show that people—even philosophers and public orators—are hopelessly ignorant even when they are addressing the most basic and important aspects of moral life, such as love, virtue, justice, truth, and goodness.

Here is how he puts the matter to the jury at his trial:

For let me tell you, gentlemen, that to be afraid of death is only another form of thinking that one is wise when one is not. It is to think that one knows what one does not know. No one knows with regard to death whether it is not really the greatest blessing that can happen to a person, but people dread it as though it were the greatest evil, and this ignorance, which thinks that it knows what it does not, must surely be ignorance most culpable. (*Apology* 29a–b)[4]

Later in his speech he continues:

I have often noticed that some people . . . go to extraordinary lengths when they come up for trial [with a possible death sentence], which shows that they think it will be a dreadful thing to lose their lives— as though they would be immortal if you did not put them to death! (*Apology* 35a)

He goes on to give his own view of what happens at death: "Death is one of two things. Either it is annihilation, and the dead have no consciousness of anything, or, as we are told, it is really a change—a migration of the soul from this place to another" (*Apology* 40c). Socrates doesn't think either option is fearful—quite the contrary: both are attractive and to be embraced. On one hand, if at death the person becomes unconscious, it will be like a very deep, dreamless sleep. And who does not enjoy that? In that case "death must be a marvelous gain"—the best rest and relaxation anyone has ever had (*Apology* 40c).

If it is the alternative, the removal to the realm of the dead where others also reside, "what greater blessing could there be than this?" (*Apology*

40e). Socrates himself would love to be transported to another world where he could meet all the greats of his Greek civilization: Orpheus, Hesiod, Homer, and others. Indeed, "I am willing to die ten times over if this account is true" (*Apology* 41a). Moreover, as he points out with a twinkle in his eye, he assumes that in this other world no one will ever be executed for crimes against the state, since "they are now immortal for the rest of time, if what we are told is true" *(Apology* 41c).

This last phrase is characteristic of Socrates's reflections on death, as we will see in a later context. He states what it may be like—or even probably will be like—but then he hedges his bet, claiming that he is simply propounding what others have said, with the clear implication that he is not certain himself that it is at all true, but that instead it may represent a useful "myth" that can teach important lessons. In this case, if it is true that death brings you into the presence of those who came before (and he is not at all sure it is; in fact, he rather doubts it), then that would be a tremendous good, and death is nothing at all to fear but something to embrace. And for Socrates, the alternative is good as well—a deep and lasting sleep with no pains, worries, or concerns, nothing to bring any disturbance of any kind.

So, with respect to the question of how to live in the face of death, one must not cower in fear at what will eventually happen to us all. More important, one must not do anything known to be wrong in order to escape death: it is better to do what is right, regardless of the consequences, than to do what is wrong to avoid what is both inevitable and good.

The Death of Socrates

Plato believed that Socrates lived out this conviction to his dying breath. The account of his last day and hours, up to when he calmly and willingly drinks the hemlock apportioned to him in his state-mandated suicide, can be found in Plato's dialogue, the *Phaedo*. There we learn that Socrates's apology came to no effect, and, as expected, he received a death sentence. After a delay, the fateful day arrived. The time was set for the evening, and so, for the bulk of the dialogue, Socrates spends the day with a group of friends and pupils, engaged, as was his wont, in philosophical discourse. One of those present is named Phaedo, and it is he who allegedly tells the tale that Plato relates.

Socrates decides that the most appropriate topic of the day would be the "immortality of the soul"—that is, the idea that even though the body dies, the soul is deathless and will survive. For Socrates it is obvious that, since only the body is destined to perish, the soul is the more important of the two, requiring by far the greater care and attention.

It is important to bear in mind that here, as in all of the dialogues, when Socrates speaks, we are hearing the words of Plato, even if, as suggested above, they may reflect traces of Socrates's own thought. Plato championed an essentially dualistic anthropology in which the body and soul are more or less at war with each other, with each one wanting what is at odds with the other. That is why, for Plato, physical pleasure is not the great good most people take it to be but the ultimate enemy. Pleasure ties a person to the body. When people feel pleasure, they want more. They focus on getting it. They live for it. But to what end? The body that feels pleasure will die. Then what? The pleasure brings no good in the long term.

Far more important than the temporal, pleasure-experiencing body is the soul that will live on. One should overlook the needs and desires of the body to focus on the soul. That means actually abstaining from intense pleasure, or at least being indifferent to it. The goal of life is to escape the body by centering all thought and action on the part of the human that is immortal and comparable to the gods. When philosophers put this view into practice, they allow their souls to transcend their bodies while still living, and in that sense they are already practicing death.

Since dying entails the ultimate separation of the soul and the body, philosophers—and all who think rightly—should "die daily," escaping the confines of their bodies by focusing on the welfare of their souls.

Moreover, if dying is how one is supposed to "live," then obviously there is nothing to fear in actual, physical death. Instead, it is to be embraced: it brings to completion what philosophers have been trying to do all along, escape the confines of their physical mortality. As Socrates says early in the dialogue:

> I want to explain to you how it seems to me natural that a man who has really devoted his life to philosophy should be cheerful in the face of death, and confident of finding the greatest blessing in the next world when his life is finished . . .
>
> Ordinary people seem not to realize that those who really apply themselves in the right way to philosophy are directly and of their own accord preparing themselves for dying and death. (*Phaedo* 63e–64a)

Plato realizes that this entire view presupposes that the soul does in fact live on after death, and that is precisely what needs to be proved. Most of the *Phaedo* involves Socrates's various attempts to marshal arguments for the immortality of the soul. Some of these proofs are advanced tentatively, explained, examined, critiqued, and found to be wanting; others are rather long, complicated, and defended in the face of possible objections. As invariably happens in these dialogues, Socrates manages, in the end, to convince his initially dubious and less-than-keen-witted pupils. As he summarizes near the end of the dialogue: "If what is immortal is also imperishable, it is impossible that at the approach of death soul should cease to be. It follows from what we have already said that it cannot admit death, or be dead . . ." (*Phaedo* 106b). As he states more baldly to one of his companions, Cebes: "Then it is as certain as anything can be, Cebes, that soul is immortal and imperishable, and that our souls will really exist in the next world" (*Phaedo* 106e–107a). Cebes gives the expected response: "Well, Socrates . . . for my part I have no criticisms and no doubt about the truth of your argument" (*Phaedo* 107a).

As I already suggested, and as we will see in a later chapter, it is not clear that Plato or even Socrates himself was completely convinced, although his listeners allegedly were. Recall, he also considered another completely plausible option: that at death the soul was annihilated with the body, leading to a kind of interminable dreamless sleep. Moreover, whenever he talks about what comes after death to the immortal soul, he hedges his bets by saying that such things "are said" by others. Plato's views of death and afterlife were really more about life in the present than about the great beyond. His philosophical views were directed to how we are to live now. In the case he makes in the *Phaedo*, no one should fear what will happen at death or do anything unethical in order to avoid it. One should bravely face their mortal end knowing it is not evil and that it is never right to do what is wrong in order to try to escape it.

At the end of the *Phaedo*, Socrates implements this very lesson, putting into practice the view he has just espoused. He lived by practicing death—that is, by focusing on his soul rather than his body—and he dies as he lived. In addition, he does so with a good bit of humor. When the friends' discussion about immortality ends, the time comes for Socrates to drink the state-administered hemlock. He does so calmly, and as the poison takes its effect, numbing his body from his feet upward, he lies down. As the numbness begins to reach his heart, he covers his face with a cloth. But then he takes it off and, in his last recorded words, instructs one of his companions, Crito, to "offer a cock to Asclepius; see to it, and don't forget" (*Phaedo* 118).

Asclepius was the Greek god of healing. Sacrificing a cock meant thanking him for bringing recovery from an illness. This was Socrates's way of expressing thanks that he now had finally been "healed." He had done what is right to the very end, and had either entered into an eternal dreamless sleep or escaped his body to enjoy everlasting life with his immortal soul.

This is a lesson that comes to us from over two millennia ago, but it is one that we can still learn from today. Whatever we think of death—whether it brings extinction or a life beyond—we do not need to face it with terror. Plato's ultimate point is that there is nothing to fear.

CHAPTER THREE

Life After Death
Before There Was
Life After Death

The fear of death for many people in antiquity differed from the terrors of torment or horrors of actual nonexistence experienced by so many in the West today. It was instead the dread of losing out on everything a full life has to offer, everything that makes living pleasant. As we will see in this chapter, for many ancients there was indeed a kind of non-tortured existence after death, but it was bleak, dreary, and completely uninteresting—not just for some, but for everyone. As one great scholar of antiquity has summed up this widely attested view: "Nothing is so hateful to [a person] as death and the gates of Hades: for when death comes it is certain that life—this sweet life of ours in the sunlight—is done with, whatever else there may be to follow."[1]

This banal and purposeless existence after life is attested in the Western tradition as far back as our earliest sources of information, some three centuries before Plato, in the *Iliad* and *Odyssey* of Homer.

Death in the *Iliad* and the *Odyssey*

The traditional author of the *Iliad* and *Odyssey* was a blind bard who put into verse a large number of oral traditions about part of the ten-year war the Greeks fought by the walls of Troy (the *Iliad*), initially caused by the Trojan prince Paris's seduction of the Greek beauty Helen, "the face that launched a thousand ships" (in the words of Marlowe's *Doctor Faustus*), and the ten-year escapades of one of the Greek heroes in the war, Odysseus, in his attempt to return home to his wife, Penelope, on the island of Ithaca (the *Odyssey*). Scholars have long debated who actually produced the epics and when. It is now generally thought they were composed more or less as we have them in the eighth or seventh century BCE, but the author is anonymous.

That death figures prominently in both works comes as no surprise: the first recounts part of a prolonged war with numerous casualties, and the second a series of perilous escapades involving a giant Cyclops, sirens, witches, shipwreck, and lots of other threats to life and limb. In the *Odyssey*, just about all the humans—barring the protagonist and his relatives—are eventually killed off.

In the various reflections on death in these books, one point is crystal clear: death is uncompromisingly final. There is no coming back. The point is made already in the *Iliad* by its central figure, Achilles, the greatest of the Greek warriors, who laments what he has seen on the battlefield:

> *But a man's life breath cannot come back again—*
> *No raiders in force, no trading brings it back,*
> *Once it slips through a man's clenched teeth.* (Iliad,
> Book 9, lines 495–97)[2]

The Greek term rendered here as "life breath" is *psychē*, often translated by the word "soul." It may be related to the verb *psychō*, which means to breathe. When a person stops breathing—that is, dies—the *psychē*, the "life breath" or soul, leaves the body through the mouth, never to return. Once that has happened, there is no military or bartering solution: you can't fight or buy your way back into the body.

But where does the life force go? For Homer and other ancient Greek authors, it goes to the underworld, where souls (*psychai*) have the form but not the substance of human life, and none of its goodness. The soul appears in the shape of the human it had left—bodily defects and wounds included. But there is nothing substantial or tangible about it. In that state, forever and ever, it does not experience any physical torment or pain—or pleasure either. Instead, the *psychē* exists as a mere "image" or "shade" (Greek: *eidōlon*) of the person.

Nowhere is Homer's understanding of the state of the "soul" after death expressed more clearly than in a fascinating tale at the halfway point of his second epic, an account that describes the protagonist Odysseus's terrifying visit, while still alive, to the realm of Hades to meet and speak with some of the shades who have preceded him in death.

Odysseus's Visit to the Underworld

The background to the story is an intriguing tale of its own. In Book 10, Odysseus and his men have sailed to the island of the enchanting nymph Circe. Odysseus sends half his men to explore the island. They meet Circe, who hosts them and treats them to a magical meal, which turns them into pigs. Charming. One of the men escapes, however, and runs to inform Odysseus. The hero of the story stalks off to Circe, sword in hand. On his way, he meets the god Hermes, who has come to warn him and provide an antidote for Circe's witchy cuisine. When Odysseus does meet her, he eats her foul food but proves immune to its swinish effects. She in her amazement realizes he has received divine assistance and, in a somewhat unexpected move, promptly tries to bed him. He refuses her sexual advances until she agrees to release his mates from their swinish captivity. She does so, hero and nymph go to bed, and the men end up so enjoying the hospitality she provides, and Odysseus the sex, that they stay for a year.

They finally decide to continue on their journey home. As they prepare to leave, Circe instructs Odysseus that before sailing for Ithaca he must go to the "House of the Dead" and to the "awesome one Persephone," the goddess who rules over the underworld with her husband Hades, in order to:

> consult the ghost of Tiresias, seer of Thebes,
> the great blind prophet whose mind remains
> unshaken.
> Even in death—Persephone has given him wisdom,
> Everlasting vision to him and him alone . . .
> The rest of the dead are empty, flitting shades.
> (Odyssey, Book 10, lines 541–45)

Tiresias is a famous but deceased prophet, and Circe is telling Odysseus to learn from him how he can successfully complete his voyage. In doing so, she provides an apt description of the dead. Apart from Tiresias, they are all "empty, flitting shades." Everyone, with very few exceptions, is the same. There is no differentiation between the wicked and the righteous, religious and nonreligious, valiant and coward.

The narrative continues in Book 11 as Odysseus follows closely the instructions that Circe had given for contacting the dead. He and his men set sail to the end of the ocean, beyond where even the sun shines, where "an endless deadly night overhangs those wretched men" (Odyssey, Book 11, line 21). When they arrive to the place Circe indicated, just outside the realm of the dead, Odysseus does exactly as he had been told. He digs a trench and pours out libations for the dead: milk, honey, wine, and water, sprinkling it all with barley. He then utters a vow that on his return to Ithaca he will slaughter a heifer for the dead and load up a pyre with treasures. To Tiresias himself he will offer a black ram.

He then cuts the throats of a ram and a black ewe. This draws ghosts up from the realm of the death, thousands swarming on all sides, eager to drink the blood. As bodiless souls, they lack the blood of life and all the sensations that come with it. They are desperate for a drink.

Odysseus pulls a sword to keep the shades away from the blood. The narrative seems internally incoherent at this point: it is not clear why, if the shades are in fact immaterial vapors, they would be afraid of a sword. In any event, what follows are a number of encounters of Odysseus with various dead people—not just Tiresias, but also his own mother, the hero Achilles, and others. The descriptions of these encounters are powerful and moving.

One of the overarching points made throughout the scenes that follow is that the afterlife is not life. It is death. Those who have departed life are joyless, bodiless shades, with no possibility of pleasure or vibrancy of any kind. Tiresias calls the underworld "this joyless kingdom of the dead" (*Odyssey*, Book 11, line 105). Achilles later says that it is "where the senseless, burnt-out wraiths of mortals make their home" (*Odyssey*, Book 11, line 540). It is the realm of the "breathless dead." Shades have no bodies, no strength, no knowledge of anything happening in the world above. And—an important point—they are not immortal. The term "immortal" for Homer is synonymous with "divine." Only gods are immortal. Deceased humans are dead, not alive. As described by historian of ancient Greek religion, Erwin Rohde:

Down in the murky underworld they now float unconscious, or, at most, with a twilight half-consciousness, wailing in a shrill diminutive voice, helpless, indifferent. . . . To speak of an "immortal life" of these souls, as scholars both ancient and modern have done, is incorrect. They can hardly be said to *live* even, any more than the image does that is reflected in the mirror. . . . The *psyche* may survive its visible companion, but it is helpless without it.[3]

Odysseus's Encounters with the Dead

Even though meeting with Tiresias is the entire raison d'être of Odysseus's harrowing trip to Hades, their encounter is disappointingly brief and anticlimactic. Tiresias comes to the pit and drinks the blood on offer before delivering his prophetic speech. Odysseus, he knows, wants a safe and quick journey home, but this is not going to happen. He has angered one of the gods, who will make life difficult for him. Here Tiresias is referring to one of Odysseus's earlier escapades, when he encountered and eventually blinded the giant cyclops Polyphemus, whose father, the sea god Poseidon, vowed vengeance; and since Odysseus's only way home is on the sea, this will create problems.

Even worse, Tiresias prognosticates an absolute disaster that could come from a different divine source, and later does: if the companions of Odysseus, out of desperation, eat the cattle dear to the sun god, Helios, they will incur his irreversible wrath and be slaughtered to a man. Moreover, even though Odysseus will survive and return home, he will find a completely fraught situation. His palace will be filled with wife Penelope's suitors (hoping he has died), desperate for her hand and eating her out of house and home while she decides whom to choose.

In the narrative of the *Odyssey* these predictions seem somewhat superfluous, since after his return from Hades Odysseus learns the same information from Circe herself. She could have saved him the trip. But readers of the epic are nonetheless glad he took it. The story gets more interesting with Odysseus's other encounters with shades of the dead, especially the one that comes next: his deceased mother, Anticleia.

She comes to him and drinks the blood, and her memory returns: "She knew me at once and wailed out in grief" (*Odyssey*, Book 11, line 175). She is amazed that her son has managed to arrive in the realm of the dead, and then comes a scene filled with pathos. Odysseus tries to embrace his beloved mother, but to no avail. She is an immaterial shade:

> *Three times I rushed toward her, desperate to hold*
> > *her,*
> *three times she fluttered through my fingers, sifting*
> > *away*
> *like a shadow, dissolving like a dream, and each time*
> *the grief cut to the heart, sharper . . . (Odyssey, Book*
> > *11, lines 235–38)*

Odysseus cries out his deep dismay: he longs to hold his mother and take joy together, but wonders if she is just "some wraith [*eidōlon*] that great Persephone sends my way / to make me ache with sorrow all the more" (*Odyssey*, Book 11, lines 244–45).

Anticleia replies:

> *"My son, my son, the luckiest man alive!*
> *This is no deception sent by Queen Persephone,*
> *this is just the way of mortals when we die.*
> *Sinews no longer bind flesh and bones together—*
> *the fire in all its fury burns the body down to ashes,*
> *once life slips from the white bones, and the spirit*
> > *[psychē]*
> *rustling, flitters away . . . flown like a dream"*
> > *(Odyssey, Book 11, lines 247–53)*

Heart-wrenching for Odysseus and awful for his readers. After death there is no flesh, there are no bones, or there is no body. What survives is simply the "breath," the "soul" [*psychē*], which escapes the body and lives on as a shade. It rustles and flitters like a dream in the appearance of the body but with no possibility of physical sensation or pleasure of any kind.

This gloomy outlook is confirmed when Odysseus encounters the shade of the greatest warrior of the Greek armies, Achilles himself. When they meet, Odysseus pronounces that Achilles is more blessed than anyone who has ever lived: because of his military prowess, the Greeks honor him "as a god." And now, Odysseus exclaims, "you lord it over the dead in all your power" (*Odyssey*, Book 11, line 552). He tells the valiant hero he has no reason to grieve at having died.

Achilles protests with the most memorable and moving words of the entire chapter:

> *"No winning words about death to me, shining*
> > *Odysseus!*
> *By god, I'd rather slave on earth for another man—*
> *some dirt-poor tenant farmer who scrapes to keep*
> > *alive—*
> *than rule down here over all the breathless dead."*
> (Odyssey, *Book 11, lines 555–58*)

How awful is it to be dead? It would be better to be the lowest, most impoverished, slave-driven nobody on earth than to be the king of the dead in gloomy Hades. And there is no turning back and no way to improve one's lot. That is the fate of virtually all who die.

There are, however, two kinds of exception: several extraordinarily few and fortunate people who, because they have family connections with gods, enjoy a better fate after death; and many who have it even worse because of the circumstances of their deaths.

Exceptional Dead That Prove the Rule

A better afterlife is not available to mere mortals, but the *Odyssey* recounts two exceptions for those with divine relations. Odysseus sees in Hades the god-man Heracles, who, according to Greek myth, had a mortal mother but whose father was actually Zeus. As it turns out, probably because of this mixed parentage and his resultant split personality, Heracles's fate is binary as well:

> And next I caught a glimpse of powerful Heracles—
> his ghost [eidōlon], I mean; the man himself
>   delights
> in the grand feasts of the deathless gods on high,
> wed to Hebe. (Odyssey, Book 11, lines 90–93)

It's not clear exactly how Heracles can be two places at once, but apparently his mortal self has the fate of shades while his immortal person—his real being—is having a grand ol' time in marital bliss at the heavenly banquets.

Another exception is the Greek king Menelaus, a central figure in the earlier epic, the *Iliad*, as it was his wife, Helen, who had been seduced away to Troy, leading to the ten-year conflict in the first place. In an earlier part of the *Odyssey* we learn that, unlike other mortals, Menelaus will have a pleasant happily ever after in the glorious "Elysian Fields" because of his divine connection: he is technically a divine son-in-law, since his espoused Helen, like Heracles, was born of Zeus (hence her incredible beauty). As Menelaus himself is told in Book 4 by the sea god Proteus:

> But about your own destiny, Menelaus,
> dear to Zeus, it's not for you to die

and meet your fate in the stallion-land of Argos,
no, the deathless ones will sweep you off to the
    world's end,
the Elysian Fields, where gold-haired Rhadamanthus
    waits,
where life glides on in immortal ease for mortal man;
no snow, no winter onslaught, never a downpour
    there
but night and day the Ocean River sends up breezes,
singing winds of the West refreshing all mankind.
All this because you are Helen's husband now—
the gods count you the son-in-law of Zeus (Odyssey,
    Book 4, lines 631–41)

A nice life if you can get it. But almost no one else can. It is not that Menelaus will die and his shade will go to heaven. Because he is a son-in-law of the king of the gods, he will never die but will instead be taken to the utopian Elysian Fields. These are not up in heaven, where, for example, the semi-divine Heracles resides, but on earth, in a place that is fantastically pleasant for all time.

In addition to these incredibly rare lucky exceptions, there are a large number of pathetically unlucky ones. You might think nothing could be worse than the banal, boring, and pleasure-less existence of the shades in Hades bemoaned by Anticleia and Achilles. As it turns out, there *is* something worse—not eternal torture but being refused admission into the realm of the dead at all, a fate endured in particular by those who have not received proper burial rites upon their deaths.

Odysseus sees thousands of these on his otherworldly journey, unburied shades who bemoan and curse their fate. Their horrible situation is expressed most clearly during Odysseus's encounter with one of his former companions, a soldier named Elpenor. Before Odysseus and

his men had set sail from Circe's island, the night before their sched-
uled departure, Elpenor, the youngest of the crew, drank himself virtually senseless, climbed up on Circe's roof to sleep, leapt up at dawn not
knowing where he was, fell off the roof, and broke his neck. His "soul
flew down to Death" (*Odyssey*, Book 11, line 72).

Apparently Odysseus hadn't known this, because when he comes to
the realm of the dead, the first one he meets—even before encounter-
ing Tiresias—is, to his surprise, "the ghost of Elpenor" (*Odyssey*, Book
11, line 57). The shade is deeply distressed, not because he has died but
because his corpse has not been given funeral rites of passage to the
underworld. He has been "unwept, unburied" (*Odyssey*, Book 11, line
60). Elpenor begs Odysseus not to leave him on Circe's islands without a
proper funeral:

> *I beg you! Don't sail off*
> *and desert me, left behind unwept, unburied, don't,*
> *or my curse may draw god's fury on your head.*
> *No, burn me in full armor, all my harness,*
> *heap my mound by the churning gray surf—*
> *Perform my rites, and plant on my tomb that oar*
> *I swung with mates when I rowed among the living.*
> (Odyssey, *Book 11, lines 79–87*)

Death is awful, but even worse is dying and being caught in a
no-man's-land between the living and the dead. Only the properly buried
are fully dead. Those who are not are in eternal agony, displaced forever.[4]

Of all the people who have ever died, there are only three mentioned
during Odysseus's trip to Hades who have it even worse than the displaced (*Odyssey*, Book 11, lines 660–89). These are the eternally tortured.
Such torments, it needs to be stressed, are not among the options for
most mortals. It is not clear why these three unfortunates were chosen in

particular.[5] It is true that all of them did something particularly offensive to the gods, but then again, so do a lot of people. Possibly the three stand in for everyone who fits that rather dire category. They are Tityus, the Titan who had tried to rape the goddess Leto, and who is sprawled out over nine acres while vultures eternally eat his liver; Tantalus, who had sacrificed his own son and cooked him in a meal provided to the gods, who for his torment has lovely food and drink kept barely outside his reach forever and ever; and Sisyphus, who had captured Death when it had been sent to him and locked it up, preventing people from dying, and who, as punishment, is compelled to push a boulder uphill only to have it roll down again over and over and over again without stopping.

Unlike everyone else, for these three, death is not death. They are being forced to make never-ending atonement in the afterlife for what they had done while living. These three will become the prototypes of hell as it develops later in Western traditions. [6]

The Influence of Homer

It is impossible to overrate the importance of Homer on the culture and religion of ancient Greece. It is not that the *Iliad* and the *Odyssey* were "the Bible" the way the Hebrew Scriptures or the New Testament were for later Jews and Christians. No one thought these epics were "the inspired and infallible Word of God." But they were thoroughly known and deeply influential for people in the Greek and Roman worlds as they thought about their lives and the nature of the divine realm. In particular, the views of the afterlife propounded by Homer were massively influential for centuries to come.

Evidence comes from the much later satirist Lucian of Samosata—some eight hundred or more years after Homer's day—who could lament the ongoing credulity of many in his own world, among "the general herd . . . [who] trust Homer and . . . other myth makers in these matters, and take their poetry for a law unto themselves. So they suppose that there is a place deep under earth called Hades, which is large, and roomy and murky and sunless."[7]

Not many people hold that view today. Most believe that when we die we either cease to exist or receive our due rewards. The latter too, though, is an ancient view, even if not set forth by Homer. It is not a view that originated in Jewish or Christian circles but in pagan ones—somewhat oddly, among the heirs of Homer. In fact, some such view can be seen in rather graphic terms in the writings of the most famous and talented imitator of Homer in the later Roman world, the great Latin poet Virgil (70–19 BCE), who like his Greek predecessor some seven centuries earlier, tells the story of a descent to the underworld.

Aeneas En Route to the Underworld

Virgil is best known for his epic the *Aeneid*, named for its main character, Aeneas, a fugitive from the Trojan War who, in the wake of Troy's disastrous defeat, through Greek deception and duplicity (the Trojan Horse), journeyed to Italy to found the city that would eventually lead to the emergence of Rome. The long epic, in short, is the history of the origins of the Roman people, told with all the disinterested observation of any nationalistic propaganda.

For our purposes, the key incident occurs in Book 6, a descent to Hades modeled on the account of Homer we have already considered. In the preceding book Aeneas and his men have left Sicily, where they celebrated the anniversary of the death of Anchises, Aeneas's father, and have arrived at Cumae, a port on the western coast of Italy. Aeneas is eager to visit the cavern of the famous Sibyl who lives there. The Sibyl was an ancient semi-divine prophetess who could predict the future when driven into a state of inspired prophetic ecstasy by the god Apollo. Aeneas wants to know his fate and whether he will ever reach his destiny. The Sibyl is the one, filled with the deity, who can tell him.

Aeneas finds the prophetess in her cave, and she immediately is overtaken by the god:

> *Suddenly all her features, all*
> *her color changes, her braided hair flies loose*
> *and her breast heaves, her heart bursts with frenzy,*
> *she seems to rise in height, the ring of her voice no*
> > *longer*
> *human—the breath, the power of god comes closer,*
> > *closer. (Aeneid, Book 6, lines 59–63)*[8]

The Sibyl cries out to Aeneas to pray; he does so, promising a glorious temple to Apollo and Diana if he can reach his destiny safely. The Sibyl—out of control and in the power of Apollo—warns of many dangers and disasters lying ahead of him. But he will reach his goal.

Aeneas then tells the Sibyl that he has heard that nearby "are the gates of Death's king / and the dark marsh where the Acheron [the river in the realm of the dead] comes flooding up" (*Aeneid*, Book 6, lines 126–27). He desperately wants to visit the realm of the dead to see his father. Can she tell him how to reach it?

The Sibyl informs him that it is, in fact, quite simple to get to the world of the dead. The problem is getting back:

> *Man of Troy, the descent to the Underworld is easy.*
> *Night and day the gates of shadowy Death stand*
> > *open wide,*

> *but to retrace your steps, to climb back to the upper*
>   *air—*
> *there the struggle, there the labor lies. Only a few,*
> *loved by impartial Jove or born aloft to the sky*
> *by their own fiery virtue—some sons of the gods*
> *have made their way. (Aeneid, Book 6, lines 149-*
>   *55)*[9]

But she instructs him on what he needs to do to undertake a journey to the underworld. He follows her instructions, and she accompanies him on the terrifying journey into a vast deep and dark cave that leads to the nether world.

> *There in the entryway, the gorge of hell itself,*
> *Grief and the pangs of Conscience make their beds,*
> *and fatal pale Disease lives there, and bleak Old Age,*
> *Dread and Hunger, seductress to crime, and grinding*
>   *Poverty,*
> *all, terrible shapes to see—and Death and deadly*
>   *Struggle. . . . War . . . raging Strife . . . (Aeneid,*
>   *Book 6, lines 312–19)*

Before he crosses over to the underworld itself, at the river Styx, Aeneas sees the soul of one of his erstwhile companions, Palinurus, the pilot of his ship, who, unknown to the protagonist, had been swept to sea and, coming to shore, been murdered by brutes who left him unburied. He pleads with Aeneas to find his corpse and provide the necessary burial rites, else he will never be allowed to cross the river to enter the realm of the dead. The curse of Elpenor lives on. The Sibyl, to Palinurus's relief, prophesies that he will indeed be buried with ceremony, and he departs in less anguish.

Aeneas and the Sibyl are allowed passage across the Styx. They pass the three-headed hound from hell, Cerberus, and encounter those who have died badly—that is, those who passed away in infancy, suicides, and lovers who died of a broken heart. They come to a place for the heroes of the upper world, who, as in the *Odyssey*, are nothing but powerless wraiths, "in terror before a fully armed man still alive." Virgil emphasizes the completely feeble state of the dead, even the greatest warriors on earth, once they encounter the vibrant Aeneas:

> *But the Greek commanders and Agamemnon's troops*
> *in phalanx,*
> *spotting the hero and his armor glinting through the*
> *shadows—*
> *blinding panic grips them, some turn tail and run*
> *as they once ran back to the ships, some strain*
> *to raise a battle cry, a thin wisp of a cry*
> *that mocks their gaping jaws.* (Aeneid, Book 6, lines
> 567–72)

Rewards and Punishments in the Afterlife

Most of the inhabitants of the underworld, however, are not to be found in one of these preliminary places. This is the very big difference from Homer. Now, in Virgil's telling, most of the souls in Hades are either being punished for their sins or rewarded for their upright lives.

Aeneas and the Sibyl come to a fork in the road. The right path leads to Elysium, the place of eternal happiness, but "the left-hand path torments / the wicked, leading down to Tartarus, path to doom" (*Aeneid*, Book 6, lines 631–32). Aeneas looks to his left and sees a cliff and an enormous fortress, around which rages a "blazing flood of lava, / Tartarus' River of Fire, whirling thunderous boulders" (*Aeneid*, Book 6, line 640). Contrary to what a modern reader might expect, this flaming river is not the place of torment; it is a burning moat to prevent escape from the fortress: the tormented have no choice but to remain.

Above the river is an enormous iron gate, so massive it can be moved by no one, not even the gods. Above it looms a high tower on which one of the three divine "Fates" crouches to keep watch over the entrance. We are not told exactly what is happening within this fortressed torture chamber, but what Aeneas hears from the distance should strike terror in the heart:

> *Groans resound from the depths, the savage crack of*
> > *the lash,*
> *the grating creak of iron, the clank of dragging*
> > *chains.* (Aeneid, Book 6, lines 647–48)

He asks the Sibyl why there are such punishments. She tells him that no pure soul can go to that place. Rhadamanthus, the divine judge of the underworld, rules there

> *with an iron hand*
> *censuring [people], exposing fraud, forcing*
> > *confessions*
> *when anyone up above, reveling in his hidden*
> > *crimes,*
> *puts off his day of atonement till he dies, the fool,*
> *too late . . . (Aeneid, Book 6, lines 658–62)*

If one departs life without making amends for whatever sins have been committed, there is no turning back. She then gives a litany of the relevant transgressions: hatred of brothers, killing of fathers, fraud, avarice, adultery, breaking of oaths, treason, incest. As to the fate of those guilty of such ill-advised transgressions:

> "Don't hunger to know their doom,
> what form of torture or twist of Fortune drags them
>   down.
> Some trundle enormous boulders, others dangle,
>   racked
> to the breaking point on the spokes of rolling wheels."
>   (Aeneid, Book 6, lines 710–13)

There are in fact innumerable crimes and commensurate torments. As the Sibyl reveals:

> "No, not if I had a hundred tongues and a hundred
>   mouths
> and a voice of iron too—I could never capture
> all the crimes or run through all the torments,
> doom by doom." (Aeneid, Book 6, lines 724–27)

Hell is not a happy prospect. But some avoid its torments, and those who do so can expect glorious ecstasies that beggar description. Aeneas and the Sibyl make their way to Elysium:

> They gained the land of joy, the fresh green fields,
> the Fortunate Groves where the blessed make their
>   homes.
> Here a freer air, a dazzling radiance clothes the fields
> and the spirits possess their own sun, their own stars.
>   (Aeneid, Book 6, lines 741–44)

They find people engaged in sport, dance, singing, and feasting. Among them are soldiers killed while fighting valiantly for their country, pure priests, faithful poets, and "those we remember well for the good they did mankind" (*Aeneid*, Book 6, lines 765–69). None of those living there has a fixed residence. They all "live in shady groves, / . . . settle on pillowed banks and meadows washed with brooks" (*Aeneid*, Book 6, lines 779–80). A glorious utopian existence.

And yet here, as in Book 11 of the *Odyssey*, there are some ambiguities that are hard to explain—or at least that have not been carefully worked out by the poet. Just as Odysseus's sword could threaten shades impervious to touch, so too here the souls feasting and playing sport have no physical existence. This becomes clear when Aeneas encounters his deceased father. Like Odysseus before him, he makes three fruitless attempts to embrace his parent:

> . . . *Aeneas pleaded, his face streaming tears.*
> *Three times he tried to fling his arms around his*
>   *neck,*
> *three times he embraced—nothing . . . the phantom*
> *sifting through his fingers,*
> *light as wind, quick as a dream in flight.* (Aeneid,
>   Book 6, lines 807–11)

Then Virgil departs from Homer by introducing an innovation. Most of the souls in the underworld are destined to live again. Virgil endorses the idea of reincarnation.

After his failed parental hug, Aeneas sees an enormous crowd of souls:

> *numberless races, nations of souls*
> *like bees in meadowlands on a cloudless summer day*
> *that settle on flowers . . .*

> . . . *and the whole field comes alive with a humming*
> *murmur.* (*Aeneid*, *Book 6, lines 815–19*)

Aeneas's father tells him these are "the spirits / owed a second body by the Fates" (*Aeneid*, Book 6, lines 823–24). They are allowed to drink from the river Lethe (i.e., Forgetfulness: those who drink from it lose their memory) and are set free from their cares. But before that can happen, they have to pay for the sins they committed in their bodies.

> *And so the souls*
> *are drilled in punishments, they must pay for their*
> *   old offenses.*
> *Some are hung splayed out, exposed to the empty winds,*
> *some are plunged in the rushing floods—their stains,*
> *their crimes scoured off or scorched away by fire.*
> *Each of us must suffer his own demanding ghost.*
> *Then we are sent to Elysium's broad expanse,*
> *a few of us even hold these fields of joy*
> *till the long days, a cycle of time seen through,*
> *cleanse our hard, inveterate stains and leave us clear*
> *ethereal sense, the eternal breath of fire purged and*
> *   pure.* (*Aeneid*, *Book 6, lines 854–64*)

Others, however, must return to life after a thousand years in order to have a second chance at it, in the hope they will do better this time.

The Invention of Hell and Heaven

There are obviously numerous similarities between the voyages to the afterlife of Odysseus and Aeneas, but one cannot help but be struck especially by the impressive differences. Some six or seven centuries after the Homeric epics, Virgil does not populate Hades with shades that all experience the same boring and pleasure-free existence. He writes of hellish torments for some and heavenly glories for others. Most have to be punished for their sins before being given a second chance at life. Why such a change from Homer? What has led to this invention of heaven and hell?

It is hard to say what among the enormous changes in the political, social, and cultural worlds between seventh-century Greece and first-century Rome might have effected the shift in thinking. But it is relatively easy to see what happened in the realm of ethical thought. Equity had become an issue. Thinkers came to believe that no one can live a life of sin, hurting others, offending the gods, pursuing only self-aggrandizement, enjoying, as a result, wealth, influence, and pleasure, and then die and get away with it. No: everyone will have to face a judge. The wicked, no matter how powerful and revered in this world, will pay a price in the next. Those who have done what is right, however, will be rewarded.

By the time of Virgil, these ideas had been around for centuries, popularized most importantly by the greatest philosopher of antiquity, Plato.

CHAPTER FOUR

Will Justice Be Done?
The Rise of Postmortem Rewards and Punishments

There were obvious problems with the concept of Hades imagined in the writings of Homer. If everyone has the same fate after death—whether noble or lowly, righteous or wicked, valiant or cowardly—then where is justice? Doesn't this life, in the end, make any sense? Isn't good behavior to be rewarded and evil punished? Won't I get a better hereafter than the brutal tyrant who tortures and kills for his own sadistic pleasure, or even that obnoxious fellow who lives across the street?

We have seen some hints of what we might call "differentiated" afterlives even in Homer. Three particularly wicked sinners are punished forever, and a very few individual humans, or semi-humans, related to the gods are rewarded. This differentiation is far more pronounced in Virgil's *Aeneid*, which portrays fantastic rewards for the upright and horrible punishments for sinners. In the centuries between Homer and Virgil, more than any other thinker and writer, it was Plato who developed the notion of postmortem justice for both the virtuous and the wicked.

Plato himself did not invent the idea of rewards and punishments in the afterlife. He was building on earlier views, as he himself tells us. But it was Plato who most influenced later thinking, leading ultimately to the views of heaven and hell that developed centuries later in the Christian tradition.

The Afterlife in Plato

The twentieth-century philosopher Alfred North Whitehead once said that the entire European philosophical tradition consisted of "a series of footnotes to Plato."[1] Among Plato's long-enduring contributions to Western thought, one stands out as unusually significant for later understandings of the afterlife: his view of the immortality of the soul, as articulated especially in the dialogue we have already examined, the *Phaedo*.

Today, when people reflect on the distinction between body and soul, they tend to think of the body as a material, visible object but of the soul as completely immaterial and invisible. It cannot be experienced by our senses in any way. Many ancient thinkers did not see it quite that way. In part that is because they lived long before the writings of the seventeenth-century philosopher René Descartes (1596–1650). Descartes passed on to Western posterity the dualistic idea that body is made up of matter but the soul is inherently immaterial. Before his time, however, it was believed that the soul was indeed material, but of a vastly different *kind* of material from the realities we normally encounter through our senses.[2]

In this older view, shared by many Greeks and Romans, some material entities are rather coarse and rough, and susceptible to sense perception—including rocks, trees, lions, and human bodies. But other material is very much more refined—literally finer—and therefore of higher quality. The soul is made up of that kind of material. It may be rarified "stuff" but it is still stuff. That can help explain some of the paradoxes you may have already noticed in our discussions of the after-life. If souls are completely immaterial in the modern sense, how can they have material sensations? How can they experience physical tor-ment or pleasure if they have no physical qualities? How can souls in the afterlife see, hear, taste, smell, or feel either pain or pleasure if they have no eyes, ears, tongue, nose, or nerve endings?

In modern understandings of the afterlife, that continues to be a real problem—and believers in postmortem rewards and punishments there-fore have to come up with additional explanations for how, in the afterlife, God allows or forces people to feel bodily pleasure or pain without a body. Many of the ancients would have had fewer problems with the paradox, because they believed the soul was made up of real substance. It may be refined, but it is still substance. That's why in Hades the shades can be seen.

But why can't they be touched? Why can't Odysseus hug his mother? It is because the stuff of the soul is far more refined than the coarse stuff that makes up the human body. This makes sense even in our post-Cartesian understanding of "stuff." Your hand is firmer "stuff" than either air or water, and so can pass through them. Since air and water, on the other hand, are less firm, they cannot pass through the hand. For some ancient Greeks the soul was more refined than the body, and so Odysseus's and Aeneas's arms pass right through the stuff. But since the soul is still made of stuff—highly refined as it is—it can hear, taste, speak, and so on. And that's why souls can feel pleasure and pain, and, after Homer, experience heaven and hell.

In the *Phaedo* the coarse material of the body is said to die but the refined soul is immortal and so lives on. And so Socrates says at one point that death is nothing other than "the release of the soul from the body" (*Phaedo* 64e). Or, as Plato says in another of his works, the *Laws*:

What gives each one of us his being is nothing else but his soul, whereas the body is no more than a shadow which keeps us company. So 'tis well said of the deceased that the corpse is but a ghost; the real man—the undying thing called the soul—departs to give account to the gods of another world, even as we are taught by ancestral tradition—an account to which the good may look forward without misgiving, but the evil with grievous dismay. (*Laws*, Book 12, 959a–b)[3]

This is an unusually interesting passage. For one thing, it seems to put the views of Homer in complete reverse. For Homer, the "real person" was the embodied flesh; the departed soul was simply a shade, the shadow of a person. For Plato it is the soul that is the real person; the body is the gross material that is to be sloughed off and left behind. Moreover, once that happens, when the soul leaves the body, it goes off to either a happy or a miserable fate.

What are these blessed and awful fates awaiting the person after death? When Plato discusses the ultimate fate of the soul, most commonly he shifts from his logical discourse to regale his readers with myths. Plato admits that his tales about the afterlife are in fact myths: stories meant to convey deeper truths. They are not literally true. They portray truths that are difficult to put into rational, logical discourse. Similar to what we have already seen in other texts, these Platonic myths are less about what really happens after death than about how someone should live in the present. Plato's overarching concern is not to give the geography and temperatures of heaven and hell but to show people how they should live in the present life as they pursue virtue and truth for the well-being of their souls.[4]

Plato's Basic Myth

The most straightforward statement of Plato's myths comes to us in the *Phaedo*. As always happens, in the back-and-forth Socrates hedges on the literal character of this myth by saying, "This is what we are told." The fact that Plato doesn't subscribe to the word-for-word accuracy of the account is shown by the fact that in different dialogues he actually tells different myths—for example, in the *Gorgias* and the *Republic*. But all his myths move toward the same point: the soul that is virtuous is rewarded and the one that is wicked is punished. The tales he tells about the afterlife are therefore meant to convey something he thinks is true in the present life. People should live virtuously, concerned not for the pleasures of the body but for the good of the soul.

Here is the myth from the *Phaedo*. When people die, Socrates says, their guardian spirits take them to the place of judgment, where they undergo the "necessary experiences" as long as required to rid them of their impurities. Souls that are impure are shunned by everyone in this other world and wander about "in utter desolation until certain times have passed." But those who are pure and sober enjoy "divine company" (*Phaedo* 107c).[5]

Socrates then goes into detail about various postmortem fates reserved for different kinds of persons (*Phaedo* 113d–114c). People who have lived a "neutral" life—that is, not being overly righteous or wicked— go to a place of purification, the Acherusian Lake, where they are both punished for their sins and rewarded for their good deeds. Others who are great sinners judged to be incurable, such as murderers, are sent off to Tartarus, never to be released. Those who have committed lesser sins—for example, violence against their parents—are sent to Tartarus for a year before being regurgitated into the Acherusian lake, where they shout out to those they have killed or harmed. Only if and when their victims agree can they be released from their torment. Finally, those who have lived lives of surpassing holiness are released at death and pass up to the pure realm above. "And of these such as have purified themselves sufficiently by philosophy live thereafter altogether without bodies."

After detailing the myth, Socrates hedges again: "Of course, no reasonable person ought to insist that the facts are exactly as I have described them, but that either this or something very like it is a true account of our souls and their future habitations." That is, his description is largely figurative. What is literal is the meaning conveyed by the myth: one should live a life of virtue, and that will bring its own reward. Wickedness leads only to misery.

The Myth of Er

Such teachings are embodied in more explicit myths in Plato's other writings. The most famous is the Myth of Er, which comes at the very end of Plato's longest dialogue, the *Republic*, a work which sets out at length Plato's understanding of the ideal state. Plato believed that the political state should be designed to help people live optimally through a life of philosophy. The ideal state was therefore to be led by a group of philosopher-kings who promoted lives that were good, just, and virtuous. After spending many, many pages laying out what that utopian state would be like, Plato ends his dialogue by moving from logical discourse to myth, in this case a myth that entails a near-death experience. In its immediate context, the function of the myth is to show that people need to work to live good and just lives (*Republic* 613a–b). It is by the "practice of virtue" that a person can be "likened unto God so far as that is possible" (613b). The rewards for righteous living are great during life—and even greater after death (614a). That is what this "tale" is to convey.[6]

The myth is about a man named Er, a brave warrior from Pamphylia, who is slain in battle but who revives twelve days later on his funeral pyre. After coming back he tells his near-death experience. When Er died, his soul went from his body and came with a large company of others to a mysterious region that had two openings side by side in the sky and two others in the earth. Judges were sitting between these openings and were sending souls either up above through one of the holes in the sky or down below though a hole in the earth, depending on whether they were just or unjust. Er was an exception. He was told that he was to be a messenger to people back on earth of what took place in these places of judgment.

The other two holes—one coming from above and the other from below—were for souls returning from one fate or the other. Dirty and dusty souls appeared out of the lower hole and pure and clean ones from the upper. All of these went together off to a meadow as if to a festival, and there they regaled one another with the stories about what they had experienced over the past one thousand years, one group wailing and lamenting their horrific experiences below and the other reveling in the fantastic pleasures they had enjoyed above. All the sins that had been committed in life by the souls in the underworld were punished ten times over; the good deeds of the pure souls were correspondingly rewarded. But the worst of sinners—tyrants and others guilty of great crimes—were not allowed to leave the place of punishment even after a thousand years. Instead, "savage men of fiery aspect" bound them, threw them down, flayed them, dragged them over thorns, and hurled them into Tartarus (616a).

After the souls had spent seven days in the meadow telling each other what they had experienced during the preceding millennium, they were taken to another place where the divine Fates resided. All souls now were to be sent back to earth to live again in new incarnations, as either humans or beasts. Lots were cast and according to which was drawn, the soul could decide its next life. Some souls chose to become the wealthiest and most powerful people, not realizing, apparently, as rather slow learners, that this would lead to punishment later. Others were thoroughly disgusted with the possibilities of human life and chose to become animals. A full range of choices was possible.

As might be expected, those souls that had suffered most under the earth were circumspect in their choice. Among them, those who chose lives of wisdom chose best. They would be rewarded later. Once all the choices were made, the souls were directed to drink from the River of Forgetfulness before entering their new bodies. Er was not allowed to drink, but he returned to life, not knowing how, to tell the tale.

Socrates concludes the myth by drawing its lesson:

> And so . . . if we are guided by me we shall believe that the soul is immortal and capable of enduring all extremes of good and evil, and so we shall hold ever to the upward way and pursue righteousness with wisdom always and ever. . . . And thus both here and in that journey of a thousand years, whereof I have told you, we shall fare well. (*Republic* 621d)

It should be clear that Plato does not literally believe the myth he has just told any more than he believes there was a historical Er who actually had a near-death experience. He calls the tale a "fine story" and admits that anyone listening to him will probably think the story is a "myth." For him the tale is "true," but not literally true. It is true in the sense that it conveys the truth that people should prefer to suffer injustice than commit it, that they should actually be good instead of simply seeming to be. In short, the myth of Er is about how we should live: focused not on the body and its desires, passions, and pleasures but on virtue, justice, and wisdom.

It should be stressed, however, that to make his points about how to live, Plato employs common conceptions, with his own twists, of what will happen after death. That shows that even if he invented this particular myth of Er, he is not making up the idea of postmortem rewards and punishments on which it is based. He is using an understanding of the nature of the afterlife that would have been perfectly believable to a Greek audience in the fourth century BCE.

This understanding is embedded in numerous other writings of

Greek and Roman antiquity, and we can probably assume that whatever Plato thought about their literal truth, they were accepted by many or even most people at the time.

Going to the Underworld with Aristophanes

Sometimes authors express these views of the afterlife with dead seriousness. At other times they are recounted with a lively sense of humor. There have always been thinking people who are not afraid to laugh at death, one of whom was Plato's older contemporary, the very funny comic dramatist Aristophanes (circa 450–circa 388 BCE). Of direct relevance to our interests here is one of Aristophanes's most humorous plays, *The Frogs*, an account of a descent to the underworld—not by a mere mortal but by the god Dionysus, along with his sidekick slave Xanthias. The play obviously involves satire, but for satire to be effective it needs to spoof views that are widely held. Some of the play's descriptions of life below therefore would certainly have resonated with many in the play's audience.

There is a very serious undertone to this funny play, connected with the immediate context within which it was produced. At end of the fifth century, Athens was experiencing a very serious political and military crisis at the climax of the Peloponnesian War, and was desperately in need of leadership and sage advice. Thus the plot of the play: Dionysus wants to go to the underworld to bring back from the dead the greatest tragic playwright to provide the necessary direction to the state, possible only from the lips of one of its great intellectual figures. Dionysus proposes to interview the two leading candidates: Aeschylus and Euripides, known still today, along with Sophocles, as the great dramatists of the fifth century. The second half of *The Frogs* is taken up with the interviews. But the first half is about the trip to Hades and what Dionysus and Xanthias find there.

As almost always happens—as we have seen with both Odysseus and Aeneas—the journeyer needs some instruction about how to contact the dead in their place of residence. And so the play begins with Dionysus and Xanthias paying a visit to Heracles, the demigod who, for one of his famous Twelve Labors, had had to make a descent to Hades. Heracles tells them how to get there and what to expect when they arrive. They will find places of punishment and blessing.

The former will include "the Great Muck Marsh and the Eternal River of Dung."[7] These will be the abodes of "pretty unsavory characters floundering about." Specifically, such punishments will be reserved for those who have wronged a guest (thought to be an unforgivable sin for much of antiquity), not paid a young partner in pederasty (pederasty itself was widely approved of, but the elder partner needed to take care of the youth), struck one of their parents, or committed perjury.

Other punishments are not specified in this allusive text, although at one point the judge of the dead, the divine Aeacus, mistakenly thinks that Dionysus is Heracles making a return journey and, offended at what Heracles did the first time—when he stole the hellhound Cerberus—threatens to "have you flung over the cliff, down to the black hearted Stygian rocks, and you'll be chased by the prowling hounds of Hell and the hundred headed viper will tear your guts and the Tartessian lamprey shall devour your lungs and the Tithrasian Gorgons can have your kidneys." A variety of creative and horrifying torments awaited those on the wrong side of divine justice.

On the other hand, before embarking, Dionysus and Xanthias are told they will also find a bright and happy place, with "plantations of myrtle, and happy bands of revelers, men and women, tripping around and clapping their hands." These are said to be the "initiates," by which Aristophanes means people who had been inducted into what scholars commonly call the "mystery cults." These are religions that had become increasingly popular in Greek antiquity, which required initiation into the secrets of the god or goddess; those initiated would enjoy a particularly intimate relationship with the divine being and be guaranteed a much improved situation in the afterlife.

When Dionysus and Xanthias arrive at the place of blessing, they do indeed find a group of initiates singing their joy:

> *Let us hasten to the meadow, where the roses are so*
> *sweet,*
> *and the little flowers grow in profusion at our feet;*
> *with the blessed Fates to lead us we will laugh and*
> *sing and play,*
> *and dance the choral dances in our traditional way.*
> *Oh to us alone is given, when our earthly days are*
> *done,*
> *to gaze upon the splendor of a never-setting sun;*
> *for we saw the holy Mysteries and heard the god's*
> *behest,*
> *and were mindful of our duty both to kinsperson and*
> *to guests.*

Obviously this is far better than dwelling forever in the Muck Marsh or the River of Dung. But it is striking that such ecstasies are reserved not for those who focus on philosophy and the good of the soul rather than the pleasures of the body, as in Plato, but for those who have been initiated into a mystery religion.

A Not-So-True Story

From centuries later, and in the Roman world rather than in Greece, we come back to one of the great humorists of antiquity we have met before, the satirist Lucian of Samosata. Lucian's dialogues tend to be very short—unlike those of Plato—and filled with fictional creatures. A number of them narrate visits to the underworld, always told tongue-in-cheek, not meant to explain what one can really expect but using widespread assumptions to paint humorous pictures that convey serious points—principally about how not to live. Lucian especially delights in showing the afterlife torments of the very wealthy and the very powerful.

One of Lucian's longer works is called, with full irony, "A True Story." In fact, at the outset of the tale, Lucian tells his reader that in it "I've told all sorts of lies with an absolutely straight face." Later he indicates that "the one and only truth you'll hear from me is that I *am* lying; by frankly admitting that there isn't a word of truth in what I say, I feel I'm avoiding the possibility of attack from any quarter."[8] The story is about Lucian's own alleged adventures on his travels, some of the time in outer space—spoofing travel narratives and histories found in older writers such as Herodotus and Thucydides. Along the way Lucian has a journey to the afterlife, described in terms that are patently more fictional even than anything found in Plato. As Lucian says, "I'm writing about things I neither saw nor heard of from another soul, things which don't exist and couldn't possibly exist. So all readers beware: don't believe any of it!"

The story begins with Lucian and his companions taking a sea journey past the Straits of Gibraltar, where their ship gets caught up in a whirlwind and ends up airborne, eventually landing on the moon, which is inhabited by "moon people" who are at war with "sun people." What ensues is a space battle worthy of later science fiction. When Lucian's ship returns to earth, it is swallowed by a whale that is 150 miles in length, in which Lucian and his companions meet others who have been stranded inside for years. When they emerge, after several adventures, they sail on to the realms of the afterlife.

First they pass by "five enormous islands" with "huge flames . . . spurting from their summits." Obviously these are places of torment, but unlike the roughly contemporary Christian author of the *Apocalypse of Peter*, Lucian does not describe the various tortures being experienced by their inhabitants. Instead, in this work at least, he wants to focus on the blessings reserved for those who are rewarded after death. The ship comes to a low, flat island that wafts scents of perfume and is filled with harbors, crystal clear rivers, meadows, woods filled with songbirds, sweet-blowing breezes, and people at a banquet with music and singing. After they make landfall, they wander up to a meadow filled with flowers and are captured by the inhabitants, who, instead of shackling them, garland them with roses and take them to the ruler of this "Isle of the Blessed." They are allowed to stay on the island and attend a banquet for the great people who live there.

Lucian describes the city where these greats dwell. Anyone familiar with the biblical description of the New Jerusalem in the world to come in Revelation 21 cannot help but be struck by the similarities: the city is made of gold and surrounded by walls of emerald; it has seven gates made with cinnamon wood; its foundation and streets are made of ivory; there are temples to the gods made of beryl, inside each of which is an altar of amethyst; around the city flows a river of myrrh two hundred feet wide and deep enough to swim in. As to the inhabitants of the city,

[they] are disembodied, i.e., they are without flesh or substance. They have a discernible outline and form, but no more than this. In spite of having no body they stand and move, think and talk; in short, it's as if their naked souls were walking about clad in the semblance of their bodies. Without testing them by touch you would never know you weren't looking at actual bodies; they're like shadows, but shadows that stand erect and have color; they never grow old but remain the age they were when they arrive.

The island itself is covered with a soft light at all times and experiences eternal spring. The countryside is lush with all varieties of flowers and fruit trees. The vines and trees bear fruit twelve times a year and so are harvested monthly. The wheat stalks do not produce grain but full loaves of bread at their tops, making them look like giant mushrooms. Around the city are 365 springs of water, 365 of honey, 500 of myrrh, 7 of milk, and 8 of wine.

The banquet for the deceased greats is held in a lovely meadow called the Elysian field; its inhabitants are sprawled out on mounds of flowers. They are served by the winds, with much music and singing—mainly of the Homeric epics. All the demigods are there, along with the veterans of the Trojan War and Socrates, everyone making love, publicly, with others of both sexes, sharing sexual partners with no shame.

Obviously the account is meant to be humorous, but there is a very interesting aspect to it as well: the ecstasies are very physical and bodily— precisely the opposite of what Plato wants to emphasize. To stress the idea, with pointed irony Lucian places Socrates there amid all the food, wine, and random sex, enjoying with all others the eternal pleasures of the flesh.

The Naysayers and Skeptics: Epicurus

Some ancient philosophers found such views of postmortem blessings and curses very disturbing and disruptive—not for themselves personally but for people at large. There was a strong minority position that maintained that tales of the afterlife, and the beliefs based on them, were damaging to a person's well-being, since they corresponded to no reality. In this alternative view, the horrors of the afterlife in particular were pure fictions that not only terrorized innocent people but forced them to behave in ways contrary to their health and happiness. Of those who held such skeptical views, none was more important than the Greek philosopher Epicurus (341–270 BCE).

Throughout history Epicurus has had a completely undeserved reputation as a hedonist, interested only in promoting physical pleasure. This, in fact, is a mischaracterization of his views. Like many philosophers in antiquity, Epicurus was interested in knowing how a person could lead the best life with the greatest amount of happiness. It is true that, in his view, the happiest life was one that avoided pain and promoted pleasure. But not wild licentious pleasure. Quite the contrary, intense pleasure only leads to pain, as human experience abundantly shows: binge drinking produces blackouts and nasty hangovers; sexual abandon can lead to social trauma, not to mention some rather serious physical effects; massive culinary overindulgence can make a person a corporeal wreck; and so on. Instead, Epicurus argued for the simple pleasures: moderate food and drink, good friends, intelligent discussions on important and compelling topics.

Happiness also requires people to understand what it means to be human and not to allow baseless and irrational fears to overwhelm their mental lives. No fear, for Epicurus, is more irrational than the fear of death, based as it is on a profound misunderstanding of what it means to be human, specifically about what it means to have a soul.

Epicurus firmly believed that the soul is a corporeal entity, made up of a kind of matter. It consists of a large number of fine particles dispersed throughout the body. Only when the soul is united with the body is sense perception possible. When at death the soul separates from the body, its atoms are simply dispersed into the air. At that point, the body, lacking its soul, can no longer feel anything. But neither can the dissipated and therefore no-longer-existing soul.

Epicurus points out in his writings that when a person loses a body part—say, a hand by amputation—the body as a whole can still have feeling. The soul has not departed. But "when the whole [body] is destroyed, the soul is scattered and no longer has the same powers" . . . including the power of "sense-perception."[9] Since a departed and therefore dispersed soul no longer exists, it cannot be rewarded or punished. It simply disappears.

That is why Epicurus repeatedly insists there is nothing to fear in death. As he says most trenchantly in one of the preserved fragments of his works, quoted by his ancient biographer Diogenes Laertius, "Death is nothing to us. For what has been dissolved has no sense-experience, and what has no sense-experience is nothing to us" (Diogenes Laertius, *Lives of Eminent Philosophers*, 10, 139).[10] Or as he writes to a man named Menoeceus, in one of the few letters that is preserved:

> Get used to believing that death is nothing to us. For all good and bad consists in sense-experience, and death is the privation of sense-experience. Hence a correct knowledge of the fact that death is nothing to us makes mortality of life a matter for contentment, not by adding a limitless time [to life] but by removing the longing for immortality. (*Diogenes Laertius*, Book 10, 124)

Or, in a clear summary of his views:

> So death, the most frightening of bad things, is nothing to us; since when we exist, death is not present, and when death is present, then we do not exist. Therefore, it is relevant neither to the living nor to the dead, since it does not affect the former, and the latter do not exist. (*Diogenes Laertius*, Book 10, 125)[11]

For people who enjoy thinking about the glories of the hereafter, these notions will not seem to be particularly good news. But they are especially intended for those who fear the afterlife and live in dread of it. Epicurus insists there is nothing to fear. You won't feel a thing and will not even know that you do not feel a thing. This is the long, deep, dreamless sleep of Socrates.

Lucretius on the Nature of Reality

Not many philosophers in antiquity were persuaded by Epicurus's views. In some ways, the deeply rooted human sense that this life cannot be all there is proved too strong. So far as we know, humans have always imagined there must be life beyond. Possibly, in part, that is because individual humans have always—as long as they have been able to think—known nothing other than existence, making it very difficult indeed to imagine a never-experienced state of nonexistence. But, for whatever reason, the understanding of death that made such brilliant sense to Epicurus did not catch on, either among professional thinkers or the population at large.

There were some notable exceptions, however, the most famous of whom appeared in Roman circles over two centuries later: Epicurus's latter-day disciple Lucretius (circa 98–55 BCE). Unlike Epicurus, for whom we have only a few scant literary remains, Lucretius has bequeathed to us an entire philosophical work, openly and proudly indebted to the views of the one he considered the greatest philosopher of all time. The book, called *On the Nature of Things*, tries to accomplish nothing less than to explain the nature of reality. In it Lucretius develops a theory that may sound remarkably prescient. Everything in the world, all that we experience and do not experience, is made up of atoms that have come together in chance combinations over infinite amounts of time as they run into each other in infinite reaches of space. We ourselves are the products of matter, time, and chance. As such, we will eventually dissipate as our atoms dissolve their connections. Dissolved with them will be not only our bodies, which obviously disappear eventually, but also our souls.

In many ways, Lucretius's entire treatise on the atomic basis for all reality is meant to accomplish a specific aim: to dispel the fear of death and destroy any foolish notions of life beyond the grave. As he says at one point in the book, he seeks to "drive out neck and crop that fear of Hell which blasts the life of a person from its very foundations, sullying everything with the blackness of death and the leaving no pleasure pure and unalloyed."[12] He profoundly realizes the grip the power of death can hold over a person: "As children in bland darkness tremble and start at everything, so we in broad daylight are oppressed at times by fears as baseless as those horrors which children imagine coming upon them in the dark." He goes on to explain how to deal with such baseless fears: "This dread and darkness of the mind cannot be dispelled by the sunbeams . . . but only by an understanding of the outward form and inner workings of nature."

As with many ancient philosophers, Lucretius believed that a correct understanding of physics—in his case, the atomic basis for all reality—could have moral and spiritual consequences. He thus has a lot to say about the relationship of a person's mind and body. In his view, both grow together as a person matures, and therefore, naturally, both decay together. He points out that just as "our hand or eye or nostrils in isolation from us cannot experience sensation or even exist . . . so mind cannot exist apart from body and from the person who is, as it were, a vessel for it."

In other words, if your eye is gouged out, or your index finger amputated, it no longer has any feeling, since it is no longer connected to the rest of your body. So too if your soul leaves your body, it can experience no sensation. Indeed, when the soul parts from the body, it does not even exist as some kind of unified entity. "When the body has perished there is an end also of the spirit diffused through it."

The practical conclusion strikes Lucretius as inevitable: a person who no longer exists cannot suffer—any more than she or he suffered *before* coming into existence, or had any sensation at all. Lucretius points out that the wars that devastated Rome in the generations before he was born did not concern him at the time; he knew nothing about them, since he didn't exist. Nor will he exist after his death, so nothing will concern him then either. Or, as he says even more graphically: "Look back at the eternity that passed before we were born, and mark how utterly it counts to us as nothing. This is a mirror that nature holds up to us, in which we may see the time that shall be after we are dead."

Such views were held by others of the most highly educated and philosophically inclined authors from Greek and Roman antiquity. As just one example, the great Roman orator Cicero declared: "If souls are mortal, we can have no doubt . . . that destruction in death is so complete that not even the faintest vestige of sensation is left behind." He then draws the natural conclusion that if the soul dies, "what evil can there be in this, seeing that death does not appertain to the living or to the dead? The dead do not exist and the living it will not touch."[13]

Varieties of Belief Among the Masses

But what did people who did not dwell in the rarified world of the philosophical elite think? As it turns out, it is nearly impossible to know, and for a simple reason: the common folk have left us no writings. Unlike today, when almost everyone you know is literate and able to write, say, a reasonably legible and sensible letter, the vast majority of people in Greek and Roman antiquity—85 to 90 percent of the population—was illiterate.[14] So how can we know what they thought and believed?

One obvious way is to see what the upper-crust elite who did write say about these voiceless others. The problem is that we can never fully trust that a wealthy aristocrat will fairly represent the views of people he considers low-lifes and outcasts—that is, everyone but his family, friends, and people like them. Still, there are some references to widely held views that appear to be reasonably on target, since the author who mentions them is not simply summarizing what he imagines others are thinking but is trying to convince people they should think differently. That presupposes that he knows what they commonly said, or thinks he does. That could be the case, for example, with the second-century philosopher-priest Plutarch, who wrote a treatise attacking those in the general population who were inordinately "superstitious," who feared the "undying evils" of the afterlife, torments that "never cease":

> Rivers of fire and offshoots of the Styx are mingled together, darkness is crowded with specters of many fantastic shapes which beset their victim with grim visages and piteous voices, and besides these, judges and tor-turers and yawning gulfs and deep recesses teeming with unnumbered woes. (*On Superstition* 4)

Clearly, people with views like these could use a good dose of Epicu-rus. But were such notions widespread? My guess is that they were—just as they are today or, probably, even far more so then. But it's a guess.

Since we have so little literary evidence for knowing the views of hoi polloi, scholars have looked to nonliterary evidence, the material remains from antiquity that might give us clues to what regular ol' folk who were not among the educated upper classes may have believed.[15] On first reflection, this would seem to be a helpful approach. If we could see what kinds of goods were left around grave sites, for example, possibly these would be indicators of what people thought happened to the body after death. On this score archaeologists have indeed made remarkable progress, showing that, broadly throughout the Greco-Roman world, it was common for family members to leave personal belongings and cooking vessels in or near tombs. Wouldn't that suggest that the survi-vors believed the departed would want some of their beloved possessions on the other side, and possibly need to cook their meals?

It certainly *could* mean that. But the problem with material remains is that they are silent: they don't provide their own interpretations. And that means various interpretations are possible. When my family buried my father with his favorite pipe, it was not because we thought he'd be wanting a good smoke in the world to come. The same may have been true in antiquity: favorite or useful objects may simply have been left as memorials.

So too with a phenomenon not widely attested in the modern world. Archaeologists have uncovered numerous tombs from Greco-Roman antiquity with feeding tubes coming up to the surface, where sustenance could be poured down for the deceased. That may seem very odd, but doesn't it suggest that the deceased were understood to be hungry and thirsty and would appreciate their favorite consumables on occasion? Again, that is perfectly plausible, but it is not necessarily right. Even today people are known to pour libations on tombs, for example—not so much to indicate a belief that the departed would like a bit of their favorite whiskey on occasion as to engage in a memorial rite.[16]

Among the material remains that have come down to us from ancient Greece and Rome, the most useful are epitaphs: inscriptions placed on tombstones.[17] We have hundreds of thousands of inscriptions from antiquity, and as it turns out, epitaphs make up the majority of them. These indeed can be helpful, but there are also complications. Many of the inscriptions have worn out and can no longer be read. Among those that can be read, most of them comprise only a few identifiable letters or, at most, the name of the deceased. Very few give us any concrete indication about what the survivors believed had happened to the person; those that do mention an afterlife are highly formulaic, simply giving generalized phrases (ancient equivalents of "Rest in Peace"). And those that do give us more are usually susceptible to various interpretations.

But still, there are some useful specimens. Those that refer explicitly to an afterlife for the person (the tiny minority of inscriptions) almost always assume that the body dies and the soul goes somewhere else to live. Lots of inscriptions say things like "the soul . . . has fluttered away" or "your soul has escaped the body" or "air has taken their soul and earth their body" and so on. As you might expect from reading modern obituaries, only rarely—very rarely—does the inscription, set up by the mourning survivors, say anything negative. If any tone at all can be detected, it is invariably hopeful and positive. And so there are inscriptions that talk of the person going off to "the company of the blessed" or to "the worshipful house of Zeus" or "to the immortal abode in the sky" and so on.

It is worth noting that even though inscriptions do not talk about the departed roasting in hell, there are a number that side with Epicurus in denying there is an afterlife at all. Often these inscriptions are set up, ironically, as words coming from the deceased to the living. For example, one brief inscription simply says:

If you want to know who I am, the answer is ashes and burnt embers.

Another is more expansive:

> *We are nothing.*
> *See reader, how quickly*
> *We mortals return*
> *From nothing to nothing.*[18]

One of the fullest and most interesting of such inscriptions makes a rather emphatic denial of any life to come, addressed to anyone walking by the tomb:

Wayfarer, do not pass by my epitaph, but stand and listen, and then, when you have learned the truth, proceed. There is no boat in Hades, no ferryman Charon, no Aeacus keeper of the keys, nor any dog named Cerberus. All of us who have died and gone below are bones and ashes:

there is nothing else. What I have told you is true. Now withdraw, way-farer, so that you will not think that, even though dead, I talk too much.[19]

The one inscription I have always found even more amusing (and moving) is a seven-letter Latin abbreviation that was as widely used in antiquity as "R.I.P." ("Rest in Peace," itself from the Latin *requiescat in pace*) has been in the modern world. The abbreviation is "n.f. f. n.s. n.c." Translated, it provides a most trenchant summary of the materialist views endorsed and promoted by Epicurus, Lucretius, and their followers: *non fui, fui, non sum, non curo*—"I was not. I was. I am not. I care not."

CHAPTER FIVE

Death After Death in
the Hebrew Bible

I t is often said, and widely believed, that views of the afterlife in
ancient Israel were quite different from those found in the surrounding pagan world. After all, the Israelites had a fundamentally different religion, a monotheistic faith in the one Creator God who had called
Israel to be his people. And there are indeed many distinctive features
of Israelite understandings of the afterlife. But there are also numerous
similarities with Greco-Roman views.

One thing they held in common was the deeply rooted sense of the
inevitability and finality of death, a view that can be found in a number
of passages of the Hebrew Bible. Thus, in the book of 2 Samuel, which
records events that would have occurred in the early tenth century BCE,
an anonymous woman is depicted as urging the great king David to for-
give the heinous transgression of his son Absalom by reminding him that
death is the end of the story: "We must all die; we are like water spilled on
the ground, which cannot be gathered up" (2 Samuel 14:14). An accepted
truism in a brilliant image, an ancient expression of the law of entropy:
once dispersed, life can never be retrieved.

Another striking image comes in the words of the famous skeptic Job:

> *As waters fail from a lake*
> *and a river wastes away and dries up, so mortals lie*
> > *down and do not rise again;*
> *until the heavens are no more, they will not awake*
> *or be roused from their sleep. (Job 14:11–12)*

For this great poet of the ancient Israelite tradition, life comes no more once a person is dead. There is no life after death. Only death after death.[1]

The Nature of Death

Even if death is inevitable for the ancient Israelites, what is it? For most of the Hebrew Bible, death is what happens when life leaves a person. And so we have the prayer of the psalmist, lamenting to God what is certain to come: "When you take away their breath, they die and return to the dust" (Psalm 104:29). Here the person does not "go someplace"—other than back to the dust they came from. Humans were originally made from dust (Genesis 2:7) and that is where they return.

This is one key difference from the Greek thought represented best by Plato. Ancient Israelites did not subscribe to the view of the immortality of the soul. Souls are not inherently deathless, destined for an eternal existence. In ancient Hebrew thought, there was no "soul" in the Greek sense. This can be seen by the different terms used. The closest equivalent to the Greek *psychē* is the Hebrew *nephesh*. The *nephesh*, though, is not a soul, set in contrast to the body. Hebrew anthropology was not dualistic (body and soul) but unitary. *Nephesh* means something like "life force" or "life" or even "breath." It is not a substance that can leave a person and exist independently of the body. It is the thing that makes bodies live. When the body stops breathing, it becomes dead matter. In modern terms, when you stop breathing, your breath doesn't go somewhere. It just stops. So too with the Hebrew *nephesh*. The person is then dead.

But does the person then live on in any sense? It depends on which part of the Hebrew Bible you read.

Locations of Death in the Hebrew Bible

The Jewish scriptures contain a variety of views about what happens to a person at death. Most commonly, a person who dies is simply said to have gone to "death"—a term used some thousand times in the Bible. Better known but far less frequent, a person's ultimate destination is sometimes called "Sheol," a term whose meaning and etymology are debated. It occurs over sixty times in the Hebrew Bible, and there is unanimity among critical scholars that in no case does Sheol mean "hell" in the sense people mean today. There is no place of eternal punishment in any passage of the entire Old Testament. In fact—and this comes as a surprise to many people—nowhere in the entire Hebrew Bible is there any discussion at all of heaven and hell as places of rewards and punishments for those who have died.

Probably most people who read the Bible think of Sheol as a Jewish kind of Hades, a shadowy place where everyone goes and all are treated the same, a banal and uninteresting netherworld where nothing really happens and people are, in effect, bored for all eternity. But in fact, in most passages of the Bible where Sheol is mentioned, it may well simply be an alternative technical term for the place where an individual is buried—that is, their grave or a pit.

This can be seen throughout the poetic books of the Hebrew Bible, such as the Psalms, where most of the references to Sheol can be found. To make sense of what I want to say about the matter, it is important to recognize a significant literary feature of Hebrew poetry. Poetry in books such as Psalms, Proverbs, Job, and extensive passages of the prophets did not use rhyming schemes as in much English poetry. Instead of rhyming "sounds" at the end of lines, Hebrew poetry could be said to have rhymed "ideas." There were various ways a poet could set up an idea-rhyming scheme, but the most common was to express the same idea in parallel lines using different words. In this scheme the second line simply rephrases the idea of the first. You can see this use of "synonymous parallelism" throughout any poetic section of the Hebrew Bible. Consider some verses from Psalm 2, for example.

> *Why do the nations conspire*
> *and the peoples plot in vain? (Psalm 2:1)*

As you can see, the second line reinforces the first by restating the idea in different words, with possibly a slight amplification: Nations/people; conspire/plot. So to the next lines:

> *The kings of the earth set themselves,*
> *and the rulers take counsel together. . . .*
> *[But] He who sits in the heavens laughs;*
> *the LORD has them in derision. (Psalm 2:2, 4)*

Thus in parallel lines we have "kings"/"rulers"; "set themselves"/"counsel together"; "He who sits in the heavens laughs"/"the LORD has them in derision."

I want to stress this point because it is a key to interpretation of Hebrew poetry. In synonymous parallelism, the ideas of the two lines are fundamentally the same, even when put in different words. And that is significant for understanding how the Israelite poets understood "Sheol."

It is often parallel precisely to terms such as "pit" and "grave," the place where the body is buried. In these places it does not appear to be used to refer to a gathering spot for souls destined for eternal banality. For example, in one place the psalmist thanks God for preserving him from premature death:

> For you do not give me up to Sheol
> or let your faithful one see the Pit. (Psalm 16:10)

Another place provides a reflection on the foolish who do not obey the LORD:

> Like sheep they are appointed for Sheol;
> Death shall be their shepherd;
> Straight to the grave they descend. . . .
> Sheol shall be their home. (Psalm 49:14)

Here the synonyms for Sheol are "death" and "the grave."

I do not want to insist that every ancient Israelite author thought of Sheol simply as the burial place for a corpse. Some may well have extended the idea into a broader metaphor as the "place" that people go.[2] And so some of the Patriarchs of Israel talk about "going down to Sheol" (e.g., Genesis 37:35; see 42:38), and a rebellious band of Israelites is swallowed up by the earth and taken down, while still alive, to Sheol (Numbers 16:30–33). It is certainly possible that some of these authors were imagining Sheol as an actual holding pen for the dead, a pen never to be escaped. On the other hand, perhaps these uses were also meant to be metaphorical, simply to refer to the fact that people die and are buried: hence they "go down."[3]

The Nature of Sheol

Whether Sheol was a place or, as seems more likely to me, simply in most instances the grave, the Hebrew poets say a good deal about it, and none of it very good. It clearly was not a place of reward for the righteous. On the contrary, Sheol was the realm of death, to be avoided as long as possible. It is not that it was boring; it was that it was a complete diminution of life, to the point of virtual nonexistence. And if one does not exist, one cannot enjoy the good things in life. For ancient Israelites, that meant one could not enjoy all that the LORD provided for his people; could not even enjoy praising God and thanking him for all that he does, since what he does no longer applies to the dead. His interactions are entirely with the living.

Thus the terms used to describe Sheol are bleak, not because there is any pain involved, but because there is *nothing* involved. It is a realm of "forgetfulness" (Psalm 88:12); "silence" (Psalm 115:17), and "darkness" (Job 17:13). God is not even present there and, since the deceased are dead, none of them can worship him: "The dead do not praise the LORD, / nor do any that go down in silence" (Psalm 115:17). No one can experience the love and presence of God in Sheol/the grave, since they are cut off from the land of the living:

> I am counted among those who go down to the Pit;
> I am like those who have no help,
> like those forsaken among the dead,
> like the slain that lie in the grave,
> like those whom you remember no more,
> for they are cut off from your hand. (Psalm 88:4–5)

Since in the grave one literally has no life, God does not even think about them or remember them anymore. His love is not found among those who have died (Psalm 88:11). That is because God is the god of the living, not those who reside in Sheol: "For in death there is no remembrance of you; / in Sheol who can give you praise?" (Psalm 6:5); "[T]hose who go down to the Pit cannot hope for your faithfulness" (Isaiah 38:18). Or, as is stated in the apocryphal book of Ecclesiasticus (otherwise known as Sirach):

> Who will sing praises to the Most High in Hades? . . .
> From the dead, as from one who does not exist,
>   thanksgiving has ceased;
> those who are alive and well sing the Lord's praises
>   (Sirach 17:27–28)

All this is why it is important to live a long and full life, and to avoid Sheol for as long as possible—as seen in the Hebrew poets who regularly praise God for saving them from it. It is not that they are hoping to go to heaven and avoid eternal flames: the Old Testament says no word about either eternal bliss for the righteous dead or everlasting punishment for the wicked. The poets praise God, instead, for allowing them to stay alive for a while longer, making it possible for them still to praise him. And so we read:

> For great is your steadfast love toward me;
> You have delivered my soul from the depths of Sheol.
>   (Psalm 86:13)

and:

> But he did not give me over to death. (Psalm 118:8)

and:

> *O LORD, you brought up my soul from Sheol,*
> *restored me to life from among those gone down to*
> *the Pit. (Psalm 30:3)*

The prophet is relieved that God has kept him from premature death, allowing him a long and full life. Those who do so can die content. They have received all that they could expect.

For some authors, the reality of death seems to have served as motivation to prolong life as much as possible. One gets this sense in the book of Ecclesiastes, one of the most skeptical works of the Hebrew Bible, where the author, allegedly King Solomon, expresses himself with a striking image: "Whoever is joined with all the living has hope, for a living dog is better than a dead lion" (Ecclesiastes 9:4). He then gives his reason: "The living know that they will die, but the dead know nothing; they have no more reward, and even the memory of them is lost" (Ecclesiastes 9:5).

Nowhere in the Bible, however, do we get the idea that one who lives a long and full life has any regrets at dying. This is a point emphasized by Hebrew Bible scholar Jon Levenson, who reasons that if death for the elderly were a horrible fate to be avoided at all costs, the book of Job would not have ended on the high note that "Job died old and contented." More likely it would have added a comment about how he now, in death, was undergoing a horrible existence in which he was endlessly bored to tears and miserable forever.[4]

Hints of an Ongoing Existence Beyond the Grave

The Hebrew Bible is no monolith: it contains a wide range of views held by different authors over a period of many centuries. And so, not all authors of the Jewish scriptures held to the view that death was the end of the story. We find some hints, outside of the comments on Sheol in the poetic books, that the dead may, in some sense, live on after departing this life. Notably, in the portions of the Bible that describe the Law of Moses, we find several warnings to ancient Israelites that they are not, under any circumstances, to contact or interact with "the dead." And so, for example, we find the command: "Do not turn to mediums or wizards; do not seek them out, to be defiled by them . . ." (Leviticus 19:31). Mediums and wizards here do not refer to ancient precursors of Harry Potter; they are people who have powers to consult the dead for advice. This is made clear in the book of Deuteronomy: "No one shall be found among you who . . . practices divination, or is a soothsayer . . . or a sorcerer, or who casts spells, or who consults ghosts or spirits, or who seeks oracles from the dead" (Deuteronomy 18:10–11). Obviously, dead persons cannot be consulted if they no longer exist. Thus, whatever the elite and educated authors of Job, Psalms, and Ecclesiastes may have thought, other ancient Israelites believed the dead still do exist in some form and can communicate, if illicitly, with the living.

Nowhere is this made more clear than in the one and only story in the entire Old Testament of a dead person who is temporarily called back to life for purposes of consultation, the famous story of "Saul and the Medium of Endor" in 1 Samuel 28. Saul is the first king of Israel, and he is having trouble. As a young man he had been anointed king by the great prophet Samuel, but his rule has been filled with terrible problems, many of them due to his own fickle character and inconstant behavior. There is a young upstart, David, who has been receiving massive popular support, and Saul is afraid of a possible coup. Then something even worse happens. The neighboring enemy, the Philistines, have amassed an army and are preparing to attack. The military situation looks hopeless. Saul needs divine guidance to see him through the crisis.

But his trustworthy advisor Samuel has died. And when Saul prays to

God for insight, he receives no reply. He then tries to use the traditional means of determining God's will, the mysterious Urim—apparently lots that were thrown to learn God's answers to questions that were posed. But to no avail. He decides he needs to use illicit means for guidance. He will ask the deceased Samuel for help. But there is a very big problem. Not only is this kind of necromancy forbidden in the laws of Moses, King Saul himself has explicitly banned all mediums and wizards from Israel.

Still, he is desperate. The king learns of a medium in the town of Endor, near the front lines of the approaching battle. He goes to her and does so in disguise, for rather obvious reasons: it would not help matters if she were to realize the illicit request for contact with the dead is coming from the sovereign ruler who made it illegal in the first place. When approached, she is understandably reluctant: the Law of Moses orders sorceresses to be put to death. But when her potential client swears an oath that no harm will come to her, she obeys his request and holds a kind of séance, bringing Samuel up "out of the ground." Or rather, the text says that it was an "Elohim" that came up. The term "Elohim" is the Hebrew word for God—used typically for the God of Israel himself, but also applicable to other divine beings. Either this text imagines that as God's prophet, Samuel, is semi-divine, or it wants us to think that the dead, or just dead prophets, have somehow become divinized. It is his divine being that appears.

It is interesting that this divine being is specifically said to have come up from the ground. The word "Sheol" is not used in the account, and it is not clear if the text wants us to imagine that Samuel has been in some large community under the earth (doing what exactly?) or if he has been resting in his grave. The latter would make perfect sense, given the wording of the text. Moreover, it is worth noting that this divine being can readily be recognized for who he is: since he comes up as an old man wearing a robe, Saul realizes it is in fact Samuel. For this story, as for the Greek and Roman texts we have examined, the dead retain the appearance they had while living; in this case, the Samuel looks just as he did at the end of his life.

What is most striking is Samuel's own reaction to the situation: he is extremely upset that Saul has interrupted his rest: "Then Samuel said to Saul, 'Why have you disturbed me by bringing me up?'" (1 Samuel 28:15). It is hard to interpret this reproach, but it appears that Samuel had been enjoying being dead.

That does not necessarily mean that Samuel had a conscious existence in his dead state. It could equally suggest he was in a deep, even a dreamless sleep and was upset about being woken up. But either way, his death was not awful, terrible, and something to escape. It was pleasant. What was awful was being brought back to life.

Saul explains why he felt compelled to call him forth, and the roused prophet treats him harshly. Yes, he tells the king, the LORD is rejecting him—hence his refusal to answer his inquiries or respond to the Urim; yes, the LORD will take his kingdom and give it to David; yes, Saul's Israelite armies will be soundly defeated in battle with the Philistines; and—in one of the great lines of the Hebrew Bible, foretelling death without mentioning the word—the deceased Samuel tells Saul, "and tomorrow you and your sons will be with me" (1 Samuel 28:19).

Again, this does not necessarily mean that the dead all live together and Saul will soon join them in that large assembly hall beneath the earth. It could simply mean that the dead have in common the same fate: they are all dead, and Saul will soon join their ranks. It is striking, though, that the divine spirit of Samuel knows what will happen on the morrow. Apparently the dead—at least dead prophets—know the future.

Here then is an Israelite Tiresias, with some key differences. Samuel, for example, does not need to drink the blood of a sacrifice to tell the future. His mind is intact and knows not only the past but also what is to come. Is that true of all the dead? The author never says. But presumably it was believed by some people in ancient Israel at least. Unlike the psalmists, these others thought the dead could advise the living, in part by predicting what would soon happen in their lives. That this view is not unique to the author of 1 Samuel is shown by the fact that we find laws that forbid the living from consulting the dead. You don't make laws to forbid things no one ever does.

The Afterlife of the Nation

Whatever differences we can find in the passages of the Hebrew Bible we have already considered, one thing we can say for certain: in none of them can we find the traditional Christian views of the afterlife. That is true for the entire Old Testament. As one of the leading experts on after-life in the ancient world, Alan Segal, the late scholar of Judaism, unequivocally stated: "There are not any notions of hell and heaven that we can identify in the Hebrew Bible, no obvious judgment and punishment for sinners nor beatific reward for the virtuous."[5]

To the surprise of many readers today, much of the discussion of "afterlife" in the Hebrew Bible focuses not on the fate of the individual at death but instead on the ultimate fate of the entire nation. I do not mean the fate of the individual people in the nation who die but rather the fate of the nation of Israel itself. If Israel is destroyed, will it "come back to life"? Will Israel exist again? That may not be a question most of us are particularly interested in, especially when we're exploring the issue of what will happen to each of us when we shuffle off our mortal coil. Even so, for reasons we will see, the question of the afterlife of the nation came to play a significant role in shaping how ancient Jews eventually came to think of the afterlife of the individual.

Above all, Israel's life, death, and afterlife is a central and abiding concern for the prophetic writings of the Hebrew Bible—from Isaiah, Hosea, and Amos in the eighth century BCE, to Jeremiah, Ezekiel, and

Habakkuk in the sixth BCE, on through just about all the prophets. If the nation "dies," will it "live again"?

The Message of the Prophets

It is first important to clarify a common misperception about prophecy in ancient Israel. Today people think of a prophet as someone who predicts the future. And ancient Israelite prophets certainly did that. But it was not their major task. Israelite prophets understood themselves primarily to be spokespersons for God. They were the ones who spoke God's word to his people, the ones who communicated God's message to those who very much needed it, usually in times of crisis. Their overarching concerns were their present contexts, which were almost always situations of impending or manifest crisis. The prophets proclaimed why the crisis had come, what the people should do about it, and what would happen if they refused.

The Hebrew prophets, in other words, are grossly misunderstood if they are thought of as predicting the distant future, 2,500 years after their day. They were speaking to their own situation, and they need to be placed in that context if they are to be understood. To some extent they did foretell the immediate future. But they understood themselves less to be "foretellers" of the future than to be "forthtellers" of God's will. They were speaking forth the word of God that was directed to their current situation in terribly difficult, fraught, and even disastrous times.

The message of these prophets is remarkably consistent in its overall features, from one to the next. In the context of ancient Israelite religion— in a world in which religion and politics were never kept distinct—the prophets proclaimed that the social, economic, political, and/or military disaster that was at hand was being sent by God as a punishment for the sins of the people. The nation of Israel had been told by God how it had to conduct itself. And the people had disobeyed. As a result, God was going to bring calamity—or had already done so. The only way to avert it was to repent and return to the ways of God, worshiping him as he required and living as he demanded. Anything short of that would bring disaster. But if they did what God commanded, he might relent and restore the nation to a blessed state.

Death and Restoration in Amos

It would be simple to illustrate this message from nearly any of the prophets of the Hebrew Bible. Here I will do so—and show why the matter is relevant to the question of the afterlife—by considering one of the earliest prophets, the eighth-century-BCE Amos.

Amos was living at a time in which the original nation of Israel had been divided in two after a civil war, with Israel itself in the northern part of the land and the nation of Judah, with its capital of Jerusalem, in the south. The two neighbors both understood themselves to have descended from the Patriarchs and to be subject to the Law of Moses. But as often happens with close relatives, they were frequently at each other's throats. In Amos's most immediate context, however, the bigger problem was external. The mighty nation of Assyria, on the far eastern side of the Fertile Crescent, was on the rise and threatening to attack and destroy the nations of the Levant.

Amos was himself from the southern kingdom of Judah, but he came into the north to make his proclamation: the Assyrians were being empowered by God himself. God was incensed at how the northern Israelites were living their lives, oppressing the poor, ignoring the needy, perpetuating injustice. They "oppress the poor . . . crush the needy . . . afflict the righteous . . . and push aside the needy out of the gate" (Amos 4:1; 5:12). Because they had not mended their lives and turned to the ways God had commanded, by working for fairness, charity, and justice, God would direct the Assyrian armies to attack, leading to massive devastation.

And so Amos says, in powerful and gripping terms,

> They [the people of Israel] do not know how to do
>   right, says the LORD,
> those who store up violence and robbery in their
>   strongholds.
> Therefore thus says the Lord GOD:
> An adversary shall surround the land,
> and strip you of your defense;
> and your strongholds shall be plundered. (Amos
>   3:10–11)

Through the prophet, God reminds the people of all the disasters he had already brought upon them. He brought famine, but they refused to repent (Amos 4:6); then drought and they didn't repent (Amos 4:8); then crop failure and they didn't repent (Amos 4:9); then epidemic and they didn't repent (Amos 4:10). Since they hadn't learned their lesson from these "lesser" disasters, he was compelled to make the calamity complete: "Therefore, thus I will do to you, O Israel; because I will do this to you, prepare to meet your God, O Israel!" (Amos 4:12). In this context, meeting your God was not a good thing. It meant God was going to bring the entire force of his divine power down on the nation of Israel and utterly destroy it. And so Amos's famous lament: "Fallen, no more to rise, is maiden Israel; forsaken on her land, with no one to raise her up" (Amos 5:2).

Clearly Amos is principally concerned not merely with the coming death of individuals but with the destruction of the nation itself. And yet, even after destruction, there is still hope. At the end of the book—possibly in a portion that was added by a later editor[6]—Amos declares that after national death will come national restoration and new life:

> The time is surely coming, says the LORD,
> when the one who plows shall overtake the one who
>   reaps,
> and the treader of grapes the one who sows the seed;
> the mountains shall drip sweet wine,
> and all the hills shall flow with it.
> I will restore the fortunes of my people Israel,
> and they shall rebuild the ruined cities and inhabit
>   them;
> they shall plant vineyards and drink their wine,
> and they shall make gardens and eat their fruit.
> I will plant them upon their land,
> and they shall never again be plucked up
> out of the land that I have given them,
> says the LORD your God. (Amos 9:13–15)

The key point is that among some of the prophets, this idea of a future restoration of the nation after disaster is sometimes likened to a resurrection of the dead. As we will see in the next chapter, this image of a national "life after death" was eventually taken to mean a life after death for individuals within it. This was not the case for the Israelite prophets themselves. For them, the "resurrection" was not something to happen at the end of human history when individual bodies returned to life for eternal reward or punishment. It was instead a metaphor for the nation being given new life. But the metaphorical language they used to describe this great moment of national salvation was later to take on new resonances. One passage particularly open to these later resonances occurs in a key passage in the book of Isaiah.

Rising Corpses in Isaiah

Critical scholars have long recognized that the long book of Isaiah as it has come down to us is actually a combination of writings by different authors from different periods of history.[7] Most of the first thirty-nine chapters, with the exception principally of chapters 24 to 27, derive from the prophet Isaiah himself, who lived in Jerusalem in the eighth century BCE, about the time of Amos; he, like his contemporary, proclaimed a coming military disaster at the hands of the Assyrians. A century and a half later, sometime after the later destruction of Jerusalem by a different ancient Near Eastern power, the Babylonians, in 586 BCE, another prophet from Judah produced what is now chapters 40 to 55; the burden of his message was hope that God would restore the fate of the nation. Sometime later in the sixth century, yet a third prophet produced what is now chapters 56 to 66, discussing the difficulties that arose after the nation had started to rebuild itself.

Somewhat later still, a prophet wrote what is now chapters 24 to 27, and these came to be inserted into the writings of "First" Isaiah. The chapters presuppose that the nation of Judah and its capital, Jerusalem, have been destroyed. But the prophet is comforting his readers that all is not lost. God will restore the fortunes of his people and allow the nation to rebuild and start again. In a sense, it will return to life from the dead. The key verse for our purposes is Isaiah 26:19:

> *Your dead shall live, their corpses shall rise.*
> *O dwellers in the dust, awake and sing for joy!*
> *For your dew is a radiant dew,*
> *and the earth will give birth to those long dead*
> *   [literally: "shades"].*

On first reading and in isolation, the verse may seem to be saying that individuals who have died will experience a resurrection. But the context of Isaiah 25–26 makes it crystal clear that the author is talking about the redemption—the "return to life"—of the nation of Israel in metaphorical language. He says explicitly that salvation will come to Jerusalem itself after being destroyed (Isaiah 26:4–6). God will bring them peace (Isaiah 26:12) because people have prayed to God in the midst of their affliction (Isaiah 26:16–17). God will therefore bring them, the nation, back to life ("Your dead shall live, their corpses shall rise" [Isaiah 26:19]). Just as Adam came to life from the dust, so too will the nation of Judah in its "life after death." And so he says: "O dwellers in the dust, rejoice!" Why? Because the earth will "give birth to those long dead" (Isaiah 26:19).

Ezekiel and the Valley of Dry Bones

The metaphorical language of national resurrection is presented in particularly graphic and memorable terms by a writer contemporaneous with the anonymous author of Isaiah 24–27, the great prophet Ezekiel, in a famous passage describing "the valley of dry bones." Ezekiel was writing immediately after the destruction of Jerusalem at the hands of the Babylonians, and the burden of his message, in part, was that the nation would be restored. This is the context of his well-known description of the valley of bones in Ezekiel 37, a passage frequently misread by people who think the prophet is discussing the future resurrection of individuals at the end of time. He is not. He is explicitly referring to the restoration of the nation of Judah after its destruction.

In this highly symbolic passage, the Spirit of the LORD takes Ezekiel out to a valley that is filled with dry human bones (Ezekiel 37:1–2). They are dry because they are completely dead: there is no flesh on them. These are the remnants of the living. The LORD asks the prophet whether the bones can be brought to life again, and Ezekiel, clueless about the matter, gives a nonanswer: "O Lord GOD, you know" (Ezekiel 37:3). In other words, he himself has no idea.

God tells Ezekiel to prophesy (that is, "speak forth") to the bones and tell them to return to life: "Thus says the Lord GOD to these bones: I will cause breath to enter you, and you shall live. I will lay sinews on you, and will cause flesh to come upon you, and cover you with skin, and put breath in you, and you shall live; and you shall know that I am the LORD" (Ezekiel 37:5–6). Ezekiel does as he is told, and it all happens:

> As I prophesied, suddenly there was a noise, a rattling, and the bones came together, bone to its bone. I looked, and there were sinews on them, and flesh had come upon them, and skin had covered them, but there was no breath in them. (Ezekiel 37:7–8)

God then tells Ezekiel to "prophesy to the breath," telling it to come from the four winds and "breathe upon these slain, that they may live" (Ezekiel 37:9). He does so, and breath comes upon the reconstructed bodies, "and they lived, and stood on their feet, a vast multitude" (Ezekiel 37:10). Comparable to the creation of Adam in Genesis 2:7, first a body is made, then the breath of God is breathed into it and it comes to life. Only here, instead of coming to life for the first time, these are bodies that come *back* to life after having died before. It is a resurrection of the dead.

Readers who come to this intriguing passage with later Christian theology in mind can scarcely be blamed for thinking that here we have a prophetic prediction that at the end of time individuals would be raised from the dead for eternal life in heaven. But read in its context, that clearly is not the meaning. Ezekiel is unambiguous about what is being predicted: it is the restoration of the fortunes of the nation: "Mortal [the term God uses to address Ezekiel throughout the book], these bones are the whole house of Israel. They say, 'Our bones are dried up, and our hope is lost; we are cut off completely'" (Ezekiel 37:11). In other words, the people of the nation Judah are distraught that after their kingdom has been destroyed, it is like a valley of dry bones, completely dead, incapable of resuscitation. But God knows otherwise, and tells the prophet so in no uncertain terms: the people of Judah who have been taken into exile into Babylon will return to their own land and thrive again, fully alive once more, a nation under God:

> I am going to open your graves, and bring you up from your graves, O my people; and I will bring you back to the land of Israel . . . I will put my spirit within you, and you shall live, and I will place you on your own soil; then you shall know that I, the LORD, have spoken and will act. . . . (Ezekiel 37:12–14)

Resurrection and the Question of God's Justice

In many ways Ezekiel's message is a kind of theodicy—that is, an explanation for how God can be fair and just, given what happens in the world. A great evil had occurred. The nation of Judah had been destroyed and its leaders taken into exile—not by a nation that was faithful to God, but by one that was filled with pagans who had no interest in the God of Israel or his law. Is that fair? And is it right that there should be no hope, even if people turn back to God? Ezekiel explains that punishment has come for the nation's sins, but God is eminently just, and he will now restore his people to their land.

One of the reasons this prophetic message of the "resurrection" of a nation often does not resonate with many readers today is that most modern people are not particularly interested—except by way of occasional curiosity—in knowing what happened in antiquity to the northern nation of Israel or the southern nation of Judah. But, more broadly, most people in the modern world are less focused on the nation than on themselves. To be sure, we want our own country to thrive, and we want to make it the best place we possibly can in our world. But at the end of the day, am I that concerned about whether the United States will be around in three hundred years?

I suppose many of us are to some extent, and we would love to have a glimpse of the future of the world. But for most people it is not an obsession, something that keeps them awake at night. They are concerned more about the fact of their own deaths. To some extent—sometimes to a very large extent—they may be worried about their families and other loved ones and what will become of them, rather than what will happen to their city, state, or nation. But especially, in most cases, they are concerned about their own destiny: What will happen to *me* when I die?

At a certain point, that also became an obsession of some ancient Israelite thinkers, who redirected thinking about death—the grave, the pit, Sheol, and the national restoration of Israel—to their personal identities. When they did so, they began to reapply metaphorical language of national restoration to individual resurrection. People began to think they themselves might be restored, personally raised from the dead. In no context did such new thinking take hold more firmly than in times of serious persecution and martyrdom, when people who suffered for their beliefs and ancestral customs and practices came to wonder how it was fair for them to suffer and die for what they knew to be right, when the wicked prospered by living in ways opposed to God. These contexts helped pave the way for the view that at the end of time, God would reassert his sovereignty over the world and judge the righteous and the wicked, individually at the resurrection of the dead.

CHAPTER SIX

Dead Bodies That Return to Life: The Resurrection in Ancient Israel

After the period of the classical prophets, Jewish thinkers came to imagine that in fact there would be life for the individual who had died. For them, there was a possibility of life beyond the grave—real, full, and abundant life. But in this original Jewish conception, unlike widespread Christian views today, the afterlife was not a glorious eternity lived in the soul in heaven or a tormented existence in hell, attained immediately at the point of death. It was something else altogether. It was the idea that at the end of time God would vindicate himself and his people. When history and all its evil and suffering had run its course, God would reassert his sovereignty over this world and destroy everything and everyone who was opposed to him, bringing in the perfect, utopian world he had originally planned. Inhabiting this world would be the righteous who had lived and suffered throughout all of history. God would miraculously bring them back into their bodies, and they would live, bodily, without any pain, misery, or suffering, for all time, in his most glorious kingdom.

Those who were wicked would also be brought back to life. In the original understanding of resurrection, they would be raised in order to see their crimes and pay for them with a final and irreversible punishment: they would be destroyed for all time. Eventually this view developed and changed, and it came to be thought that the wicked would have to pay an even dearer price for all the injustice they had inflicted on others. They would be returned to their bodies to be tormented.

The doctrine of the bodily resurrection of the dead at the end of time originated about two centuries before the life of Jesus, and by his day it had become a common feature of Jewish thought. Later, at the hands of Christians, it came to be transformed into a teaching of postmortem rewards and punishments, the ideas of heaven and hell.

The Origins of Resurrection

It is much debated among scholars how and why this doctrine of bodily resurrection arose. It has often been argued that Jews adopted it from the dualistic Persian religion of Zoroastrianism, which understood that the forces of good and evil are in a cosmic struggle that will lead to the ultimate triumph of good and a vindication of those who sided with it in an end-of-time resurrection. One reason that a derivation from Zoroastrian thought has always seemed plausible is that the nation of Judah, after its destruction by the Babylonians in 586 BCE, came under Persian rule in 539 BCE. Surely they were influenced by their Persian overlords, no?

More recently scholars have questioned a Persian derivation for the Jewish doctrine because of certain problems of dating.[1] Some experts have undercut the entire thesis by pointing out that we actually do not have any Zoroastrian texts that support the idea of resurrection prior to its appearance in early Jewish writings. It is not clear who influenced whom. Even more significant, the timing does not make sense: Judah emerged from Persian rule in the fourth century BCE, when Alexander the Great (356–323 BCE) swept through the eastern Mediterranean and defeated the Persian Empire. But the idea of bodily resurrection does not appear in Jewish texts for well over a century after that.

Even though other external influences may have exerted some level of influence,[2] the idea of a future, personal resurrection may have arisen principally as an internal development in response to the troubling social and political situations confronting the Jewish faithful. This new belief provided an answer to the disturbing question plaguing many thinkers devoted to a monotheistic religion. If there is only one God, and he is in control of the world, why do the people who try to follow him suffer for it? The problem of suffering is not very difficult to solve for polytheists. Anyone who believes in many gods can easily say that some of them are wicked and these are the ones who create such misery in this world. But if there is only one God, and he is both thoroughly good and ultimately sovereign, why do his chosen ones suffer?

Almost everyone has an answer to this question, of course—so much so that many people don't see that the problem is an actual problem. Every week I get emails from people who want to tell me the answer to why there is suffering. It's because we have free will. It's because God is testing us. It's so we can appreciate the good times. And so on.

All of these—and the many others that are commonly held today—emerged at some time in human thought. They have been discussed, debated, refined, developed, rejected by some, and accepted by others.[3] In ancient Israel there were answers as well. We have already seen one in the writings of the Hebrew prophets such as Amos and Isaiah. Their view was held by each and every one of the prophets: Jeremiah, Hosea, Joel—take your pick. It is that the people of God have sinned and God is punishing them for it. Suffering comes from God, to penalize his people for not living as they should. This is sometimes called the "prophetic" or the "classical" view of suffering.

It is still a widely held view among Christian people today and has seeped into common parlance, as seen in some of our common complaints: "What did I do to deserve *this*?"—as if bad things happen to us because we've earned them. Most people today, of course, realize it is never that simple. Do we really want to say that birth defects, the death of a child, Alzheimer's, or any of the other mind-numbing forms of suffering in extremis are punishments from God for something we did wrong?

The Rise of Apocalyptic Thinking

That simple question is what eventually led some ancient Jewish thinkers to question the prophetic answer to why the people of God suffer. Maybe it would make sense that God ordained the destruction of the nation of Israel at the hands of the Assyrians as a punishment for the sins of the people. But if that's the case, why, when the people repented and returned to God's ways, doing their best to do what he demanded in his law—why then did they *continue* to experience social upheaval, political disaster, economic crisis, and military defeat?

Moreover, if the key to a life happy and blessed by God is keeping his law, and the path to pain and misery is breaking it, why is it that the wicked prosper and the righteous suffer? Why do some people exploit the system, oppress the poor, snub the needy, violate every commandment God has ever given, and then grow rich, influential, and deeply satisfied with themselves—only to die and get away with it? And why do other people, meek and humble, quietly live their lives by being concerned for those in need, giving what little time and resources they have to help others, yet lead lives of personal misery filled with pain, illness, poverty, and oppression, and then die lonely and in pain?

It would make sense if there were no God. Or if there were many gods, some of whom were nasty. But how can it make sense if there is only one God who is truly good and completely in control of this world? It was a problem for Jewish thinkers. And eventually, about two centuries before Jesus, they came up with a new solution. In a sense, the solution was a kind of rejection of the prophetic answer. For these new thinkers, even if some suffering could come from God—for example, occasionally to punish sin—that is not why the massive suffering that has turned the world into a place of misery has devastated even the people of God. On the contrary, it is not God who causes the problem. Instead, God has cosmic enemies. They are the ones doing it.

There developed within Jewish thinking the idea that even though God is sovereign, there are other powers in the world, superhuman beings who are responsible for persecuting and harming God's people. It was in this period that some Jewish thinkers propounded the idea that God has a cosmic antagonist, the devil. The devil went by different names in the Jewish tradition—for example, Satan and Beelzebul. You will not find him in the Hebrew Bible. To be sure, a figure known as "the satan" does appear in a couple of places, most famously in the book of Job (chapters 1–2), but there he is not the devilish opponent of God. He is one of God's divine counselors who opposes humans but who still does God's bidding. For later Jewish thinkers, however, this figure was transformed into a massively powerful being opposed to God and all who worship him.

Modern scholars use the term "apocalypticism" to describe the Jewish view that God has cosmic opponents creating havoc on earth, destined to be destroyed in the end through a cataclysmic act of divine judgment. The term comes from *apocalypsis*, the Greek word for revealing or unveiling. The revealed "secret" is that the proponents of earthly evil, whether it is obvious or not, stand under the ultimate sovereignty of God. And their days are numbered.

For now, the devil has forces who do his will, demonic powers that can wreak havoc on earth. All that is evil comes from these adversaries of God. For some reason, even though God is ultimately sovereign, he has ceded control of the world to these powers of evil. That is why there is so much pain, misery, and suffering here, and it is why the righteous suffer while the wicked prosper. They prosper because they side with the powers that are for now in control of this world. The righteous, on the other hand, bear the brunt of the forces alien to God.

But it will not go on like this forever. Evil, in the end, will not have the last word. God will.

Thus apocalypticists maintained that even though pain and suffering are rampant now, especially among the people of God, an end is coming soon, a time when God will reassert himself, intervene in history, and overthrow the forces of evil. There is a judgment day coming, and everyone and everything that is opposed to God will be destroyed. Those who side with God, however, will be vindicated and rewarded. A utopian world will arrive, the return of the Garden of Eden on earth, literally "paradise" (a Persian word for garden). There will be no more evil or corruption, pain, misery, or suffering. The followers of God will enjoy eternal bliss.

Most important for our discussion here, this judgment will affect not only those who are living at the time but all people, even those who are dead. Those who have already suffered for doing what is right and died for their pains will be raised from the dead, in their actual human bodies made immortal. In their newly embodied state they will inherit the good world God has prepared for his followers. The unrighteous, on the other hand, will be raised in order to face judgment. They will be shown the errors of their ways, be crushed by their horrible realization of what they have done, and realize that they will not receive any reward but instead be totally and painfully destroyed.

Biblical Roots for the Idea of a Future Resurrection

This, then, is the Jewish doctrine of the resurrection of the dead on the Day of Judgment. Even though the idea was first endorsed after most of the Hebrew Bible was written, it would be a mistake to think it came virtually out of nowhere, created ex nihilo by Jewish apocalyptic thinkers two centuries before the ministry of Jesus. In fact, as scholars have sometimes argued, the notion of bodily resurrection finds its roots in other, non-apocalyptic traditions found throughout the Jewish scriptures.[4]

The idea that God is the one who gives life, of course, stands at the very heart of the biblical tradition. It is the ultimate point of the creation stories in Genesis 1–2: God makes living plants, animals, and humans out of what previously was not alive. But for later thinkers, there are further implications of the divine origin of life: If God brings living creatures into being, and God is eternal, then isn't life eternal? Even for those who die?

In fact the Bible tells several instances of God's prophets restoring life to those who had died, such as Elijah in 1 Kings 7:17–24 and his disciple Elisha in 2 Kings 4:18–37. If God's prophets could do that, can't God? Indeed, God allowed Elijah to ascend to heaven without dying (2 Kings 2:1–12), as he did much earlier with the mysterious figure Enoch, seven generations after Adam (Genesis 5:21–24). If these two live forever, why not others?

And then there is the tradition we have already seen, that God would restore the nation of Israel, his chosen people, bringing it back to life after it had been destroyed by its enemies (thus Isaiah 26:19; Ezekiel 37). If God can "raise from the dead" the nation as a whole, it is not a huge leap to think he could do the same for the individuals who inhabit the nation, who have suffered not national destruction but personal death.

The Role of the Suffering Servant in Isaiah 53

One biblical text that appears to have provided support for the later idea of a future, personal resurrection is Isaiah 52:13–53:12, a passage that, comparable to Ezekiel 37 from roughly the same time, refers to the ultimate vindication and return of Israel. Eventually, however, also like Ezekiel 37, the passage came to be thought to refer, instead, to the resurrection of individuals. Later still, at the hands of Christian interpreters, it came to be understood as a prophecy of the death and resurrection of one individual in particular, the messiah Jesus. Christians have long argued that Isaiah 53 is a prediction of Jesus's crucifixion and triumph over death three days later. But that is almost certainly a misreading of the passage, at least as the author originally intended it. The passage deals with the "suffering servant" of the LORD. But in its original context the servant does not appear to be the messiah.

Of course, Jesus is not named in the passage. But even more surprising to many Christian readers who learn this for the first time, the word "messiah" never occurs in it either. There is a good reason for the surprise: it is hard indeed for Christians to read the chapter and *not* think that it is speaking specifically about Jesus.

> *He was despised and rejected by others;*
> *A man of suffering and acquainted with infirmity . . .*
> *He was despised, and we held him of no account*
> *Surely he has borne our infirmities*
> *and carried our diseases . . .*
> *He was wounded for our transgressions,*
> *crushed for our iniquities.*
> *Upon him was the punishment that made us whole,*
> *and by his bruises we are healed. (Isaiah 53:3–5)*

Not only did this unnamed servant of the LORD suffer because of others, he also is vindicated by God. Doesn't this refer to the resurrection of Jesus?

> *Out of his anguish he shall see light;*
> *He shall find satisfaction through his knowledge.*
> *The righteous one, my servant, shall make many*
>   *righteous,*
> *and he shall bear their iniquities.*
> *Therefore I will allot him a portion with the great*
> *and he shall divide the spoil with the strong*
> *because he poured out himself to death,*
> *and was numbered with the transgressors.*
> *Yet he bore the sin of many,*
> *And made intercession for the transgressors. (Isaiah*
>   *53:11–12)*

The main reason it is so difficult for Christian readers to see these words and not think "Jesus" is because for many centuries theologians have indeed argued that the passage is a messianic prophecy looking forward to the Christian savior. Anyone who is first shown this passage and told it is about Jesus will naturally always read it that way. *Of course* it's about Jesus! Who *else* could it be about? This is surely a prophecy of Jesus's crucifixion and resurrection made centuries before the fact.

Still, it is important to stress not only that the passage never uses the term "messiah" or explicitly indicates it is talking about a messiah, but also that we have no evidence that any Jew prior to Christianity ever *thought* it was about the messiah. There is a good reason for that: before the birth of Christianity, no one thought the messiah would be someone who would die and be raised from the dead.

That may seem both weird and counterintuitive to many Christian readers today. But historically it is almost certainly the case: the idea of a suffering messiah is not found in any Jewish texts prior to Christianity. The idea that the messiah had to suffer and die for others was first espoused by Christians on the basis of two facts that they "knew" about

Jesus: he was the messiah and he had been crucified. Their conclusion: the messiah had to suffer and die.

But not in traditional Judaism. Instead, Jews consistently believed the messiah would be the great and powerful ruler who delivered Israel from its oppressors. He would be a mighty general or a powerful cosmic judge come from heaven. Different Jews had different views of who or what the messiah might be, but all these views had one thing in common: they all thought of the messiah as a future figure of grandeur and might who would rule the nation with justice and power.[5]

And who was Jesus? An itinerant preacher who got on the wrong side of the law and was arrested by the enemies of Israel, tried, and publicly tortured to death by crucifixion. This was just the opposite of what the messiah would be.

Christians nonetheless came to believe Jesus was the messiah and, naturally, started looking for proofs from the Bible that could support the idea—passages that, contrary to what everyone had previously thought, might indicate that the messiah was to suffer and be raised from the dead.[6] Isaiah 53 was a natural choice. Christian thinkers picked up the passage, promoted it as a messianic text, and that has influenced its interpretation ever since.

But there are solid reasons for thinking the passage is about something else. To begin with, it is important to stress the historical context within which the passage was written. This part of Isaiah was produced after the Babylonian armies had destroyed Jerusalem and taken large numbers of the Jewish people into captivity in Babylon.[7] These exiles were suffering, and the prophet was writing in order to give them hope. Those in captivity were suffering for the sins of the people, which had led to God's punishment of the nation, but they would be returned to their land and good things would come. These suffering ones are talked about as God's "servant": they are serving God's purposes.

Some readers think the servant has to be a single person, since, after all, he is described as an individual, God's servant. But it is important to realize that, throughout the Hebrew Bible, groups of people could be and often are described as individuals. Nations are named after people. Thus the southern nation after the civil war dividing Israel is named "Judah," after one of the sons of Jacob; it is obviously a group but it is named after a person. So too with "Gog and Magog" in Ezekiel 38–39 and the fierce "beasts" that Daniel sees as ruling the earth in Daniel 7. Each is described as an individual animal, but it represents an entire national group.

Another reason for thinking Isaiah 53 does not refer to just one person, the future messiah who would die for sins, is that the passage describes the suffering of the servant as a *past* event, not future: he *was* despised and rejected; he *has* borne our infirmities; he *was* wounded for our transgressions. On the other hand—and this is a key point—his vindication is described as a *future* event: he *shall* see light; he *shall* find satisfaction; he *shall* divide the spoil. The author thus is referring to someone (as a metaphor for a group of people) who has already suffered but will eventually be vindicated.

And who is that someone, that "servant of the LORD"? The historical context of the author's writing is obviously an important factor in deciding, but there is a clincher to the argument. The author of Isaiah explicitly tells us who the servant is. Most readers don't notice this because they do not read the passage in its literary context. But as biblical scholars have long known, there are four distinct passages in Isaiah that talk about this servant. And they tell us who he is. This is most clear in Isaiah 49:3, where God directly addresses the servant: "And he said to me, 'You are my servant, Israel, in whom I will be glorified.'" The suffering servant is Israel.

In short, Isaiah 53 is not originally about a future messiah; it is about the nation of Israel taken into captivity. Some of the people were suffering horribly because of the sins of others. But God would restore them— raise them from the dead, as it were—bringing them back to the land

and allowing them to live again after their national destruction. Thus the message is very much in line with what we already saw in Isaiah 26:19 and in the famous passage about the valley of dry bones in Ezekiel 37. But it is easy to see how later readers could think it was referring to an individual, not the nation.

Some three centuries after this part of Isaiah was written, Jewish apocalyptic thinkers began to believe that evil derives from cosmic powers aligned against God who are wreaking havoc on earth and on those who dwelled on it. Anyone who tries to keep God's law is targeted by these powers of evil. These cosmic forces use others, their human minions, to oppress and punish the righteous, sometimes leading to their deaths. But in the end God will have the last word. There is a Day of Judgment coming, and all people will face the divine tribunal, to be rewarded for their righteous behavior or punished for their sins. This is true not only for those living at the time but also for the dead, who will be bodily raised, either to enter God's paradise or to be judged and destroyed. For some of these thinkers, the passage of God's servant in Isaiah 53 could be used to explain that God will eventually vindicate those who suffer for him, not just collectively, as Isaiah thought, but also individually, by raising them from the dead.

Resurrection in the Book of Watchers

The idea of a future bodily resurrection of the dead first occurs in a book that was not included in the Bible but was nonetheless one of the most popular Jewish writings in the final two centuries BCE, a book known today as 1 Enoch. The pseudonymous author of the book claims to be none other than Enoch, the first person never to have died. According to Genesis 5:24, "Enoch walked with God; then he was no more, because God took him." Who better to pen an apocalypse, an account of the heavenly secrets that could explain earthly realities? A man who actually lived with God above! The book of 1 Enoch contains a number of special revelations given to this human resident of the heavenly realms.

There are in fact five different writings that have been accumulated and placed together in this longer work. Even though they are all connected with visions and experiences of Enoch, the five sections were written by different authors at different times and only later combined into a literary whole.[8] Here we will be considering only the oldest part, found in what is now chapters 6–36 of the longer collection, a section called by scholars the Book of Watchers, written, probably, some two or two and a half centuries before the birth of Jesus (250–200 BCE).

The book provides a full exposition of one of the most mysterious short passages of the entire Hebrew Bible, not connected with Enoch but with the story of the flood in the days of Noah. In the lead-up to the story in the book of Genesis, we are told that:

> When people began to multiply on the face of the ground, and daughters were born to them, the sons of God saw that they were fair; and they took wives for themselves for all that they chose. . . . The Nephilim were on earth in those days—and also afterward—when the sons of God went into the daughters of humans, who bore children to them. These were the heroes that were of old, warriors of renown. (Genesis 6:1–2, 4)

This strange passage appears to be referring to angelic beings, "the sons of God," who came down and impregnated women, leading to a mighty clan of mixed beings who were half-divine and half-human. The flood that God sent to destroy the earth was, in part, meant to annihilate them.

The early portion of 1 Enoch contains an extensive set of apocryphal stories about these Sons of God, here called "Watchers." In one of the stories, the head angel, Semyaza, descends from heaven with two hundred others, who impregnate women and teach them the ways of magic. Their offspring, the Nephilim, are giants who wreak havoc on earth, eating crops and then, still ravenous, humans. God decides to punish them and sends the flood to wipe them out, sentencing them to eternal torment. Even then evil ravages the earth, however, as out of the Watchers' dead bodies emerge demons who continue to engage in nefarious activities.

This Book of Watchers is our first known apocalyptic text, a book filled with cosmic battles between good and evil. God intervenes to destroy the evil embodied in the Watchers so that good can return to the earth. In the course of the battles a number of visions and experiences of Enoch reveal heavenly realities, including those connected with the future judgment and resurrection of the dead.

In a key passage, Enoch is taken by the angel Raphael and shown that the souls of those who have died are held until the Day of Judgment (chapter 22). He is brought to a high mountain containing four hollows, each holding a different kind of deceased soul, destined to experience a different eternal fate. One hollow holds the souls of the righteous; these apparently will be raised from the dead on Judgment Day. A second holds the souls of sinners who did not receive their punishments on earth; these are being tormented in their temporary dwelling place in anticipation of the Day of Judgment, when they will be assigned to eternal torment. A third contains souls that were not as righteous as those in the first hollow nor as wicked as those in the second but who had been murdered by sinners. They will receive a different, unspecified judgment, presumably not as good as the first group but not as awful as the second. Finally, there is a hollow for sinners who, unlike those in the second hollow, already had experienced punishment for their crimes and misdemeanors. These will neither rise from the dead nor be destroyed on Judgment Day: they will dwell forever in the unpleasant hollow.

In comparison with later texts such as the Christian *Apocalypse of Peter*, these destinies are rather vague and lacking in graphic specificity.

But the basic ideas are here. There is a future Day of Judgment; there are more unrighteous people than righteous; and there will be different degrees of punishment and reward, depending on the degree of righteousness.

The angelic Watchers too will suffer on Judgment Day. We are told in an earlier chapter that they will be bound for seventy generations under the earth before their ultimate destiny is decided (1 Enoch 10:12). That destiny will not be good: they will be led "to the abyss of fire; in torment and in prison they will be shut up for all eternity, and then [Semyaza] will be burnt and from then on destroyed with them; together they will be bound until the end of all generations." This judgment is not reserved for the fallen angels alone, however; it will also be the fate of the humans who sided with them.

The righteous, on the other hand, will be rewarded with an existence of unbelievable pleasure forever:

> And in those days the whole earth will be tilled in righteousness, and all
> of it will be planted with trees, and it will be filled with blessing. . . . and
> the vine which is planted on it will produce fruit in abundance; and every
> seed which is sown on it, each measure will produce a thousand, and
> each measure of olives will produce ten baths of oil. (1 Enoch 10:18–20)

A literal paradise indeed, a garden for eternal life. The earth itself will then be cleansed of all sin, injustice, and iniquity: "And all the children of the people will become righteous, and all the nations shall worship and bless me . . . And the earth shall be cleansed from all pollution, and from all sin, and from all plague, and from all suffering" (1 Enoch 10:22). How good can it get? God will reassert himself and take over this world. There will be no more pain or misery. It will be a utopian existence for all time, for those who have lived righteous lives and been raised from the dead to their eternal reward.

This basic apocalyptic view can be found in a number of early Jewish texts from outside the Bible, including others that together make up the collection found in 1 Enoch.[9] But the best known reference to a future resurrection occurs in the Jewish scriptures themselves, in the last book of the Hebrew canon to be produced, the book of Daniel.

Book of Daniel as an Apocalypse

Daniel certainly does not *claim* to be the last book of the Old Testament. Its author, writing in the first person, indicates that he was one of the Jews taken into Babylonian captivity in the sixth century BCE. But critical scholars have long known this is a literary ploy. Internal evidence from the book shows clearly that it was written some four centuries later, during the time Judea, as Judah came to be renamed in the Persian period, was experiencing a dramatic period of intense persecution leading up to what is known as the Maccabean Revolt.[10]

In 323 BCE, not long after conquering the lands of the Levant, Alexander the Great died, still a young man. The territories he conquered were divided among his generals. For about a century, up to 198 BCE, Judea was controlled by the rulers of Egypt, the Ptolemies. It then passed to the hands of the rulers of Syria, known as the Seleucids. Some thirty years later things were very bad on the Judean front. The ruler of Syria, named Antiochus IV—more commonly called Antiochus Epiphanes—tried to unify his relatively vast empire by imposing Greek culture on it. Many of those in Judea welcomed this progressive thinking and supported the adoption of the Greek language, dress, culture, institutions, and even religion. Many other Jews were incensed that they were not allowed to worship according to their ancestral traditions and were even being compelled, on threat of death, to violate their kosher food laws and to stop having their baby boys circumcised.

Antiochus was, in effect, forcibly trying to stop them from being Jewish.[11]

Eventually, in 167 BCE, a revolt broke out, started by a family known as the Maccabees. It began as series of guerrilla skirmishes but eventually became a major uprising that led to the defeat of Antiochus's forces and the ouster of the Seleucid overlords from the land. Judea became an independent state, and was to remain that way for a century until the Romans came in conquest, taking over the land in 63 BCE.

It was during the time of Antiochus Epiphanes's reign that the book of Daniel was written. The first six chapters contain memorable folktales of the Judean exile, Daniel, and his companions as they resist foreign domination in Babylon, a kind of parable for how Jews of the author's own day could resist the Seleucid attempts to Hellenize the land. The final six chapters contain apocalyptic visions given to Daniel. These are striking, powerful, and bizarre narratives that not too subtly predict the future and its massive catastrophes, climaxing in the triumph of God over the forces of evil—in this case, for the pseudonymous author, the powers of the world empires troubling the Jewish homeland, in particular the Seleucids under Antiochus Epiphanes.

Critical scholars have no doubt that the author "Daniel" is in fact using a pseudonym, just as the unknown writer of the Book of Watchers had done when he claimed to be Enoch. In fact, this kind of apocalyptic literature in which a human seer experiences visions of heavenly realities—often told in highly symbolic language with, at times, quite bizarre images—is almost always written pseudonymously. A book of this sort is known as an "apocalypse," a literary genre used set to forth an apocalyptic view that explains the cosmic reasons for the horrible state of earthly affairs and/or reveals how God will eventually make right all that is wrong at the end of massive suffering and disaster, restoring his creation to its intended goodness, and bringing to justice all who have corrupted it (as, for example, in the New Testament book of Revelation, which we will be exploring later). A number of such apocalypses were in circulation for about four hundred years, beginning with the earliest portions of 1 Enoch.

There are two reasons apocalypses are typically pseudonymous. For one thing, if heavenly secrets are to be revealed, surely it makes best sense for them to come to a particularly great spiritual leader who had a highly unusual and special relationship with the God of All. And so we have apocalypses allegedly written not just by Enoch and Daniel but also by Abraham, the father of the Jews, Moses, and even Adam.[12]

The other advantage of making the author a famous religious figure of the past is that such books often purport to tell the future. They are meant to urge people who are suffering now to hold on for a little while longer, because God, very soon, will intervene to destroy the forces of evil and reward his people. One way this message is conveyed is by having the author—allegedly a person in the distant past—predict what will happen after his day, up to and beyond the time the real author is actually writing. Making these "predictions" of the future was relatively easy when the real author was living after the events he "predicted." The reader, not knowing that the author is describing his own past, rather than predicting the future, is impressed by the accuracy of the predictions and is thus led to believe that the seer had been given secret, mystical knowledge. It had all come true! And if what he predicted leading *up to* our day has come to pass, then what he says is to come next is equally certain to happen.

The pseudonymous authorship, then, is a literary ploy used by authors to convince their readers they know what was soon to happen, and so to provide comfort for them in their time of trouble. That is certainly the case with the book of Daniel, who, by extensive recounting of detailed visions about the future of Judea, allegedly written centuries earlier, discusses at length the rule of Antiochus Epiphanes, without calling him by name, and his ultimate fate. The real author is clearly living during

Antiochus's reign, and he actually predicts Antiochus's death in a final battle in the Promised Land (Daniel 11:40–45). This particular prediction did not come true, showing that the book was produced sometime before Antiochus died in Persia in 164 BCE.

From Death to Life in Daniel

Daniel is the first and in fact only book of the entire Hebrew Bible to predict that a resurrection of the dead would come at the end of time. It was to take place right after Antiochus died, foretold in Daniel 11:45. The very next passage, Daniel 12:1–3, is key to understanding this new Jewish view of the afterlife:

> At that time Michael, the great prince, the protector of your people, shall arise. There shall be a time of anguish, such as has never occurred since nations first came into existence. But at that time your people shall be delivered, everyone who is found written in the book. Many of those who sleep in the dust of the earth shall awake, some to everlasting life, and some to shame and contempt. Those who are wise shall shine like the brightness of the sky, and those who lead many to righteousness, like the stars forever and ever.

The great prince Michael is the chief archangel, head of God's heavenly armies and divinely appointed protector of the nation of Israel. After the reign of Antiochus there will be a period of terrible distress, but then a divine intervention. "Many" will be raised from the dead. It is striking that, for this text, not everyone will be. On the other hand, that is what we found in the Book of the Watchers as well, where a group of people in one of the hollows would not experience the resurrection. But the fact that Daniel indicates that "many" will be raised shows that he, unlike Isaiah 26:19 or Ezekiel 37, is not talking about the collective, the entire nation of Israel. He is talking about individuals.

And he maintains their actual bodies will come back to life. This is not some kind of "spiritual" resurrection in which people are granted eternal life as souls; it is a profoundly bodily experience. These people are "asleep," a common euphemism for "death," specifically "in the dust." This shows he is talking about bodies returning to life: that which comes to life is in the soil. And what is in the soil? The corpse.

It is debated among scholars who, exactly, these "some" are who will be given everlasting life. Is it the leaders of the Jews who were persecuted and martyred prior to the Maccabean revolt, as suggested by Daniel 11:33, 35? Is it all the faithful Jews? Is it all people who strove to live a good, righteous life? Whoever it is, they are the people especially blessed by God. This is the only verse in the entire Old Testament that uses the term "everlasting life."[13]

These people are not only raised to a new life; they are raised to a new location. No longer will they reside in the dusty grave, but they will be taken up to the heavenly realm to live like angels, shining "like the stars forever and ever." A number of ancient Jewish and Christian sources talk about the resurrected faithful becoming like stars or even, actually, becoming stars. The idea is rooted in the notion that the stars in heaven are in fact angels (see, e.g., Job 38:6–7) and that righteous humans, after death, are made into angelic beings. That is true, for example, of some ancient Jewish traditions about Enoch.[14] Daniel does not say the faithful will actually become stars, but they certainly become like them, shining in the heavens.

The wicked are not so fortunate. "Some" of them too will be raised not to be glorified but to be put to shame and experience everlasting contempt. Are these the persecutors of the faithful Jews during the reign of Antiochus Epiphanes, the violent sinners alluded to in Daniel 11:33–35? Or is it all those opposed to the Jewish people? Could it be the most wicked of all people, whether connected to Jewish persecution or not? In any event, it is striking, and possibly significant, that the author does not actually say they will undergo eternal torture; they are not said to be *tormented* forever but *despised* forever. It may well be that, instead, they will be raised, shown the error of their ways, be put to shame, and then annihilated. As those who faced such an ignominious end, they will be the sources of eternal disdain among those they oppressed and persecuted.

Bodies Raised Only to Be Destroyed

Other early Jewish texts also speak of everlasting destruction—that is, annihilation—not eternal torture. This is the case with the first-century non-canonical book known as the Psalms of Solomon, which in poetic verse refers several times to the contrasting eternal fates of the righteous and the sinners:

> For the life of the righteous (goes on) forever
> but sinners shall be taken away to destruction
> and no memory of them will ever be found (Psalms
>   of Solomon 13:11)

> The destruction of the sinner is forever
> and he will not be remembered when God looks after
>   his righteous . . .
> But those who fear the Lord shall rise up to eternal
>   life
> and their life shall be in the Lord's light, and it shall
>   never end (Psalms of Solomon 3:11–12)

> Sinners shall perish forever in the day of the Lord's
>   judgment

> *when God oversees the earth at his judgment.*
> *But those who fear the Lord shall find mercy in it*
> *and shall live by their God's mercy.*
> *But sinners shall perish for all time. (Psalms of*
> *Solomon 15:11–13)*

In this text it appears that the alternative applies to all righteous and all sinners, not just "many" of them, as in Daniel. Here there are two types of people, and they will have opposing fates. One group will find mercy and live in the presence of God's light forever and ever. Others will not. They are said to be bound not for torment but for destruction. They will be annihilated, so thoroughly that no one will ever remember them, not even God himself. The choice is not between reward and punishment but between life and extinction.

Resurrection and Immortality

It is often said that the key difference between ancient pagan and Jewish views of the afterlife is that Greeks developed the notion of the immortality of the soul but Jews came to believe in the resurrection of the body.[15] Even though there is an element of truth in this characterization, it is far too simple and, in fact, demonstrably problematic.

To be sure, there are differences between Plato's view of immortality and, say, Daniel's view of resurrection. In Plato's view the soul is *inherently* immortal. It simply always will exist because it is its nature always to exist. Unlike the body, it cannot die. This entails a kind of dualistic anthropology: humans are made up of two competing entities, the mortal body and the immortal soul, which at death separate from each other.

That is indeed different from most of the ancient Israelite and then later Jewish texts we have examined so far. These assume a unitary understanding of the human being. The soul is not a separate essence or substance that can exist independently of the body. The person is a body that can be alive, but when the breath of life leaves it, it is dead. At that point neither the body nor the breath is living. The body disintegrates and disappears and there is no soul to live on.

In the later Jewish doctrine of the resurrection, God reverses death by bringing the breath of life back into the body, ensuring it will never die again. Unlike in the Greek tradition, here the person is *made* immortal. Immortality is an act of God, not an innate nature of the real essence of the human. Moreover, in these Jewish texts, the idea is not that people cannot die but precisely that they do die. God needs to raise them from the dead because they really are dead.

That certainly is not the doctrine of immortality. But in reading this description you may be puzzled by one of the texts we have already considered. If people are really dead in Jewish traditions, and the soul does not live on after death, how does one explain 1 Enoch 22, where there are four holding places—"hollows" in a giant mountain—for "souls" being kept for the future judgment?

As it turns out, the neat differentiation between pagan and Jewish views does not always hold. There were pagans who had no trouble imagining that bodies could live forever—for example, Menelaus in the *Odyssey*.[16] And there were Jews who believed in the immortality of the soul, as possibly hinted at in 1 Enoch and as more explicitly affirmed in texts we will examine later. The characterization of the sharp lines between pagan immortality of the soul and Jewish resurrection of the body is therefore too simplistic. Historical reality was much muddier than that.

That is not to deny the unique importance of the doctrine of resurrection as it developed in Judaism in the years leading up to the life of Jesus. Indeed, it is fair to say that by the time of Christianity, *most* Jews held to some version of this doctrine, believing in a future restoration and resuscitation of the body that did not involve simply a temporary return to life but an entrance into life eternal, not lived as a disembodied soul but as a unified person, body and soul. That, as we will see, was also the view of Jesus and his followers, who, as a consequence, did not maintain that when a person died their soul separated from their body and went to heaven or hell. On the contrary, they were Jewish apocalypticists. They believed it was the body that would be raised on the Day of Judgment, when the righteous would be given eternal life and the wicked would be annihilated for all time.

CHAPTER SEVEN

Why Wait for the Resurrection?
Life After Death Right After Death

We have seen that the notion of individual resurrection, developed at the tail end of the Hebrew Bible period, arose principally in response to questions of theodicy. How is it fair—or, rather, how can God be just—if the wicked prosper and then die and get away with it? Or if the righteous suffer for doing God's will and then perish in misery? Surely there must be some kind of recompense when we pass from this world of mortality. As evidenced in the non-canonical book of 1 Enoch and then the canonical Daniel, Jewish thinkers developed views of the afterlife that explained it all. At the end of time God will make right all that is wrong. He will reassert his sovereignty. The dead will be raised and God will vindicate his people, rewarding them for their pious deeds and punishing their enemies.

It is this idea of ultimate vindication that later drove another shift in the understanding of the afterlife. Eventually Jewish thinkers came to wonder why justice—involving divine rewards and punishments—would come only at some future time. Shouldn't justice be not only severe but also swift? Driven by such questions, some Jews came to believe there was life after death immediately after death, with no waiting period prior to the resurrection. This shift in afterlife thinking proved essential for later developments, including the later formation of Christian views of heaven and hell. Moreover, just as the original doctrine of the resurrection arose in periods of uncertainty, trouble, and persecution, so too did the later idea, that rewards and punishments would come immediately at death.

We can actually see the transition by considering two Jewish texts that present the same stories but by authors living two centuries apart. The first of these texts assumes that God's justice will be served on the future Day of Judgment; the other maintains it comes when a person dies. Both of them focus on a small group of Jews who fiercely clung to their ancestral traditions in the face of torture and death: eight of the most famous martyrs of ancient Jewish history.

The Role of Martyrdom in Understandings of the Afterlife

Our best sources of information of the events themselves come from the Jewish apocryphal books known as 1 and 2 Maccabees. These books are named after the family of the Maccabees, which started the Jewish revolt against Syria and its ruler Antiochus Epiphanes in 167 BCE, a revolt that eventually led to the establishment of Israel as a sovereign state in the Promised Land.

The Maccabean literature describes Antiochus's violent actions against the Jews as he raided Jerusalem, purloined the treasures of the beloved Jewish temple, murdered numerous people, burned the city, and passed legislation requiring Jews to practice Greek religion rather than follow the laws of Moses (see 1 Maccabees 1). In his attempt to Hellenize the various parts of his realm—that is, to make it adopt Greek culture and religion—Antiochus forbade the centuries-old Jewish worship of God in the temple, built altars and shrines for pagan idols, forced Jews to sacrifice to pagan gods, placed a pagan statue in the temple precincts, ordered Jews to eat pork, and forbade circumcision of baby boys. Anyone who violated his commands was to be put to death. Women who circumcised their infants died with their children hanged around their necks.

For our reflections on Jewish views of the afterlife, 2 Maccabees is particularly important. The book dates to 124 BCE and provides a fervent defense of Jewish customs and religion, written to show the pious, stout, and passionate resistance to Antiochus's attempt to stamp out the Jewish faith.[1] The book is not an "apocalypse" like 1 Enoch or Daniel. It is a historical narrative. But it contains numerous apocalyptic themes, especially concerning the future Day of Judgment. There is no idea here yet of rewards that come immediately at death; instead they are granted at the resurrection.

The book is best known for its description of seven brothers and their mother, all of them devout and passionately faithful Jews who in the face of horrific tortures and gruesome deaths refuse to recant their faith and ancestral customs, even if it means simply taking a bite of pork (2 Maccabees 7). Antiochus has them all arrested and threatens to torture them with "whips and thongs" if they will not yield and taste the forbidden food (2 Maccabees 7:1). They are steadfast. One of the brothers acts as the spokesperson for all and asks, "What do you intend to ask and learn from us? For we are ready to die rather than transgress the laws of our ancestors" (2 Maccabees 7:2).

This infuriates the king, and what follows is one of the most gruesome accounts of torture you will find in ancient literature. Antiochus orders his soldiers to heat up an enormous metal pan over a large fire. He then has them take the first brother, cut out his tongue, scalp him, and cut off his hands and feet "while the rest of the brothers and the mother looked on" (2 Maccabees 7:3). Then, while the man is still living, he has him thrust onto the red-hot pan to be fried alive. As the smoke spreads, the remaining brothers and their mother do not shrink in fright or rethink their decision. Instead they assure each other: "The Lord God is watching over us and in truth has compassion on us . . ." (2 Maccabees 7:6). One might wonder what would make them think so, but we find out as the narrative proceeds: they are firmly convinced that if they remain faithful through unfathomable torture and death, they will be rewarded on the Day of Judgment.

This becomes clear when the second brother is taken by the soldiers. Before he dies he says to Antiochus, "You accursed wretch, you dismiss us from the present life, but the King of the universe will raise us up to an everlasting renewal of life, because we have died for his laws" (2 Maccabees 7:9). Pain now will lead to vindication later, at the resurrection. So too the next brother, when threatened with having his tongue and hands cut off, stretches them out and declares: "I got these from Heaven, and because of his laws I disdain them, and from him I hope to get them back again" (2 Maccabees 7:11). The resurrection will bring restoration, health, and wholeness.

When his turn comes, the fourth brother not only affirms the good that will come to the faithful at the future resurrection but contrasts the fate of the upright with that of those who are in power now: "One cannot but choose to die at the hands of mortals and to cherish the hope God gives of being raised again by him. But for you there will be no resurrection to life!" (2 Maccabees 7:14). It is important to note: the man says nothing about any punishment to come to the king on the Day of Judgment. The righteous will be rewarded but the wicked will not be raised to new life. The choice is life after death or death after death.

On first reading, however, portions of this chapter may seem to suggest that eternal punishment, as opposed to annihilation, is awaiting the wicked. The fifth brother, for example, tells the tyrant, "Keep on, and see how his mighty power will torture you and your descendants!" (2 Maccabees 7:17). This may indeed look like a threat of postmortem agony for the king, but on closer examination the brother says nothing about the future torture coming after death, no word about the wicked being raised for judgment. He may instead be making a prophetic prediction, as commonly occurs in ancient Jewish writings: anyone who mistreats the righteous in this life will pay a price eventually in this life. God will have his revenge. The torturers themselves will die in misery. Only in later texts does this divine threat come to be transferred to the life after death.

Afterlife Immediately After Life

It is striking to compare the events recorded in 2 Maccabees with the accounts of the same events in our second book, written two centuries later, called 4 Maccabees.[2] Particularly important are the different understandings of the afterlife. The author of this later text used the work of his predecessor as one of his sources of information, but he had a very different purpose for writing. 4 Maccabees is less interested in detailing the unmovable faithfulness to the law found among devoted Jews in the times of persecution than in making a philosophical argument: people, in general, should use reason, not passions, to guide their actions. The author makes his point by offering the Maccabean martyrs as a model. They preferred bodily pain to pleasure because they knew it would be to their profit in the long run. He thus provides a kind of ancient cost-benefits analysis. Pain now will lead to pleasure later.

4 Maccabees not only shifts its focus to a philosophical point, it also presents a different understanding of the afterlife. Jewish thinking, at least among some writers, had shifted by this time. Now the emphasis is not on what would happen at some indefinite point in the future on Judgment Day, when the righteous would be raised. Instead this author believes that rewards come immediately at death. No one has to wait. What is more, the wicked too will have a postmortem fate. They

will not simply stay dead but will be punished, tortured just as those who remained faithful to the law were tortured. What you give is what you get.

And so 4 Maccabees relates the same episode of the seven brothers and their mother but presents it in a different light, stressing a message that ultimately derived from Plato as much as from any Jewish author. It is the soul that matters, not the body. Bodily torments are temporary, but the soul of those who disobey God will be tormented in the afterlife forever. As the brothers now say to one another at one point: "Let us not fear him who thinks he is killing us, for great is the struggle of the soul and the danger of eternal torment lying before those who transgress the commandment of God" (4 Maccabees 13:14–15).

And so the account focuses not on the future life of the tortured bodies but on their souls and the vengeance God will wreak on the persecuting tyrant: "For these crimes divine justice pursued and will pursue the accursed tyrant. But the sons of Abraham with their victorious mother are gathered together into the chorus of the fathers, and have received pure and immortal souls from God" (4 Maccabees 18:22–23). There is no need to wait for a future resurrection. The seven sons and their mother, after their deaths, are *already* gathered together with their ancestors and have received souls that will enjoy everlasting life. The difference from Plato is that these Jewish souls are not inherently immortal; they are given immortality as a gift from God. But the focus is Platonic nonetheless: soul instead of body. And it is eternal life now, not in some vague future time.

That is why the mother can be praised for her endurance and insistence that her sons undergo torture rather than recant. The one who had given them birth was making it possible for them to be born again, immortal. And so the account extols her: "As though having a mind like adamant and giving rebirth for immortality to the whole number of her sons, she implored them and urged them on to death for the sake of religion" (4 Maccabees 16:13). Death is just a transition to immortality for those who are faithful.

But it leads to eternal disaster for the persecutors. God's retribution will not come in temporary punishments in this life, as argued by the ancient Hebrew prophets and suggested by the author of 2 Maccabees. Instead, it will be eternal in the life to come. And so the first brother says:

> "We, through this severe suffering and endurance, shall have the prize of virtue and shall be with God, on whose account we suffer; but you, because of your bloodthirstiness toward us, will deservedly undergo from the divine justice eternal torment by fire." (4 Maccabees 9:8–9)

Here then is true justice: the harm done to the righteous in this life will be visited on the wicked in the life to come. The tormentors will be tormented, and in familiar ways. The tyrant who fried the brothers in a pan will himself be fried, but not only for a few minutes until he is unconscious. On the contrary, he will experience "eternal torment by fire." God is eternal, and so will be his justice. And so the third brother declares to the godless king: "You, because of your impiety and blood-thirstiness, will undergo unceasing torments" (4 Maccabees 10:10–11). The seventh brother emphasizes the point: "You profane tyrant, most impious of all the wicked . . . were you not ashamed to murder his servants and torture on the wheel those who practice religion? Because of this, justice has laid up for you intense and eternal fire and tortures, and these throughout all time will never let you go" (4 Maccabees 12:11–12).

Changes in the Afterlife

It is important to reflect back on how understandings of the afterlife shifted over time in ancient Israel. It is not necessarily the case that there was a straight linear development, that every Jew everywhere thought the same thing at the same time. On the contrary, the developments were undoubtedly uneven, taking place in different places at different times, with some thinkers never changing their views at all and others holding various views in their heads simultaneously. But, roughly speaking, some authors see death as the end of the story; for them there is death after death but no life after death. Others focus on the life of the nation and speak of it coming back to life after being destroyed. Yet others shift the focus to the individual, and begin to imagine a resurrection not of the nation but of the individual, at the end of time, on the Day of Judgment. And later some begin to think that justice comes not at the end of time but at the point of death, when the righteous are rewarded with immortal souls and the wicked are punished with eternal punishments. It is quite a set of transitions, from the postmortem nonexistence of the person whose breathless body lies in the grave to the joyous life of the eternal soul in heaven.

Why did the final shift occur, from a belief in the bodily resurrection at the end of time to the view that rewards and punishments come immediately at the point of death? I would suggest two factors, one internal to Jewish thought and the other external.

It is easy to imagine that a simple shift in thinking played a significant role. For the doctrine of a future resurrection to work as an explanation for how God can be just, given all the pain and misery his people are suffering, it was not enough that he would later vindicate those who suffered for his sake—that he would later raise them from the dead and give them an eternal reward. Apocalypticists thought the suffering had gone on long enough—that it had gotten just as bad as it possibly could. And that led them to think that the future resurrection would happen soon. Very soon. That was certainly the view of our first canonical apocalyptic text, Daniel, which foresaw that it would occur immediately after the death of Antiochus Epiphanes (see Daniel 11:45–12:1). Many subsequent apocalypticists followed Daniel's lead, maintaining that judgment and resurrection were coming imminently, possibly sometime next month.

But what happens when it doesn't come? What happens when things just keep getting worse? And the wicked thrive more than ever? And the sufferings of the righteous only increase? Where is God? Why doesn't he act?

These questions led to a shift in thinking about the afterlife: justice occurs not in some vague, distant future but immediately after death. It comes right away. A person who dies faces judgment. Those who are wicked will face punishment for the crimes they have committed. Those who have lived lives of love, caring for others, doing what is right, trying to serve God, will be rewarded. Neither the punishment nor the reward will be short-term, for, say, the period of a lifetime. God is eternal, and so are his rewards and punishments. Eternal life or eternal torment is the choice set before all people. This shift in thinking obviously became key to the Christian formation of the doctrines of heaven and hell.

But there was probably more than an internal thought process involved in the shift. I have pointed out that the author of 4 Maccabees seems very much at home with some simple form of popular Platonic thought, which emphasized the importance of the soul over the body. The afterlife he envisions focuses on the blessed state of the immortal soul, not merely the revivification of the corpse for an eternal life lived in the fleshly body. Of course, the eternal soul has physical properties. That much is clear from the opposite state, eternal punishment, which presupposes the capacity to be tortured and tormented. Nothing suggests that the author is imagining only mental anguish forever, even if that is part of it. He appears to think the tortures endured by the martyrs in this life will be replicated for their tormentors in the life to come for all eternity. Even so, the emphasis has shifted to a more Platonic understanding of the distinction between soul and body, and the superiority of the former to the latter. What explains this shift? The obvious answer is: the increased Hellenization of the ancient Mediterranean.

After Alexander the Great swept through the eastern Mediterranean, he and his successors brought Hellenistic culture to the lands they conquered. Antiochus IV Epiphanes was not unique in wanting to stress Greek practices, institutions, and culture. This kind of Hellenization was happening widely throughout the eastern Mediterranean, and it had an enormous effect on all sorts of peoples who dwelled in all sorts of lands. Despite the Maccabean revolt, it had a huge effect on the people living in Israel, many of whom, even while trying to remain faithful to the Law of Moses, began to be influenced by Greek thought. This included the Greek philosophical distinction between the soul and the body.[3]

The text of 4 Maccabees and its view of the afterlife therefore present an intriguing irony that was almost certainly lost on the author. While celebrating the passionate Jewish resistance to Hellenistic culture, the author champions Hellenistic philosophy, especially its stress on the superiority of reason to passion and its prioritization of soul over body.

It is important to emphasize that the history of the afterlife did not involve a clear and straightforward shift from one view, resurrection of the body, to another, immediate rewards and punishments for the soul. It was in fact possible for different Jewish writers to affirm both views, at one and the same time, just as many Christians do today. We can see that in a number of early Jewish texts, most strikingly in a pseudepigraphic work known as 4 Ezra.[4]

Having It Both Ways: Judgment in 4 Ezra

Like both 1 Enoch and Daniel, 4 Ezra is an apocalypse, a pseudonymous description of a series of bizarre and symbolic visions given to a famous holy man of Jewish antiquity, meant to explain the heavenly secrets that can make sense of the horrible situations facing people here on earth. In this case the unknown author claimed to be Ezra, an important figure in the history of Israel after the Babylonian captivity. The historical Ezra was one of the key leaders of the nation after he and others returned from exile; he was especially known for his deep and profound knowledge of the law of Moses, which he and other returnees vowed to follow diligently as they attempted to rebuild Jerusalem and reestablish themselves in the land (see Nehemiah 8–9 and Ezra 7–10). In the absence of a king, the returnees turned to Ezra as an authoritative leader for direction, advice, and leadership.

The book of 4 Ezra narrates seven encounters of "Ezra" with the angel Uriel and several apocalyptic visions, allegedly thirty years after the Babylonian destruction of Jerusalem (586 BCE). The guiding question behind the account involves the prophet's distress that God has abandoned his own people, who have been destroyed by a foreign power. He is told in the various settings in the book that God is in fact just and will execute his justice soon. The end, and the final judgment, are near.

Scholars are unified in seeing this apocalyptic text as coming not in Ezra's own day, three decades removed from the Babylonian destruction of Jerusalem, but over six hundred years later, thirty years after the second destruction of Jerusalem, this time by the Romans (in 70 CE).[5] The author, pretending to live in a situation from earlier times, writes to the people of his own time, providing them hope that God is still almighty and cares for his people. One of the clear foci of the text is the justice of God. This justice is manifest in large part after death. The author certainly believes there will be a future resurrection of the dead. But before then, those who die receive an immediate judgment. That is to say, for this writer there is an *interim* state of rewards and punishments, to be followed by a day of judgment that will have permanent effect.

Theodicy issues are front and center from the outset of the book. The author cannot understand why Israel, God's chosen nation, is oppressed by nations of foreigners, when God has said these other nations "are nothing, and they are like spittle" and has "compared their abundance to a drop from a bucket" (4 Ezra 6:56). The angel replies that even though Israel has been destroyed, God will eventually triumph over the nation's enemies. That will happen at the end of time, when "the earth shall give up those who are asleep in it" (4 Ezra 7:32). God will then appear on a seat of judgment, and there will no longer be a chance for compassion and patience. Instead, justice will come: "The pit of torment shall appear, and opposite it shall be the place of rest; and the furnace of hell shall be disclosed, and opposite it the paradise of delight" (4 Ezra 7:36).

Here, unlike the prophets of the Hebrew Bible, it is not the nation that will be restored to greatness. The focus is on individuals. Those who have opposed Jews will be punished in the flames of hell. The faithful Jews will enter the garden of paradise. And so the author makes a stark contrast between the "fire and torments" awaiting some and the "delight and rest" coming to others (4 Ezra 7:38).

Ezra is happy at the prospect but also a bit alarmed, wondering how many will face eternal torment. The numbers are disproportionate: "There are more who perish than those who will be saved, as a wave is greater than a drop of water" (4 Ezra 9:15–16). Indeed, the saved are like a plant in the forest and the condemned like all the rest of the trees. For "the Most High made this world for the sake of many, but the world to come for the sake of the few" (4 Ezra 8:1).

Even though these are Ezra's enemies, he has trouble understanding it. But the angel explains that "silver is more abundant than gold, and brass than silver, and iron than brass, and lead than iron, and clay than lead" (4 Ezra 7:56). Which metals are the most desirable? The most rare. God will rejoice in the few, not the many. Moreover, in the case of judgment, people get what they deserve: "Those who dwell on earth shall be tormented, because though they had understanding they committed iniquity, and though they received the commandments they did not keep them . . ." (4 Ezra 7:72).

But to relieve Ezra's apparent anxiety, the angel intimates that even if rewards are eternal, punishment has an end: "I will not grieve over the multitude of those who perish; for it is they who are now like a mist, and are similar to a flame and smoke—they are set on fire and burn hotly, and are extinguished" (4 Ezra 7:61). It appears, then, that there is no eternal torment. Punishment entails a fire that kills and destroys the wicked. After that, they simply disappear into nonexistence.

Thus Ezra learns there will be a future resurrection and a time of reckoning. But what about in the meantime? Ezra inquires explicitly about an interim state between death and resurrection, asking: "Whether after death, as soon as every one of us yields up his soul, we shall be kept in rest until those times come when you will renew the creation, or whether we shall be tormented at once?" (4 Ezra 7:75). The angel indicates that torments in fact come at death:

> As the spirit leaves the body to return again to him who gave it . . . if it
> is one of those who have shown scorn and have not kept the way of the
> most High, and who have despised his law, and who have hated those
> who fear God—such spirits shall not enter into [good] habitations, but
> shall immediately wander about in torments . . . (4 Ezra 7:78–80)

So too with the righteous. When they are "separated from their mortal body" they will be given rest. In fact, in a reflection of the resurrection of the righteous in Daniel 12, 4 Ezra says they will "be made like the light of the stars, being incorruptible from then on" (4 Ezra 7:97). Those who "behold the face of him whom they served in life" will "receive their reward when glorified" (4 Ezra 7:98). Here, then, is the beatific vision, in a Jewish text from the time of the rise of Christianity.

Yet other Jewish texts of the period also subscribe to both postmortem justice and a future resurrection of the dead, even if the balance of emphasis shifts to the former. That is the case with another pseudonymous apocalypse associated with one of the greats of Israel's past, this time the father of the Jews himself, Abraham.

Full-Blown Immediacy:
The Testament of Abraham

The Testament of Abraham was produced at about the same time as 4 Ezra and like it is concerned with the nature of the afterlife. In contrast with 4 Ezra, however, this text focuses almost exclusively on the rewards and punishments that come immediately after death, with far less emphasis on resurrection and judgment to come at the end of time.[6]

The narrative begins with a humorous tale of Abraham, the father of the Jews, steadfastly refusing to die when his time has come. God sends his "Commander-in-Chief," the archangel Michael, to the 995-year-old Abraham to tell him that his soul must now depart from his body in death. When Michael arrives, Abraham entertains him with a feast, putting Michael in a bit of a bind, since, as an incorporeal angel, he cannot actually eat or drink. After the meal, Abraham announces he is unwilling to go with Michael to his heavenly reward, and as a delaying tactic asks to be shown the entire world while still in the body.

Michael takes him up in a flying carriage, and as they look down on the earth, Abraham sees numerous people committing transgressions. In righteous anger he calls upon God to destroy them, and the Lord, compliant to the request of his most holy creature, does so. But the slaughter goes on to such a ridiculous extent that God decides Abraham had better not be shown too much of the rest of the human race, or no one will be left. So Michael instead takes Abraham to see the realms of the afterlife.

When they come to the "first gate of heaven," Abraham sees two paths, one broad and spacious on which a large number of "souls" are driven by angels, the other straight and narrow, on which only a few are led. The narrative, to this point told in the third person, now shifts to the first person as Abraham relates what he sees.

Between the gates leading to the paths is a terrifying throne, flashing with fire. Seated on the throne is a wondrous man, bright as the sun. Later we learn that this is Abel, the first righteous man ever to live (see Genesis 4). Before him is a table on which sits a book that is nine feet thick and fifteen feet across. An angel stands to the right of the table with ink and papyrus to write the righteous deeds of each soul; another angel stands to the left, recording the sins. In front of the table is a third angel with scales in his hand to weigh the sins and acts of righteousness of each soul, to determine its ultimate fate. On his left, just to make things confusing, is yet another angel, with a trumpet that contains fire that is to test the sinners (somehow).

One by one souls are judged by the enthroned man, with the angels recording in the book their deeds; the angel with scales weighs these deeds; the one with the trumpet tests them. By the time a soul has passed these evaluations, a determination is made: souls that are righteous are given a heavenly reward; sinners are sent to a place of torment, "a most bitter place of punishment."

The whole proceeding is relatively straightforward. Whoever has committed more sins than acts of righteousness is doomed; those with more righteous deeds than transgressions are saved. But as Abraham looks on, a soul is brought forward who has precisely the same number. The angels are not sure what to do, because to be saved or damned requires more of one kind of deed than the other. Abraham urges Michael to pray with him for the soul, and when they do so, it is saved.

This creates in Abraham a more merciful frame of mind, making him feel remorse for having asked God to destroy so many people on earth. He prays for them, and they return from the dead to live out the rest of their mortal existence. God then informs Abraham that anyone he destroys prematurely on earth will not be punished further after death.

Even though the text is principally concerned with life immediately after death, the author does not neglect the now well-established idea of a future judgment. In fact, he refers to *two* further judgments. In the end, all people will be judged by the faithful of Israel (although we are not told the mechanics of how it will work), then, ultimately, by God. Thus every soul faces three "last" judgments: one by a human (Abel), one by Israel (the faithful among them), and one by God. That very last of the last judgments really is final. After that there is no court of appeal.

The narrative ends with God sending Death itself to Abraham. Even it has to resort to a bit of supernatural trickery to convince him to die. When he does so, his body is buried and his soul enters paradise. This ending is important because it reaffirms what has been intimated throughout the text. Even though this author does embrace the idea of a future judgment, there is no resurrection of the dead. When a person dies, their body is buried, and that's the end of their physical story. It is the soul that lives on, to enter paradise or torment.

It is not completely clear, however, that the torments of sinners are to last forever. As we have seen, God determined that anyone who had previously been punished—on earth—would not have to be punished again. That suggests that that "eternal" punishment is not perpetual torment but annihilation at the last judgment. Those who were already killed on earth for their sins do not need to be punished for their sins after death; that will happen only to the wicked who died through other causes.

The rewards, however, are assumed to be eternal. The righteous will live forever in paradise, always enjoying the presence of God in the company of the saints.

What Did Jews Believe at the Time of Jesus?

We have the same problem knowing what the average Jew believed at any one time that we had with the pagans. All of our surviving literary texts come from the highly educated—that is, the cultured elite. You can never know whether the upper intellectual class can be trusted to represent fairly the views of those who were uneducated, who have not had the time or, more important, the resources to be exposed widely to the thoughts, views, ideas, prejudices, and assumptions of others. Most lower-class people (that is, most people) probably believed pretty much whatever their parents did. But since we don't know for certain what that might have been, we are in the dark about what people in general thought about the afterlife.

Again, we do have material remains uncovered by archaeologists: gifts and cooking utensils discovered in or nearby grave sites, for example. And some scholars have written impressive overviews of this evidence and drawn wide-ranging conclusions.[7] But the problems have been noted by other scholars: these material goods are not self-interpreting, and we don't have anyone to interview, or any text to read, that can tell us what people were thinking when they placed them close to the corpses of their deceased loved ones. Various interpretations are possible.

Moreover, we also have Jewish inscriptions, and these are of some use, but not much, since the evidence is so sparse. The most informative study is by historian Pieter Willem van der Horst, who puts the matter in striking terms.[8] He estimates that some 165 million Jews lived during the thousand-year period he examines. We have about 1,600 epitaphs from the period. Six hundred of these have only barely legible letters, or are badly damaged, or do nothing except mention the name of the deceased. That means we have about 1,000 inscriptions for 165,000,000

Jews. Would these thousand be representative? Do the math and take a guess. That's all we can do.

Even more disheartening, after examining these thousand, van der Horst draws this conclusion: "Most of our epitaphs yield disappointingly little information concerning the ideas of either the survivors or the deceased about life after death," and, what is worse, "the evidence often defies interpretation."[9] Some inscriptions do suggest an ongoing existence beyond death but do not give specifics. A few indicate the possibility of a future resurrection. Others urge the deceased to have courage, apparently as they move into their postmortem existence. Some suggest astral immortality—that the soul will become a star shining in the firmament. Yet others suggest that, at death, the person simply ceases to exist.[10]

These relatively few data do give us one important piece of information: there were different understandings of the afterlife in the Jewish world throughout the period. This was certainly true in the days of Jesus, even in his homeland of Galilee and in Judea to the south. That much is confirmed explicitly by one of the leading Jewish figures of the first century CE, the famed historian Josephus (37–100 CE).

Josephus was an upper-class, highly educated Jew who was well-connected and deeply involved with affairs in Palestine—social, cultural, religious, political, and military. He produced a large number of books, including a seven-volume account of the Jewish War against the Romans (66–70 CE), an uprising in which he himself participated as military commander, and a twenty-volume history of the Jewish people extending all the way from the beginning (with Adam!) up to his own day. In both these works he discusses different Jewish groups who influenced the thinking of Jews in first-century Palestine, and he points out that among their differences were variant understandings of the afterlife.[11]

The group called the Essenes, known to us from other sources, are usually thought to have been responsible for producing the famous Dead

Sea Scrolls.[12] They were a very pious separatist sect who believed in maintaining their own purity, in isolation from other, sinful Jews if possible, sometimes in monastic-like communities. According to Josephus, the Essenes held a very Greek view of the afterlife: that the body was impermanent and destined to disintegrate, but the soul was immortal and imperishable. After the death of the body, the soul would be released, and those who were virtuous would enjoy a very pleasant happily ever after.

The Pharisees are known to us from the New Testament and later rabbinic writings; they were focused on interpreting the Jewish law for their own times, providing detailed explanations of the ancient words of Moses for life in the present and working to preserve the holiness that the law demanded. According to Josephus, the Pharisees believed that after death good souls pass "into another body." This may sound to modern ears like reincarnation, but it is usually thought that Josephus means they held to the doctrine of resurrection: the soul would not remain naked but would be re-embodied. Wicked souls, on the other hand will "suffer eternal punishment."

We are less well-informed about the third group Josephus mentions in this context, the Sadducees, even though in Jesus's day they were the real power players in Judea. Unfortunately, none of them left us any writings. But from the remarks of others it appears they were particularly focused on worship in the Temple of Jerusalem and determined to adhere to the prescriptions for worship laid out in the Mosaic law. Josephus is quite clear that this focus on present worship was accompanied by a denial of any life to come: "As for the persistence of the soul after death, penalties in the underworld, and rewards, they will have none of them." The soul for them, evidently, does not live on and there was to be no resurrection. This life is what matters, a view resonant with Ecclesiastes and other texts we have examined.

It is impossible to know if Josephus is completely right in what he says about the beliefs of these three groups, and difficult to know what the person on the street actually thought, in no small measure because the vast majority of the Jewish population did not belong to any of these or any other groups. But the views Josephus lays out make a good deal of sense as three leading options among Jews of Jesus's day: annihilation, immortality, or resurrection. If our other texts are any guide, it was the last of these that was most widely held, the view that at the end of history God would intervene in the world to bring about a resurrection of the dead.

That almost certainly was the view of the historical Jesus and his earliest followers. They did not believe that at the time of death a person's soul went to heaven or hell. On the contrary, they thought that at the end of time—which was coming soon—God would enter into judgment with this world, destroy the forces of evil, and raise all the dead bodily back to life, some to enter God's utopian kingdom here on earth, others to perish with no chance of return.

CHAPTER EIGHT

Jesus and the Afterlife

O ver two billion Christians in our world follow Jesus, and most of them believe that, because of their faith, they will have a glorious afterlife. But how many of them know what Jesus's own views of the afterlife actually were? My sense is: very few indeed.

Knowing the Views of Jesus

There are massive complications in knowing Jesus's views. He obviously is the most important figure for Christianity as a whole and for Christian views of the afterlife in particular. But he is also virtually the only figure we will be discussing in this entire book who did not leave us any writings. When we have wanted to know what the authors of the Psalms, Isaiah, and Ecclesiastes thought about the afterlife—or when, later, we will want to know the views of Paul, the Gospel of John, or the book of Revelation—we can simply read what they have to say. Not so with Jesus. We do not have a word from his pen. If words attributed to him come to us only in the accounts written by others at a much later date—even if they are allegedly quoting him—how can we know they are things he really said?

In part the problem is that some sayings attributed to Jesus are almost certainly things he did not say. Some of these have come to light only in modern times.

One of the most intriguing, and certainly amusing, first appeared in a scholarly article published in a respectable academic journal in 1950 by a professor of classics at Princeton University named Paul R. Coleman-Norton. In the article Coleman-Norton explained how he discovered this previously "unknown saying" of Jesus. He was stationed in French Morocco during the Second World War, and when there was a break in the action, he had occasion to visit a mosque in the town of Fédala. There he was shown an old thick book written in Arabic, inside of which was an inserted page written in Greek—one of Coleman-Norton's own academic specialties.

When he glanced through the page he realized it was something important: it appeared to come from an ancient Greek commentary on the Gospel of Matthew. Coleman-Norton had no facility to photograph the page, so he copied it carefully to be studied later. When he had the leisure to do so, he was most surprised to find a previously unknown saying of Jesus connected with the afterlife.

The commentary was discussing the famous "Parable of the Faithful and Unfaithful Servant" in Matthew 24 and was dealing with the final verse in which Jesus indicates that the wicked and disobedient servant was to be cut to pieces and cast into the outer darkness "where there is weeping and gnashing of teeth" (Matthew 25:30). But in the Greek commentary Coleman-Norton had copied, the passage did not end there. The dialogue continued. In the additional verses, Jesus's disciples, perplexed by Jesus's words, raised a possible objection: "But Rabbi, how can this happen for those who have no teeth?" Jesus is then said to reply, "Oh you of little faith! Do not be troubled. If some have no teeth, then teeth will be provided."

It is a humorous story, almost too good to be true. As it turns out, it *is* too good and is *not* true. One of Coleman-Norton's graduate students prior to the war had been Bruce Metzger, later to become one of the world's foremost experts on the Greek manuscripts of the New Testament. Years after Coleman-Norton published his article, Metzger produced a scholarly response that showed it was all a hoax. There never was a Greek manuscript that Coleman-Norton had discovered. Not only had no one ever verified the existence of the text; but in addition Metzger clearly remembered that even before the war began, back in the 1930s, Coleman-Norton used to regale his classes with this very saying of Jesus as a joke. Metzger showed that his former teacher had made the whole discovery story up. But why would he publish a learned article on it? Maybe he thought that it would also be a good joke to play on his colleagues in the field of biblical studies.[1]

This would not be the first or last time someone made up a saying of Jesus. Some of Jesus's other comments on the afterlife are almost equally amazing and are also likely inventions of someone else—including sayings from Christian antiquity. A good example appears in the writings of a second-century church father named Papias. It is much to our regret that we do not actually have a complete set of Papias's works. Around 130 CE or so—only a few decades after the Gospels of the New Testament were produced—Papias published a five-volume work called *Exposition of the Sayings of the Lord*. The book was not preserved for posterity. We know of it only from scattered quotations from later church fathers, some of which are quite fascinating.[2]

In one place Papias recounted a saying of Jesus, which he allegedly heard from impeccable authorities, in which Jesus expostulated on the glories of the afterlife in the coming Kingdom of God, where people would live in an amazing paradise, luxuriating in the abundance provided by the earth. Jesus says that in the kingdom every grapevine would have ten thousand boughs; every bough would have ten thousand branches; every branch ten thousand shoots; every shoot ten thousand clusters; every cluster ten thousand grapes; and each grape, when pressed, would produce twenty-five measures of wine. Let the good times roll. So too with stalks of wheat. Each would have ten thousand heads, and every head ten thousand grains, and every grain would yield ten pounds of flour.

Did Jesus really believe this is what the kingdom would be like? I suppose it is possible, but most interpreters think these are later exaggerations placed on Jesus's lips by his overly exuberant followers, anticipating the glories that were soon to be theirs.

These alleged teachings of Jesus obviously occur outside the New Testament. That is not normally where a person would turn for knowing what he taught. If we want to know what Jesus really said—about the afterlife or anything else—why not simply read the Gospels and see what they have to say? Even the most critical scholars of the New Testament agree that Matthew, Mark, Luke, and John are by far our best sources of information for knowing about the historical Jesus. But they are not perfect. On the contrary, since the nineteenth century, scholars have recognized why these books can sometimes be highly problematic as guides to the actual words of Jesus.

Methods for Getting Around the Problems

The first point to stress is that the Gospels were originally published anonymously. Their authors do not claim to be apostles of Jesus—or in fact to be anyone at all. They wrote their accounts without disclosing their identities. They are traditionally attributed to two of Jesus's own disciples, Matthew the tax collector and John the "Beloved Disciple," and two later companions of the apostles, Mark the secretary of Peter and Luke the traveling companion of Paul. But scholars have long adduced reasons for thinking these centuries-old traditions of authorship are not correct.[3]

For one thing, there are problems with the dates of these works. It is now widely acknowledged that the earliest Gospel was Mark, written around 70 CE; the last was probably John, around 90–95 CE. If, as just about everyone thinks, Jesus died around 30 CE, this would mean that the very first surviving accounts of his words come from forty to sixty-five years after he spoke them. To complicate matters further, the Gospels were not produced by Aramaic-speaking lower-class, uneducated persons living in Palestine (such as Jesus's disciples); they were written by highly educated Greek-speaking Christians of two generations later, living in other regions of the Roman Empire.[4]

How did these authors know what Jesus actually said? Almost certainly they had sources of information. Most of these would have been oral traditions. That is, the authors of our Gospels heard stories of what Jesus had said, so many decades earlier, by people who had been repeating his words year after year for forty or sixty years.

You might think that people living in oral cultures would make sure that, when telling accounts of what famous teachers said, they would preserve those words accurately, without changing a thing. But research into both oral cultures of today and ancient modes of telling stories shows that this in fact was not the case. Words change as they come to be transmitted—they always have changed and always will change.[5]

There can be no doubt that as ancient Christian storytellers recounted the sayings of Jesus they sometime altered them by shortening, expanding, modifying, and even inventing them. We know this for a fact because we have sources from outside the New Testament with sayings of Jesus that no one can seriously argue he said. Where did they come from? Someone made them up. What about within the New Testament?

Critical scholarship is unified in thinking that the same is true even for some sayings of Jesus in the New Testament. Not all of them, of course. A number of Jesus's recorded sayings almost certainly are good approximations (in a different language) to what Jesus really said, and are reasonably reliable guides to what he thought and taught. Others have probably been modified, either a little or a lot. Yet others were probably placed on his lips by Christian storytellers who wanted Jesus to say things that they themselves believed, to provide heightened credibility to their views.

One reason we know that even the New Testament Gospels contain altered or even invented words of Jesus is that we can compare Jesus's words from one Gospel to the next. When we do so, we find there are differences, sometimes significant, that are very difficult to reconcile.[6] So what is the historian to do? If some of Jesus's recorded words are not what he said, how can we know what Jesus taught, about the afterlife or anything else?

Scholars have devised a series of critical methods that can help us determine which sayings of Jesus in the Gospels (or in any other source) are ones that he most likely said. These methods involve rather obvious and commonsensical rules of evidence that you would use today if you wanted to know if *anyone* in the past actually said things attributed to him or her.

Thus, for example, if you have a number of conflicting sources of information about what a person said, you would obviously favor those that are nearest to the time the person lived. As greater amounts of time pass, sayings are increasingly likely to change (or be invented). When it comes to the words of Jesus, the earliest Gospel of Mark and possibly Mathew are probably to be preferred, for example, to such later Gospels as Luke and John. But one cannot simply accept everything in these earlier Gospels—or in any of the Gospels—uncritically. It is important to evaluate each and every saying of Jesus and mount reasons for thinking it is something he really said.

If, for example, Jesus is reported to have said something in a number of independent sources, then obviously no one of them made the words up, since, as independent, none of them borrowed the saying from another. That would increase the likelihood that such words are the sort of thing—if not precisely the thing—a person said.[7] Moreover, if some of the words the person allegedly spoke are not the kinds of things that the biased reporters who record them would have wanted him to say—if the words contradict what the reporters themselves personally believe, for example—then such words have obviously not been invented by those people themselves and so are more likely things the person actually said. On the flip side, if a reported saying makes no sense in the person's own historical context—if, for example, a cook from 1920 is reportedly complaining about her microwave—then obviously such a saying is not authentic.

Scholars, in short, have a number of methods they apply to sources to establish the actual sayings of a person that are reported only later. Most critical scholars over the past century have agreed that if you apply these methods to the historical Jesus, it becomes clear that, if nothing else, Jesus subscribed to the Jewish apocalyptic views we discussed in the previous chapter. Evidence for this view is abundant and discussed in a number of other studies, so there is no need to detail it here.[8] Suffice it to say that like so many other Jews of his time, Jesus believed the world was controlled by forces of evil, the devil and his demons who were causing immense suffering in the here and now. But he also believed that God would soon intervene to destroy these alien powers and bring in a good kingdom on earth. It is safe to argue, in fact, that this coming Kingdom of God was the very core of Jesus's teaching and belief. His very first recorded words are found among the opening lines of our oldest Gospel: "The time has been fulfilled; the Kingdom of God is at hand. Repent and believe the good news" (Mark 1:15).

This is an apocalyptic image. This evil age has a set amount of time appointed to it by God. That time is now up. God's kingdom, in which there will be no more pain, misery, or suffering, is almost here. People need to repent in preparation for it. Jesus believed a day of judgment was coming, and when it arrived it would bring a serious reversal of fortunes. Those who sided with God now and suffered for it (since the rulers of this world are empowered by the forces of evil) would be vindicated when God's power reasserted itself; those who had prospered now and enjoyed corrupt lives of wealth and influence would be destroyed. Then the first shall be last and the last first; the exalted shall be humbled and the humble exalted (see, e.g., Matthew 20:16; 23:12).

Jesus believed this would happen very soon. As he told his disciples directly, "Some of those standing here will not taste death before they see that the Kingdom of God has come in power" (Mark 9:1). Jesus is not saying that people will go to heaven. He is saying that some of his disciples will still be alive when the end comes and God's utopian kingdom arrives on earth. Or, as he says elsewhere, when his disciples asked when the end of the world would come: "Truly I tell you, *this generation* will not pass away before all these things take place" (Mark 13:30, emphasis added).

Jesus did not teach that when a person died they would go to heaven or hell. He taught that the Day of Judgment was soon to come, when God would destroy all that is evil and raise the dead, to punish the wicked and reward the faithful by bringing them into his eternal, utopian kingdom.

With that general teaching in mind, we can look more deeply at what Jesus has to say about the new life that would come in that new Kingdom of God.

The Kingdom for Some
but Destruction for Most

Jesus did not think the coming kingdom was for faithful Jews only. It was for all those who did God's will. Many Jews, in fact, would not be allowed to enter. As Jesus says in Matthew's Gospel, "many will come from east and west" to enjoy the heavenly banquet with the Jewish patriarchs in "the kingdom of heaven." but many of those from Israel "will be cast into the darkness where there is weeping and gnashing of teeth" (Matthew 8:10–12). It is important to note that he does not say that those excluded from the kingdom will be tormented, and he says nothing here about eternal fires. Instead it is a realm of darkness. This is surely a figurative statement: outside the kingdom lies the world of the unenlightened (who are "in the dark"). There is such grief there—weeping and teeth grinding—because those on the outside have realized too late the eternal joys they have missed out on. What will happen to them? In this passage, Jesus doesn't say. Do they simply end up dying, and that is the end of their story?

One of my theses is that a close reading of Jesus's words shows that in fact he had no idea of torment for sinners after death. Death, for them, is irreversible, the end of the story. Their punishment is that they will be annihilated, never allowed to exist again, unlike the saved, who will live forever in God's glorious kingdom.

For example, earlier in the Sermon on the Mount Jesus says there are two gates through which a person can pass. One is "narrow" and leads to a difficult path. That is the way of life and there are few people who take it. The other gate is "broad," leading to an "easy path." Most people take that route, but it is the road that leads "to destruction" (Matthew 7:13–14). Jesus does not say it leads to eternal torture. Those who take it will be destroyed, annihilated. But even so: you don't want to go that way.

Most of Jesus's teachings about the coming judgment focus on this idea of ultimate and complete destruction. In this he was very much like his predecessor, John the Baptist, who urged people to live lives pleasing to God, bearing "good fruit" (see Matthew 3:10). Those who failed to do so, John declared, would be like bad trees that, when judgment comes, would be "cut down and thrown into the fire." What happens to trees that are felled and burned? They are consumed out of existence. They don't keep burning forever.

Jesus himself thought something similar: the end of sinners will be destruction. As he says in the "Parable of the Weeds" in Matthew 13:36–43, at the end of the age God will send a mighty angelic being to judge the earth, whom Jesus calls "the Son of Man" (see Daniel 7:13–14 for this figure); this one will send out his angels to gather up all who sin and do evil and "throw them into the furnace of fire." There they will weep and gnash their teeth. But presumably not forever: those who are burned to death die. That stands in contrast to the righteous, who will "shine like the sun in the kingdom." As in Daniel 12, at the end the faithful who side with God become like shining heavenly bodies whose light will never be extinguished.

In another image in the same chapter of Matthew, Jesus compares the coming judgment to a fisherman who brings in his haul of fish and separates the good fish from the bad (Matthew 13:47–50). What does he do with the bad ones he doesn't want? He throws them away. He obviously doesn't torture them. They simply die. So too, Jesus says, at the final judgment angels will separate the righteous from the wicked and toss the latter into the furnace. They will go up in flames. For first-century listeners, this "destruction by fire" would not conjure up images of eternal hellfire but rather a house fire—or the execution of criminals by burning. Someone burned at the stake weeps and screams in anguish while dying. But they don't weep and scream for ten days or ten millennia or ten billion years. They die.

Often Jesus expresses this image of "destruction" in even more repugnant terms, indicating that sinners who are excluded from God's kingdom will not only be killed but will be refused decent burial—which, as you will recall, is the worst fate one could have in the ancient world. Even worse than that, Jesus indicates that sinners will be cast, unburied, into the most unholy, repulsive, godforsaken place that anyone in Israel could imagine, the valley known as Gehenna. Thus, for example, Jesus says that anyone who calls someone "a fool" will be liable to be cast into Gehenna (Matthew 5:22); later he says that it is better to gouge out your eye or amputate your hand if it sins, and enter the kingdom maimed, than to be tossed into Gehenna with eye and hand intact (Matthew 5:29–30). Elsewhere he says it would be better to have a millstone hung around your neck and be drowned than to make a "little one" stumble and, for your foul deed, be cast into Gehenna. There, we are told, "their worm does not die and the fire is not quenched" (Mark 9:42, 47–48).

Gehenna is obviously serious business. But what is it?

Jesus's Teaching of Gehenna

It is highly unfortunate that sometimes English translations of the New Testament render the Greek word "Gehenna" as "hell." That conjures up precisely the wrong image for Bible readers today, making them think Jesus is referring to the underworld of fiery torment where people go for eternal punishment for their sins. That is not what Gehenna referred to at all. On the contrary, it was a place well known among Jews in Jesus's day. It was a desecrated valley outside of Jerusalem, a place literally forsaken by God.

The valley is mentioned several times in the Old Testament, first in Joshua 15:8, where it is called "the valley of the son of Hinnom," which in Hebrew is *gei ben Hinnom*. We don't know who Hinnom was, but his son apparently owned the valley at one point. A later reference calls it instead Hinnom's own valley—that is, in *gei-hinnom*. Later, that term, *gehinnom*, came to be Gehenna. It is normally identified as the ravine southwest of Old Jerusalem.

Scholars have long claimed that Gehenna was a garbage dump where fires were burned—which is why its "worm never dies" and its "fires never cease": there was always burning trash in there. As it turns out, there is no evidence for this claim; it can be traced to a commentary on the book of Psalms written by Rabbi David Kimhi in the early thirteenth century CE. Neither archaeology nor any ancient text supports the view.[9] On the contrary, the place was notorious for ancient Jews not because it was a dump but because it had been a place where children had been sacrificed to a pagan god.

We are told in 2 Kings 23:10 that the Canaanite deity Molech was worshiped in "Topheth, which is the valley of Ben-hinnom" (= valley of the son of Hinnom = Gehenna), where even some Israelites had made "a son or a daughter pass through fire as an offering" to him. Human sacrifice occurred elsewhere in the ancient world, but it was obviously anathema to the writers of the Hebrew Bible, and Gehenna was the place best known for the hideous practice. And so, according to the passage, when the good king Josiah instituted a religious reform, bringing the people of Judah back to the worship of Yahweh, the God of Israel, he "defiled" the place, making it impossible for child sacrifice to be practiced there.

In many ways this desecrated valley represented the polar opposite of what was on the heights right above it: the Temple of God dedicated to Yahweh, where God himself was believed to dwell, in the Holy of Holies. Gehenna, by contrast, was the place of unfathomable cruelty and nefarious practices connected with a pagan divine enemy of the God of Israel, literally an unholy, blasphemous place.

The Israelite antipathy for Gehenna is captured in the Old Testament book of Jeremiah, which makes numerous woeful predictions of the coming destruction of the nation of Judah. At one point the prophet declares that God was determined to destroy his people because Judeans had put up an altar in "the valley of the son of Hinnom" in order to "burn their sons and their daughters in the fire." Jeremiah announces that now the name will be changed. It will be called "the valley of Slaughter: for they will bury [there] until there is no more room.

158

The corpses of this people will be food for the birds of the air, and for the animals of the earth; and no one will frighten them away" (Jeremiah 7:29–34). This most unholy of all places will be where God will slaughter those who are disobedient among his own people. Animals would feed on their bodies. Think about the "worm [that] never dies." (See also Jeremiah 19:6–9.)

The earliest evidence from outside the Hebrew Bible for Gehenna as a place of divine punishment comes in 1 Enoch 27, written, as we have seen, at least two centuries before the days of Jesus. In one of his encounters with the angel Uriel, Enoch asks why such an "accursed valley" lies in the midst of Israel's "blessed land." The angel tells him:

> The accursed valley is for those accursed forever; here will gather together all those accursed ones, those who speak with their mouth unbecoming words against the Lord. . . . Here shall they be gathered together, and here shall be their judgment in the last days. There will be upon them the spectacle of the righteous judgment, in the presence of the righteous forever.

And so, well prior to Jesus, Gehenna was seen as a desecrated place of slaughter for God's enemies at the Last Judgment. This judgment is said to last "forever." So too for Jesus: the dead corpses of God's enemies will be cast into this horrible, ungodly place, where they will be destroyed, permanently separated from God and his goodness.

Jesus combines this notion of desecrated Gehenna with another passage of Scripture that speaks of the dead being despised by the living righteous. This is the final verse of the great book of Isaiah, in which God says of his people that, after the judgment, "they shall go out and look at the dead bodies of the people who have rebelled against me; for their worm shall not die, their fire shall not be quenched, and they shall be an abhorrence to all flesh (Isaiah 66:24). These corpses are *dead*; they are not being tormented. The righteous who look with great satisfaction on these destroyed enemies will see them being consumed with worms and fire, completely desecrated, without burial, left to rot and burn. That will never be reversed. For those destroyed by God, there will be no salvation—ever. So too when Jesus teaches about Gehenna, he is thinking of annihilation, not torment.

And so, for example, in Matthew 10:28, Jesus says that people should not fear anyone who can "kill the body but cannot kill the soul." In other words, they should have no fear of physically dying. We will all die, one way or another; we should not fear those who can make it happen sooner rather than later. Instead, he continues, "fear the one who can annihilate both the soul and body in Gehenna." It is important to note that Jesus here does not merely say that God will "kill" a person's soul: he will "annihilate" (or "exterminate") it. After that it will not exist.

This stands in contrast to those Jews who could expect a future resurrection. For them, the "soul" or "breath" that enlivens their body is taken away at death. But at the resurrection it will be returned, bringing the body back to life. That, however, would only come to those whose bodies have died but whose life force is restored. If the life force is destroyed as well, there will be no resurrection into God's coming kingdom. There will only be death. God alone can destroy the life force. When he does so, the person is not just physically dead but completely dead—destroyed, exterminated out of existence.

Worse than that, these enemies of God would be cast, unburied, into Gehenna, infamous as a place of utter desolation, a place despised and abandoned by God. This was worse even than not being buried—not because it implied future torment, but because it precluded any possibility of a place of rest, a place of peace. Sinners would end up as cadavers gnawed by worms and burned by fire. For them there would never again be any hope of life.

Rewards for the Saints in the Words of Jesus

It is easier to document Jesus's words about the dreaded fate of sinners in Gehenna than about the blessings of the saved in the Kingdom of God. Even so, we have seen one teaching that is repeated in the Gospels: the coming Kingdom will entail a fantastic banquet where the redeemed eat and drink at leisure with the greats of the Jewish past, the Patriarchs. This is a paradisal image of great joy.

Another key passage involves Jesus's discussion of what life will be like once the resurrection has occurred. The earliest account is in Mark 12:18-27. In the immediate context, Jesus has come to Jerusalem to celebrate the Passover, and a group of opponents, the Sadducees, want to confound him with a verbal trap. The non-apocalyptic Sadducees, as we have seen, did not believe in a future resurrection of the dead or, apparently, in any afterlife whatsoever. But since the core of Jesus's teaching was an apocalyptic message, these naysayers thought they could publicly reveal the error of his ways.

They come up to Jesus and propose a situation. According to the law of Moses, if a man who is married dies without leaving any children, his brother is supposed to marry the widow and raise a family in his brother's name (see Deuteronomy 25:5-6). This was to keep the man's bloodline alive. In the Sadducees' cunning hypothetical situation, there was once a man who had six brothers. He was married, but he died childless, so the oldest remaining brother took his widow as his own. But he too died childless. And so it went, until all seven brothers had been married to the poor woman. Finally she herself died. Then the Sadducees spring their trap, thinking they've identified an obvious absurdity in Jesus's view of the coming resurrection: if all seven had married the woman, which one of them will be her husband when they are raised from the dead?

Jesus was not fazed by the question but, as was his wont, turned it against his opponents. First he tells them they simply don't understand the Scriptures that predict a resurrection or God's power that will make it happen. What they don't realize is that at the resurrection no one will be married. Instead, those who are raised will be "like the angels in heaven"—unmarried and, presumably, eternally happy about it. She won't be anyone's wife.

Jesus goes on to point out that in the Hebrew Bible, when God addresses Moses out of the burning bush, he tells him: "I am . . . the God of Abraham, the God of Isaac, and the God of Jacob" (Exodus 3:6). These three patriarchs had lived centuries before Moses, and Jesus wants to make a point about the verb "to be," which God uses in the present tense: I *am* their God. He does not say he *was* their God. For Jesus the fact that God said he *is* their God indicates that they were still alive. They had not been annihilated in death. They were being kept until the future resurrection. Sometimes it really does matter what the meaning of the word "is" is.

Moreover, for Jesus, when the Patriarchs were raised, they, along with all the righteous, would not simply be revivified and brought back from a very long near-death experience only to lead another life leading up to a second death. They would be given a glorified, immortal existence comparable to that of the angels. Here Jesus is endorsing the view that we have seen elsewhere, starting with the book of Daniel. The resurrection of the dead meant being given an exalted existence for all eternity; it would not be a mere replication of life people have now in this world of sin and suffering. It would be like the lives of God's powerful and glorious angels, an eternal life blessed by God in a world where there would no longer be any traces of evil.

Jesus, the Sheep, and the Goats

Jesus's view of the afterlife is stated most fully in his teaching about "separating the sheep from the goats" at the Last Judgment (Matthew 25:31–46). Even though the account is found only in the Gospel of Matthew, we will see there are reasons for thinking it is something Jesus actually said.

The passage comes at the tail end of Jesus's "apocalyptic discourse" (Matthew 24–25), two chapters of Jesus's discussion of what will happen at the end of time and of how people need to prepare for it. To conclude the discourse, Jesus describes the coming Day of Judgment, when the great cosmic judge, the Son of Man, sits on his throne, judging all the nations of the world gathered before him (Matthew 25:31–46). This is not merely the judgment of the righteous and wicked in Israel but of all the pagans as well. The Son of Man separates all the peoples into two groups, the sheep to his right and the goats to his left. He then addresses the sheep, welcoming them into the amazing kingdom God has prepared for them as a reward for all the good they did during their lives, because "when I was hungry you gave me something to eat, when I was thirsty you gave me drink, when I was a stranger you welcomed me, when naked you clothed me, when sick you visited me, when in prison you came to me" (Matthew 25:35–36). The sheep are completely confused and ask what he can possibly mean. They have never even *seen* him before. How could they have done any of these things for him? He replies, "Truly I say to you, as much as you did these things to the least of these, my brothers and sisters, you did them to me" (Matthew 25:40).

He then turns to the goats, and words of salvation shift to condemnation. He lambasts them, sending them away: "Go away from me into the eternal fire that has been prepared for the devil and his angels" (Matthew 25:41). Why? They had not helped him when he was in need: hungry, thirsty, a stranger, naked, sick, or in prison. The goats too don't understand: they've never seen the Son of Man before and so had no opportunity to provide him with help. But he replies to them, "Just as you did not do such things to the least of these, you did not do them to me" (Matthew 25:45).

One good reason for thinking some such words were actually spoken by Jesus involves the very point of the passage. People will enter the glorious Kingdom of God, or be painfully excluded from it, because of their ethical activities and for nothing else. Living a good life by helping those in need will earn a person salvation. This is why the passage—or something very much like it—probably represents Jesus's actual words. The earliest followers of Jesus after his death were firmly convinced that it was faith in him—in particular, his death and resurrection—that could make a person right with God. This was the belief not only of the apostle Paul, whose writings we will consider in the next chapter, but of all the early Christians we know about, including, of course, the authors of the Gospels. If a later Christian storyteller were to make up a saying and place it on Jesus's lips about how one could be saved at the resurrection, would he indicate that salvation had nothing actually to do with believing in Jesus but instead would involve doing all sorts of good things? Remember: the sheep not only did not believe in Jesus; they had never even heard of him. It's possible, of course, that a later Christian invented the story—but we don't know of any early Christian authors who thought that "being a good person" in itself was enough to earn God's rewards at the resurrection. That means it is unlikely the passage was placed on Jesus's lips by later Christians wanting him to say what they themselves believed. That in turn means we find it in the Gospel tradition because it is something that Jesus himself actually spoke.

How, though, are we to understand these words about the afterlife? The first thing to stress is that the passage is almost certainly a parable, not a literal description of what will happen on Judgment Day. That clearly is Matthew's own understanding, as he places the passage immediately after three other parables illustrating Jesus's views about the coming end and how people should prepare for it: the parables of the faithful and unfaithful servant (Matthew 24:45–51); of the ten bridesmaids (Matthew 25:1–13); and of the talents (Matthew 25:14–30). This too is a parable, not a literal description. Jesus does not think it will literally involve sheep and goats.

Even so, it does assume that there will be some kind of final judgment in which some people will receive a reward and others will be punished. The reward is straightforward and easy to understand: the righteous will inherit the glorious Kingdom of God and live there forever in some kind of blessed existence. And what of the punishment of the wicked? Is it "eternal torment" as opposed, say, to "eternal joy"? At first glance it might appear so, as Jesus concludes the parable by summarizing the point: "These [sinners] will go away into eternal punishment, but the righteous into eternal life" (Matthew 25:46). That must mean punishment forever, right?

Possibly, but it is important to look a bit closer at the contrast Jesus draws—a point rarely noticed by interpreters. He does not contrast "eternal torture" with "eternal reward" or "eternal misery" with "eternal happiness." He contrasts the eternal punishment of the wicked with eternal *life*. What is the opposite of life? It is not torture or misery. It is death.

But how could death be an "eternal punishment"? It is certainly the ultimate punishment—just as the death sentence is the ultimate punishment for criminals still in some civilized countries. But why is it eternal? Because it is a punishment that will never end. The wicked are destroyed, never to be restored to live. Their deaths cannot be reversed. They suffer an eternal punishment.

But aren't the goats said to go into eternal fire (Matthew 25:41)? Yes indeed—but again, it is the fire that is eternal, not the sinner in the fire. The fires never go out.[10] Just as the funeral pyre burns on once the body is consumed—or, more appropriately, just as the executioner's fire continues to burn after the condemned has long since died—so too with the fires of eternal punishment. Like the worm that never dies, it goes on, but the people who are punished have expired. They will no longer exist.

Jesus and the Afterlife

Some readers of the New Testament may have questions about this summary of the views of Jesus on the afterlife. Haven't I left out some of the most important passages, such as the story of Lazarus and the Rich Man in Luke 16, which seems to support the idea that eternal life and prolonged punishment come immediately at death rather than at the resurrection, or passages in John 3 and 11 that indicate eternal life is a present reality and not just a future one?

I have indeed put those passages to one side for now, and for a very good reason. I will be arguing in a later chapter that these are among the sayings of Jesus that were placed on his lips by his later followers, rather than things he actually said himself. This decision has not been made lightly or in order to twist Jesus's words to mean something that I simply want them to mean. It has been made by following the critical methods I referred to earlier, in which the earliest forms of Jesus's sayings (e.g., many of those in Mark and Matthew) are more likely authentic, especially those that would probably not have been invented by later Christians and then attributed to Jesus.

One of the other criteria I take very seriously is the need for any saying of Jesus to fit well into his own early first-century historical context as a Jew from Galilee. I have pointed out that for over a century now critical scholars have been widely convinced that Jesus subscribed to a thoroughly apocalyptic world view. My contention in this chapter is that his apocalyptic understanding of his world extended to his view of the afterlife. Jesus did not focus on what would happen to an individual at the point of death. He was principally concerned with that great act of God that was coming soon with the appearance of a cosmic judge from heaven, the Son of Man, who would destroy the evil powers in control of this world and establish a great, utopian, and eternal kingdom. Those who lived as God wanted them to—loving their neighbors as themselves, doing good for others in need—would enter into that kingdom. Those who lived lives of self-centered sin and wickedness, on the other hand, would be destroyed, never to exist again.

Like other apocalypticists of his day, Jesus believed this day of reckoning was coming very soon. It was right around the corner. It would happen in his generation: "Some of those standing here will not taste death before they see the Kingdom of God having come in power" (Mark 9:1).

But what happens if it doesn't come? Then adjustments have to be made, and those who accept Jesus's teachings have to reinterpret and possibly even alter them—maybe a little at first but then, possibly, more thoroughly. Eventually, in the Christian tradition, Jesus's own apocalyptic views of the afterlife would fade as believers started thinking about what would happen not only on some increasingly distant Day of Judgment, but in the meantime, when they died. Later still his followers would begin to focus almost exclusively on these rewards and punishments that would begin immediately at death. It will be these later developments that lead to the views of heaven and hell still believed by so many of Jesus's followers in our day.

CHAPTER NINE

The Afterlife After Jesus's Life: Paul the Apostle

Next to Jesus himself, the most important figure in early Christianity—indeed, in Christianity of all time—was the apostle Paul. Without Paul, Christianity would never have become what it did. It is not, as some people claim, that Paul was the single founder of Christianity, the one who invented the idea that salvation came through the death and resurrection of Jesus. That was the view of the apostles before Paul and the people they converted, and it was the reason Paul persecuted the Christians before becoming one of them.[1] Paul's significance instead lay in other areas, in the fact that he, more than anyone else we know of from the early church, spread the religion among pagans, so that Christianity was transformed from being a small and obscure sect within Judaism into a religion capable of expanding throughout the Roman world—eventually, some centuries later, to become the official religion of the empire. Just as important, Paul was responsible for some of the key theological developments within the church as the followers of Jesus struggled to make sense of what it might mean to say that a crucified criminal could be the savior of the world.

Among Paul's important contributions to Christian theology was an understanding of the afterlife that differed in key ways from that proclaimed by Jesus himself.

An Introduction to Paul

As with Jesus, it is difficult to know what Paul actually thought about a number of issues. But here the problems are different. For Paul we are not reliant on sources composed only decades after his life; on the contrary, we have letters from his own pen. The problem is that a number of the letters claiming to be written by Paul, including several in the New Testament, were almost certainly not written by him but were produced by later followers who used his name to convince readers that they themselves were the apostle.[2] Even so, critical scholars are largely unified in thinking that seven of the letters of the New Testament do derive straight from the apostle himself.[3]

In addition, we have a biographical account of Paul in the New Testament book of Acts. This book also presents problems to historians, much like the problems posed by the Gospels for those interested in knowing about the historical Jesus. It was written years after the events it recounts, and there are reasons for thinking its author was not perfectly well-informed about what the apostle said and did. One reason for such doubts is that many of the words and deeds of Paul in Acts seem to stand at odds with what Paul himself says in his letters.[4]

Even so, between his own letters and the partially historical accounts of Acts, it is possible to piece together a good bit about Paul's life and teachings. It is clear from a careful reading of our sources that Paul started out as a highly devout and unusually fastidious observer of the Jewish law: born and raised Jewish and fervent in his religious faith, living somewhere in the Greek-speaking world outside of Palestine. When he originally heard of fellow Jews proclaiming that a crucified man, contrary to all expectation, was the predicted messiah, he considered the view not only ludicrous but actually dangerous. The messiah was not to be someone destroyed by the enemy, publicly humiliated, and tortured to death. He was to be a figure of grandeur and power who triumphed over Israel's oppressors and set up a new kingdom on earth. Jesus was the opposite of what the messiah would be.

Paul vigorously persecuted the Christians until he himself had some kind of visionary experience. Later he claimed Christ appeared to him, that he actually saw him, alive, years after his death (1 Corinthians 9:1; 15:8). That convinced him Jesus had come back to life. Obviously that could only have happened if God had raised him from the dead. That in turn must mean that Jesus really was the one favored by God, which surely would show that his death was not simply a miscarriage of justice or a very big mistake. Paul came to think it was all part of God's incredible plan, unknown until now. God had set Jesus up as a sacrifice for sin. Without this sacrifice there could be no salvation. Paul concluded that the death and resurrection of Christ were the means God had provided for saving the world. The only way for a person to escape judgment—either when God destroyed this world or when the person died—was to have faith in Christ.

This is not the message Jesus himself preached. As we have seen, Jesus proclaimed the Kingdom of God was coming to those who turned to God in repentance, living good lives of loving their neighbors as themselves. Paul, however, preached that salvation came only in the death and resurrection of Jesus. These, at heart, are different messages. I'm not saying they are flat-out contradictory: scholars have varying views on that question.[5] But they are not the same. And such differences led to an alternative understanding of the afterlife. In this case the differences are not absolute. As one might expect, there is both continuity and change, and it is important to see both.

The Coming Judgment in Paul

The best place to turn for an understanding of Paul's theology, including his view of the afterlife, is his letter to the Romans. Unlike his other letters, this was written to a church—in Rome, obviously—that Paul did not himself establish and that in fact he had never visited. He indicates, however, that he wants to come to them and have them support his missionary endeavors farther afield in the western parts of the empire (Romans 15:22–24). Before coming, he wants them to know what his missionary message actually is, in part because he knows they have heard a garbled version of it that has raised suspicions. He writes to set the record straight and in doing so lays out as clearly as he can his understanding of the Gospel. This "good news" involves a very real message of bad news. God is about to judge people, and those who are not prepared will be condemned. Still, on the upside, some will be saved. One of the apparent tensions in the letter to the Romans is that it is not completely clear, from what Paul says, who will be among those delivered from this coming wrath of God.[6]

Much of the opening three chapters focuses on the coming Day of Judgment. In chapter 2, Paul addresses those who believe they will be saved and who condemn others for their unrighteous lives without fully realizing that they themselves are just as wicked and culpable: "When you pass judgment on another you condemn yourself, because you who are judging do just the same things." And so, Paul asks, "Do you think . . . you will escape the judgment of God?" On the contrary, "you are storing up wrath for yourself on the day of wrath, when God's righteous judgment will be revealed" (Romans 2:1–5).

Paul goes on to lay out his view of this coming judgment: "For [God] will repay everyone according to their deeds." That is, he explains, everyone who patiently does what is good will receive "glory and honor and immortality and eternal life." But those who are disobedient to the truth and live in wickedness will be subject to "wrath and anger." It doesn't matter whether a person is Jew or gentile: if they are wicked, they will receive "anguish and distress." But if they do what is good, they will receive "glory, honor, and peace" (Romans 2:6–10).

All of this does indeed sound very much like what Jesus himself is recorded as saying—for example, in the parable of the sheep and the goats. That is the continuity. But in the very next chapter, Paul makes it clear that salvation does not, in fact, come to those who lead good lives but only to those who have faith in Christ. Why is "being good" not good enough? In no small part because Paul thinks *no one* is actually capable of living a life without sin. Quoting the Jewish Scripture, he declares: "No one is righteous—not even one; there is no one who understands, no one who seeks after God" (Romans 3:10-11). The world is filled with sin, and everyone, Jew and pagan, is infused with it, doing what God opposes.

This is a dire situation. Those who are "righteous" will be saved. But no one is "righteous"—not even Jews deeply committed to following the law of Moses, as Paul had been. One cannot make up for sin by becoming a good Jew: being circumcised (if a male), keeping kosher, observing the Sabbath, and fulfilling the other requirements of the law. The law does not help a person dominated by sin.

God, however, has provided a solution, and that is the death of his messiah, Jesus, who "reveals the righteousness of God" (Romans 3:21–22). For just as all have sinned, so too can all be made "righteous"—meaning "right," i.e., right with God—by the free gift that comes "through the redemption that is in Christ Jesus" because God "put Christ forth as an atoning sacrifice in blood." A person can receive this redemption by having "faith in Christ" (Romans 3:21–26).

It may seem to be a contradiction for Paul first to say that the good will be saved on the coming day of God's wrath and then to say no one is good and able to be saved apart from Christ. But it's not really a contradiction—at least, not in Paul's mind. Paul, like other Christians before him, believed that a person who converted to faith in Jesus would be baptized and then would join the Christian community. This initiation rite of baptism was absolutely fundamental to Paul's understanding of both salvation and the afterlife. According to Romans 6, a person who is baptized is united with Christ. Just as Christ was "buried" in death, so too the person goes "under the water" and is symbolically buried. But for Paul this is not simply symbolism. It is a real mystical experience, a participation with Christ in his death. When Christ died, he died for the sins of the world. In a sense, he put sin to death. Those who are baptized in Christ also "die to sin." Sin no longer has any control over them. They therefore will not be subject to the destruction of sin and sinners on the day of God's wrath—or, as Paul puts it, just as they have already died with Christ in baptism, they will also "be made alive with him" (Romans 6:8). For Paul this is the key to the future resurrection of the dead. Yes, in theory, as he says in Romans 2, it comes to those who "do good." But that means only those who believe in the messiah Jesus and have participated with him in his death. They are the ones who are dead to sin and therefore can actually do the will of God, and so will be saved when the divine wrath of God bursts forth at the end of the age. At that time they will be raised from the dead.

This is obviously very different from the teachings of Jesus himself. But it becomes the standard teaching of the early Pauline churches. Paul's pagan converts adopted a form of Jewish apocalyptic thought that said the end of the age would soon arrive and would involve the destruction of the forces of evil but the salvation of those who sided with God. But there has been a serious shift in this line of thinking, away from what most Jewish apocalypticists thought. For Paul and these converts, only those who believed in Jesus's death and resurrection and who were then baptized could expect this future salvation. No one else sided with God. Baptized believers in Jesus alone would enjoy the blessings of a happily ever after when the imminent Day of Judgment arrived.

But how would it all happen? Paul explains in two of the most interesting passages to be found in all his letters.

The Return of Jesus

Christians like Paul knew full well that their belief in Jesus seemed absurd to other Jews, since Jesus had not done any of the things expected of the messiah: destroy the enemies of God's people and set up a kingdom on earth. The Christians believed, instead, that the messiah had to suffer and die. But for them that was not the end of the story. Jesus would later fulfill all the messianic prophecies. He was coming back to finish the job.

Paul's first explanation of how that would happen is in 1 Thessalonians, his earliest surviving letter, which, as a result, is our oldest Christian writing of any kind. As with all his other letters apart from Romans, this one is addressed to a church Paul founded, in the city of Thessalonica in Macedonia. Paul had come to the city as a missionary, preached his gospel of the death and resurrection of Jesus, and proclaimed that Jesus was soon to return in glory to judge the world and save his followers. It is clear from the letter of 1 Thessalonians itself that his previously pagan converts had bought into the message wholeheartedly and were eager for the end of history to come. They expected it right away. But it hadn't come, and in the meantime some of the members of their Christian community had died. That caused considerable confusion and anxiety: Had those who died lost out on the salvation Christ was to bring? Would they not enter into Christ's utopian kingdom?

Paul has learned of their anxiety and he writes this friendly letter in large part to dispel their fears. The key passage is 1 Thessalonians 4:13–18. Paul begins by assuring the Thessalonians that he does not want them to remain "ignorant" about those who have "fallen asleep"—i.e., died. He assures them that just as Christ died and rose from the dead, so too he will bring with him, at his return, those who died in him.

Then Paul gives a remarkable scenario of what will happen at Jesus's return. First he indicates that "we who are alive, who are left until the appearance of the Lord, will not precede those who have fallen asleep." On the contrary, when "the Lord descends from heaven with a cry, the voice of an archangel, and the trumpet of God, the dead in Christ will rise first." Only then will "we who are left" be "snatched up into the clouds to meet the Lord in the air." And then, Paul assures them, "we will always be with the Lord."

Here, then, is a distinctively new take on the future resurrection of the dead. Paul says nothing about a resurrection of those who have lived good lives throughout the world, nor, for that matter, about the wicked. His focus is on the followers of the messiah Jesus. The resurrection will be for them. Paul's understanding involves a kind of "three-story" universe where there are distinct levels to our world. There is "up there" where God lives, along now with Jesus after his resurrection. There is "down here," where we exist on earth. And there is the "farther down below," where the dead reside.

In this scenario, Jesus lived on this earthly level before he died and went "down." He was then raised "up"—not to our level but to God's, above us in heaven. But he will come back "down," and those (deceased believers) who are down below will be raised "up," and then those (living believers) who are here on the middle level will follow them to meet the Lord in the clouds. It is usually thought that Paul does not mean that people will live forever hovering in the air between earth and heaven but that the believers in Jesus have gone up to meet him there to escort him down to earth, where he will establish his kingdom.[7]

In some ways this understanding of the future resurrection seems very much like the teaching of Jesus. Jesus too thought that a cosmic judge, the Son of Man, was coming in judgment on the earth. But now it is Jesus himself who is to be coming on the clouds. For modern interpreters, however, there is so much here left unexplained. What is happening in the meantime to those believers who have died before the event? Are they literally "asleep," in a kind of comatose state until the end? Have their souls gone up to heaven for the brief interim before Jesus's return? Do they cease to exist for a while? Moreover, when they are raised, are their bodies simply revivified or have they been altered in some way—for example, made immortal? The passage doesn't say. For Paul's answers, we need to look elsewhere.

The Glorious Transformation
of the Resurrected Body

Undoubtedly the most important passage for Paul's view of the future resurrection is 1 Corinthians 15. The chapter, in fact, is often called "the resurrection chapter." It is also one of the most misread passages in all of the New Testament. Many casual readers have thought Paul wrote it in order to prove that Jesus was raised from the dead. But that is not right. The chapter *assumes* Jesus was raised, as both Paul and his Corinthian readers know. It *uses* this assumption in order to build the case Paul wants to make for the naysayers among his readers: there will be a future resurrection for Jesus's followers, a resurrection like Jesus's own. Dead bodies will come back to life, but not in the state in which they were buried. They will be completely transformed and made into immortal, spiritual bodies. They will still be bodies. But they will be glorified, just as Jesus's body was.

To make sense of the passage, we need a bit of context. Paul founded the church in the city of Corinth, located on an isthmus on the eastern side of Achaia, sometime after his mission to the Thessalonians. As always happened, once the church was established and running, Paul left the fledgling community to move on to other missionary grounds. Sometime later he learned of problems the Corinthian church was having. These were serious indeed: massive and deep divisions in the church; considerably infighting among the factions that supported one leader or another; cases of rank immorality, including Christian men visiting prostitutes and bragging about it in church, and one man sleeping with his stepmother; chaotic scenes in the worship services, including the weekly communion supper, with some members coming early to gorge themselves and drink all the wine so that there was nothing left when the poorer members arrived later. Paul writes his letter to deal with such problems one by one.

But he saves for last the problem he considers most threatening to the life of the community. It may not seem as serious to modern readers. Paul is astounded by the theological claim of some of the Corinthian believers that "there is no resurrection of the dead" (1 Corinthians 15:12). Paul sees this as a major problem, because his entire gospel message hinges on the apocalyptic realities of the future climax of God's cosmic plan. And so he spends the entire chapter trying to prove that in fact there will be a real, physical, glorious future resurrection in which bodies come back to life and are transformed into immortal beings. It apparently was a hard sell.

Scholars have debated why this was even an issue for these believers in Jesus. It is not obvious what they thought the alternative was. Some interpreters have thought the Corinthians must have denied there was any life after death, but that can't be right. Later in the chapter Paul reminds them, in maddeningly vague terms, that they practice baptism for the dead: "If the dead are not raised at all, why are some baptized on their behalf?" (1 Corinthians 15:29). It is altogether unclear what the Corinthians were doing in these "baptisms for the dead," and there have been roughly twenty thousand interpretations over the years. Are living Christians being baptized as stand-ins for Christians who came to the faith but were not baptized before they died? Are they being baptized for unconverted dead relatives in hopes this will secure their salvation—or for dead people generally, to make salvation possible, say, to those who lived before Christ? Or for some other reason? We don't know. But the verse almost certainly shows they believed in some kind of life after death, because baptism appears to have been efficacious in some way for those who have passed on.

Then why do they reject the idea that the dead will be raised? Other scholars have maintained that the offending Corinthians do not believe in a *future* resurrection of believers because they, like other Christians we know about from later times, believed followers of Jesus were already in some sense "raised from the dead" when they came to faith in Christ and were baptized (see, for example, Ephesians 2:1–6). That may be the case, but Paul does not explicitly say anything specifically about the Corinthians believing they were already resurrected believers. These scholars may be reading a later Christian view into this early Pauline writing.

It may be simplest to think that these former pagan converts have brought their original understanding of the afterlife with them into their Christian faith. As Greek-speaking and Greek-influenced pagans, they would have been raised on the very Platonic idea that the soul is immortal and cannot die, and that life after death involves a separation of the soul from the body for a soulish existence forever. Possibly these pagan converts still think so as Christians. For them, there is no resurrection of the dead, because life in the body forever is an absurd, even repulsive idea. The body is the problem. What lives on is the soul. If this view is correct, then Paul writes to correct them. Just as Jesus was bodily raised from the dead, so too will his followers be raised, at the end of time, in the climactic moment of all of history.

Paul's Teaching of the Resurrection

To make his case, Paul begins the chapter by summarizing what the Corinthians came to believe when they first joined the Christian community:

that Christ died for sins and was raised from the dead, and after his resurrection he was seen not only by his disciples but by a large number of people, including five hundred at one time and, finally, by Paul himself (1 Corinthians 15:1–8). All these people actually *saw* Jesus. That's because he was physically raised.

For most Jews like Paul, "resurrection" always and incontrovertibly meant resurrection of the body. It involved bodies coming back to life. This Jewish notion of resurrection stood, therefore, in contrast to the Greek view of the immortality of the soul.[8]

Paul wants to insist that those who are "in Christ" will have the same experience Jesus did. If Christ was raised (bodily!), so will they be. Conversely, if they are not to be raised, then Christ must not have been. And if Christ was not raised, he did not bring salvation, and those who thought they had been made right with God in fact will not be saved (1 Corinthians 15:12–19).

But for Paul (and his original converts), Christ has been raised, and for that reason he can be called the "first fruits of the resurrection" (1 Corinthians 15:20). This is an agricultural image. The part of the harvest brought in on the first day (the "first" fruits) is like the harvest to come thereafter. The wheat harvested on day one is, in substance, no different from that on day two. Jesus thus shows what will happen to his followers. Just as he came back with a bodily substance, so too will they.

Some of the Corinthians raised an obvious objection to the idea of resurrection, which Paul states in order to answer. Over the ages, others have had similar difficulties: My body is the source of all my problems! I may not even like my body. And you are saying that I have to live in it forever? That's ridiculous. The body grows old, gets injured, sickens, dies, and corrupts. We have to live eternity like *that*? And even more: Which body, exactly, is raised? The one I had as a teenager? At the height of my physical prowess? As it is when I am old and infirm? Really? And will it have all the same physical defects, injuries, and wounds? Will blind people be blind forever? The paralyzed paralyzed? Those born with birth defects forced to have them for eternity? As the Corinthians mockingly stated the objection: "How are the dead raised? With what kind of body do they come?" (1 Corinthians 15:35).

In their own historical context, these first-century Corinthian opponents of Paul—especially those born and raised in Greek culture with ideas that had trickled down from Plato—may have had a deeper problem: for them the body was made of coarse, gross stuff that had to be dispensed with so the more highly refined and immortal soul could live on. Paul, though, has a different idea. He does not at all believe in the immortality of the soul. But when he speaks of the future resurrection, he is also not referring to the simple revivification of the dead corpse, brought back to life from a near-death experience. For Paul there are bodies and then there are bodies. The resurrected body he imagines will be utterly and completely transformed. It will be a different kind of body.

Paul argues that the human body that goes into the ground is like a "bare kernel" of some kind of grain that grows into a plant. What grows is intimately tied to and related to what went into the ground, but it is also vastly different. When you plant an acorn, it doesn't grow into a gigantic acorn but into an oak tree. So too the human. When the body comes out of the ground, it is transformed into "the body that God gives it, as he wishes" (1 Corinthians 15:38). That is because "there are heavenly bodies, and earthly bodies" and they have different kinds of glories, just as there is "one glory for the sun, another glory for the moon, and another for the stars; even the stars differ in glory from one to the next" (1 Corinthians 15:40–41).

Paul insists that this is how it will be at the future resurrection. The body that goes into the ground is corruptible and temporary; it will be raised incorruptible and eternal. "It is sown in weakness but raised in power; it is sown a natural [Greek: *psychic*] body, it is raised a spiritual [Greek: *pneumatic*] body" (1 Corinthians 15:44). It will still be a body, but it will be made up of the most highly refined "stuff" there is: *pneuma*, or spirit. And so the resurrection is a glorious transformation in which the raised body will be a spiritual body, one that can never grow infirm or die.

Paul goes on then to the most mind-stretching passage of the chapter—indeed, of the entire book—in which he describes, in greater detail than in 1 Thessalonians, what will actually occur at the resurrection, when something happens to the mortal body to make it immortal. He calls this a great "mystery":

> We shall not all sleep [that is, die], but we will be changed. In a moment, in the blink of an eye, at the last trumpet! For the trumpet will sound and the dead will be raised incorruptible, and we [the living] will be transformed. For this corruptible body must put on incorruptibility and this mortal body must put on immortality. (1 Corinthians 15:51–53)

When that happens, "death will be devoured in victory." Death, then, will no longer have its fatal "sting."

And so, for Paul, there will indeed be a resurrection. It will be bodily. But the human body will be transformed into an immortal, incorruptible, perfect, glorious entity no longer made of coarse stuff that can become sick, get injured, suffer in any way, or die. It will be a spiritual body, a perfect dwelling for life everlasting.

It is in that context that one of the most misunderstood verses of Paul's entire corpus occurs, a verse completely bungled not just by many modern readers but throughout the history of Christianity. That is when Paul insists: "Flesh and blood cannot inherit the Kingdom of God" (1 Corinthians 15:50). These words are often taken—precisely against Paul's meaning—to suggest that eternal life will not be lived in the body. Wrong, wrong, wrong. For Paul it *will* be lived in a body—*but in a body that has been glorified.*

For Paul, the term "flesh and blood" simply refers to embodied human beings who were living in this world (see Galatians 1:16). For Paul, people will certainly not enter into God's kingdom as they are now. They need to be transformed. The gross heavenly matter of their body needs to be transfigured into spiritual matter. Otherwise they cannot be immortal. And so the contrast he is drawing is not between "bodily" existence that cannot enter the kingdom and "non-bodily" that can. It is instead between "flesh-and-blood bodies" made up of the coarse stuff to which we are restricted now (to our constant dissatisfaction and even misery), and "spiritual bodies" glorified at the culmination of all things when Jesus returns from heaven.

As a result, in addition to the ancient dichotomy of "immortality" of the soul and "resurrection" of the revivified body, Paul now offers a third alternative: "resurrection of the transformed, immortal, spiritual body." That is how eternal life will be lived.

But what about in the meantime? What about all those Christians who have died before it could happen? What is happening to them?

This was never an issue with the historical Jesus, so far as we know. Possibly Jesus never spoke about what would happen in the meantime because he thought there would not be much of a meantime: the Kingdom of God was to arrive right away. But Paul had to think about it. At first he believed the end was to appear very soon with the return of Jesus from heaven: he himself would be alive when it happened. (Note how he speaks of "we who are alive" when Jesus returns [1 Thessalonians 4:17].) But he knew that others had died before that climax of history. And eventually he began to wonder if he too might die before the end came. What then?

The Interim State in 2 Corinthians

Not long after Paul wrote his first letter to the Corinthians, other problems arose in the community that he felt compelled to address in a second letter. As might be expected, Paul continues to hold the views he stated before, even if he expresses himself differently. In 2 Corinthians he speaks less of the glorious transformation of the body that will happen at the future resurrection. He apparently felt no need to repeat what he had already told his Corinthian converts. Instead, in one place, he affirms to them that everyone will stand "before the judgment seat of Christ" to receive what is due to them according to what they have done "through the body, whether good or evil" (2 Corinthians 5:10). Here, unlike 1 Corinthians, he is not referring to the future resurrection per se but to the judgment that will come to all, some to punishment and others to reward. The reward will come, obviously, to those who are raised.

But that is not the only story to be told. In fact, this particular verse comes at the end of a passage that deals not with the final Day of Judgment but with what happens to a person who dies before it comes. Even though his language is frustratingly vague, Paul suggests that the deceased believer will have some kind of pleasant afterlife existence before the resurrection. He begins the passage by indicating: "If the tent of our earthly dwelling is destroyed, we have another building from God, a dwelling made without hands, eternal in the heavens" (2 Corinthians 5:1).

On first glance this may seem to suggest that Paul imagines that the person who dies is immediately given a new body in heaven. That is one possible view, but given the fact that Paul has been so explicit and emphatic in 1 Corinthians that the new body does not come until the resurrection, it has seemed to other interpreters an unlikely meaning. Many scholars think Paul is indeed being consistent, so that here again he is referring to the transformed glorious body followers of Jesus will receive at the resurrection, even if they die before it happens. What is different in this passage is that Paul stresses that he is eager to "put on" this new body because he does not want to be "found naked"—that is, bodiless (2 Corinthians 5:2–4). But why would he be found bodiless?

A clue comes in his statement that he is groaning in this current miserably embodied state. Paul was not one of those Christian evange-lists who thought life would always be good for those who follow Christ, that the faithful would reap many rewards and benefits in this life. On the contrary, throughout 2 Corinthians Paul stresses that the current life of the true apostle of Christ is filled with persecution and suffering. Paul actually revels in the fact of his pain, because his current miserable exis-tence replicates the life of a crucified messiah. In his view, anyone who does not lead a life of intense suffering is obviously not one of Jesus's apostles. That is the thrust of most of 2 Corinthians 11, and it is a teach-ing foreshadowed in the passage we are considering here, where Paul somewhat minimizes his earthly misery as a "momentary, light afflic-tion" that will produce an "eternal weight of glory beyond all description" (2 Corinthians 4:17).

Part of the affliction experienced by all believers is that those who are "at home in the body are away from the Lord" (2 Corinthians 5:6). Paul desperately wants to be in the actual, physical presence of Christ and so would much prefer to reverse his current circumstances and be "away from the body and at home with the Lord." That suggests that Paul imag-ines that if he were to die, he would enter into the Lord's presence. But at the same time he states that he does not want to be outside the body and "found naked." So how are we to make sense of this cryptic passage? How can he have it both ways: that he wants to be away from the body but not away from the body?

To make sense of his comments, it is important to see that Paul appears to be saying that, when they die, believers in Christ are ushered into Christ's presence. Obviously they do not still have mortal bodies at that point. Their bodies have died and are rotting in the grave. But they also don't have their transformed, glorious, immortal bodies, the "dwell-ing eternal in the heavens." Those will come only at the resurrection.

And so there are two options for what he means, both of them hing-ing on what he might imply by saying he does not at all relish the thought of being "found naked"—that is, bodiless. Either he thinks that, when he dies, he will be given a temporary body to inhabit in heaven, since he cannot imagine being naked; or, possibly more likely, Paul admits that he will, for a short time, be without a body, naked. In that case he doesn't relish the idea—it's not what he wants—but the thought of being in the presence of Christ trumps the fear of nakedness, and so he would prefer to die and to be naked with Christ than to continue on in this wretched mortal body. After all, his "nakedness" will last only for a short while, until the resurrection when Jesus returns in glory.

Death as a Great Gain

There is other very strong evidence that Paul believed in some kind of interim state in the presence of the Lord between a believer's death and resurrection. It comes to us from another book, Paul's letter to the Philippians. Paul wrote his letter to his converts in the city of Philippi from prison. We do not know whether this was his final imprisonment in Rome or some other incarceration during his various missionary journeys. What is clear from the letter is that he has been in prison for a while and is contemplating the possibility that the judicial proceeding against him may not end well. In fact, he is now thinking that he might die before Jesus returns, a notion that seemed almost inconceivable to the Paul who wrote 1 Thessalonians and 1 Corinthians, who quite clearly believed he would still be living when the glorious event occurred. (He indicates he would be among those who "are alive.")

It is not that he has given up on the idea that Christ would come on the clouds of heaven and raise the dead, transforming the bodies of his saints into immortal beings. He remains quite explicit on the point, saying, even in Philippians, that he hopes to "attain to the resurrection from the dead" and later saying that the believer's "citizenship"—that is, their place of ultimate devotion and belonging—is not on earth but in heaven, since it is from there that the "Lord Jesus Christ" would come as a savior and "transform the body of our humble existence into the same form as the body of his glory" (Philippians 3:11, 20–21). The belief in the day of glorious transformation that he discussed in his earlier letters of 1 Thessalonians and 1 Corinthians is still very much alive.

But he himself may die first. Paul begins the passage in question (Philippians 1:19–26) by expressing a fervent wish that he not do anything contrary to his faith in Christ, even in prison and in the face of possibly even worse suffering. He claims as his "eager expectation and hope that I be put to shame in nothing, but that with all boldness both always and now I might glorify Christ in my body, whether through life or through death" (Philippians 1:20) He wants to do nothing shameful, nothing that Christ would disapprove of, even in the face of death.

His reason is that his entire life is dedicated to Christ, as will be his death: "For to me, to live is Christ and to die is gain" (Philippians 1:21). This short and highly memorable verse is also unusually important. Paul is not saying that death is inevitable and has to be faced bravely. It is more than that. For him it is actually an *advantage* to die, and he tells us why: "My desire is to die and be with Christ, for that is much better" (Philippians 1:23). Paul would prefer to die, because then he would be with Christ. Our understanding of 2 Corinthians 5 is confirmed here in this clear statement: for Paul, there was an interim state. Believers who die before the resurrection will immediately be taken into the presence of Christ, but not in this state for eternity. Paul continues to think that there will be a future resurrection when Christ returns. Those who are dead will be returned to their bodies, which will be transformed into glorious, immortal, spiritual bodies just like the one Christ has; and those who are lucky enough to be living at the time will undergo the same transformation. But Paul now thinks he may die before it happens.

My sense is that Paul gradually came to this view. It is not what he thought when he started out as a Christian missionary. And it is not what he thought when he wrote the letter of 1 Thessalonians. If he had thought that, he would have responded to the Thessalonians' concerns differently. They were upset about people who had died in their community, wondering if they had lost out on their blessed reward to come when Christ reappeared. If Paul had believed in an interim state at the time, he surely would have informed the Thessalonians that those who had already died were already in the presence of Christ and so were much better off not having to wait for the resurrection. He says no such thing. He probably hadn't thought of the interim state yet.

One might suppose that he came to think of it as time dragged on. Jesus never did return, and Paul realized that he too might die. As he reflected on the possibility, he came to think that maybe that would not be such a bad thing. Surely God would not abandon his saints to some kind of netherworld to wait for the end of time or allow them to sink into nonexistence for a period. Surely the blessings that come in Christ in the present age would be felt as well once one departed. They must depart somewhere. Paul came to think they would depart, for a time, to be with Christ. There was a postmortem fate for those who believe.

What about those who do not believe? We have seen that Jesus did not teach that sinners would undergo eternal torment. He appears to have thought they would face annihilation: possibly they would be raised from the dead just in order to see that they, unlike the saints, would not be inheriting the glories of God's eternal kingdom, and then in the face of that awful realization they would be painfully destroyed. Their deaths would be eternal even if they did not undergo everlasting torment.

Did Paul agree? There are hints he did. Paul speaks openly about "the wrath of God" that is already now manifest against unbelievers (Romans 1:18). He also believes God's wrath will be revealed in a major way at the end of time when believers inherit their eternal salvation. Paul stresses that the followers of Christ will not be like those who are "destined to wrath" (1 Thessalonians 5:9). What is that wrath, though? Is it eternal torture? Paul does not say so. Instead he says that the unbelievers, at the return of Jesus, will experience "sudden destruction" (1 Thessalonians 5:3). That is to say, as Jesus also taught, the wicked will be annihilated at the Day of Judgment that was coming soon.

This coincides with what Paul later wrote in 1 Corinthians as well, in his discussion of what would occur at the resurrection of the dead. When Christ returns and the dead are transformed for eternal life, Christ will then "annihilate every authority and power" (1 Corinthians 15:24). If they are annihilated, they will no longer exist. In the end, nothing at all will exist that does not exude the glory of God the Father. Most striking of all, not even death will survive. "The last enemy, death, is annihilated" (1 Corinthians 15:26). Death will be no more, and if that is so, then neither are the people who have gone to death. They simply don't exist any longer. They aren't tortured. They are taken out of existence, never to return.

This appears to have been the teaching of both Paul and Jesus. But it was eventually to be changed by later Christians, who came to affirm not only eternal joy for the saints but eternal torment for the sinners, creating the irony that throughout the ages most Christians have believed in a hell that did not exist for either of the founders of Christianity.

CHAPTER TEN

Altering the Views of Jesus:
The Later Gospels

Paul was not the only early follower of Jesus who developed and even transformed his teachings. It was inevitable that the majority of his followers would do so. The imminent end of all things that Jesus expected with the appearance of a cosmic judge from heaven never occurred. Rather than simply conclude that Jesus had been wrong, his followers believed he had been misunderstood or misquoted. And so they took his teachings and translated them into a new idiom for a new day, making them relevant for their current situation. Christians have always done this, and always will.

For this reason it is no surprise that the Christian authors who later recorded Jesus's teachings actually altered his words in places to make them reflect their own understandings, which had developed over time after his death. That included his teachings about the afterlife.

Alterations of Jesus's Teaching About the Afterlife

The Gospels of the New Testament, as we have seen, date from forty to sixty years after Jesus's death. That is a long time. If Jesus expected God's glorious kingdom to come right away, within his disciples' lifetime, but it didn't happen, then naturally later writers discussing his teachings would have been inclined to change them, either to alter his predictions of the imminent end of the age—postponing it a bit—or to change their very essence, so that he no longer preached the coming Kingdom of God in history at all but began to talk about what happens to each individual at death. For those who modified his teachings in this way, the Kingdom of God on earth became the Kingdom with God in heaven, available to everyone who believes.

Such transformations of Jesus's teachings may have been facilitated by the composition of the later Christian communities, comprised for the most part not of Jews raised on apocalyptic views of the coming judgment of God but of former pagans raised in Greek ways of looking at the world that stressed the immortality of the soul rather than the resurrection of the body. For such people, eternal life would involve rewards and punishments after death.

As it turns out, it is possible to trace a trajectory in our surviving Gospels away from the deeply apocalyptic teachings of Jesus in Mark and Matthew, to less apocalyptic teachings in the later Gospel of Luke, to non-apocalyptic teachings in the still later Gospel of John, to *anti*-apocalyptic teachings in the noncanonical Gospel of Thomas, written a couple of decades after John. In short, the words of Jesus, over time, came to be de-apocalypticized.

Jewish apocalyptic thought is essentially dualistic, stressing not only that there are two fundamental components of reality—good and evil, God and the devil—but also that all of history can be divided into two ages, the current evil age that will be destroyed and the future age in which God will rule supreme. This is a kind of "horizontal" dualism in that you can map it out on a time line across the page from left to right. When Christians de-apocalypticized the teachings of Jesus, they retained a dualistic understanding of the future but they flipped the temporal, horizontal dualism on its axis so that it became a *vertical* conception, not moving from left to right but from below to above. The emphasis now is not on time—this age and the age to come—but on space: this awful world on earth and the glorious world above in heaven. It is no longer about "now and then" but about "down and up."

This new conception is thus still dualistic, but rather than emphasizing God's kingdom to come in the future it proclaims God's kingdom now to be enjoyed in the world above. Everyone who sides with God will go to that Kingdom of God at the point of death. This is the beginning of the Christian teaching of hell below and heaven above.

We begin to see the de-apocalypticization of Jesus's teachings in the longest corpus of the New Testament, the two-volume work of Luke and Acts. These books were written by a later Greek-educated Christian who probably produced his work a couple of generations after Jesus, around 80–85 CE. The Gospel of Luke records Jesus's birth, life, death, and resurrection; the book of Acts picks up the story at that point, describing the spread of Christianity in the Roman world through the missionary activities of the apostles, most especially the apostle Paul.[1] In both books there are sayings about the afterlife, either on the lips of Jesus in the Gospel or on the lips of the apostles in the book of Acts. It is striking that throughout these two books the understanding of the afterlife differs from what was proclaimed some fifty years earlier by the historical Jesus himself.

The Beginnings of Postmortem Rewards and Punishments

The author of Luke's Gospel begins his work by acknowledging that he had "many" predecessors who, before him, had written accounts of

Jesus's words and deeds (Luke 1:1–4). His purpose in writing, he says, is to give an "accurate" account based on significant research. The implication, of course, is that those who produced Gospels before him had possibly not done sufficient research and were not altogether correct in their accounts.

Among the sources of information Luke used, one was almost certainly the Gospel of Mark, with which he has numerous word-for-word agreements.[2] But he also alters and adds to Mark's words. This is certainly true when it comes to the words Jesus allegedly spoke about the end times and the coming Kingdom of God.

When Jesus is placed on trial at the end of his life in Mark's Gospel, for example, and is being interrogated by Caiaphas the high priest, Jesus tells him that he, Caiaphas himself, will see the cosmic judge of the earth, the Son of Man, arrive from heaven (Mark 14:62). In other words, the end of history and the Day of Judgment will come in the priest's own lifetime. Luke, writing later, has the same scene but changes Jesus's words. Now Jesus says instead that "from now on the Son of Man will be seated" with God the Father on high (Luke 22:69). Thus Jesus's saying about the future (horizontal dualism) has now become a statement about heaven above (vertical dualism).

So too, throughout Luke, the kingdom is not simply a future event but a present reality. And so Jesus's famous words in Luke 17:20–21, which are so widely misunderstood by readers, where he tells the antagonistic Pharisees that the kingdom has already come among them—"The Kingdom of God is in your midst" (words found only in Luke, not in Mark). The statement is mistranslated, and misinterpreted, by those who think that Jesus is declaring that the Kingdom of God is "inside" each person. He can't mean that. He is talking to his enemies, the Pharisees, who, in his view, definitely do not have the Kingdom of God in their inner beings. Instead, he is saying that the Kingdom of God is "among" them. To Luke, what Jesus means is that while he himself is with them, they can see the Kingdom of God here on earth through what he says and does. He, and therefore the kingdom, is among them. By the time Luke is writing, decades have passed since Jesus's ministry, and his teaching of the kingdom is being transformed. It is not only a future event but a present reality.

That is not to say that Luke has jettisoned an apocalyptic message altogether. He still is a firm believer in the resurrection, both of Jesus and of believers at a later time. In the case of Jesus, Luke goes out of his way to stress that Jesus was actually, bodily raised from the dead. In fact, he insists that precisely the body that went into Jesus's tomb is the one that came out of it—a view that actually contradicts Paul. As we have seen, Paul believed Jesus's body was completely glorified and transformed, turned from a "flesh-and-blood" being to a "spiritual one." That is why "flesh and blood cannot enter the kingdom of heaven." Not so Luke. For him, Jesus's resurrected body is his revivified corpse.

This is shown in a remarkable passage after Jesus is raised, found only in Luke. Jesus appears to his disciples, who are understandably terrified, mistakenly thinking that they are seeing a "spirit" (i.e., a ghost [Luke 22:37]). The word Luke uses for spirit here, strikingly, is *pneuma*. That is the word Paul uses to describe the kind of body a person has at the resurrection (1 Corinthians 15:44). But not Luke. He wants to deny that Jesus had a pneumatic body. And so, in his account, Jesus convinces his disciples that he is decidedly not *pneuma* but a fleshly being, the corpse brought back from the dead intact. And so he tells them to look at him closely and touch him, "for a spirit (*pneuma*) does not have flesh and bones as I have" (Luke 22:39). The disciples still aren't sure, so he asks for a piece of broiled fish, which he then eats. That proves it. He is the same as he was before, a body made of flesh physically returned from the dead—presumably with an alimentary canal—not a glorified spiritual body as Paul imagined.

Just as Jesus was physically raised from the dead for Luke, so too Luke clearly believes there will be a future resurrection at the end (see Acts 17:31; 23:6; and 24:14-15). But what is most significant is that, unlike the historical Jesus himself, Luke maintains that eternity begins immediately at a person's death. Like Paul, but even more emphatically, Luke thinks that when believers in Jesus die, they go straight to heaven.

Nowhere is this indicated more clearly than in his account of Jesus's own crucifixion, in a change from what you find in Mark, Luke's main source. In Luke, while hanging on the cross, Jesus has a brief conversation with one of the two robbers crucified beside him, who makes a request: "Remember me when you come into your kingdom" (Luke 23:42). This criminal is imagining that there will be a future event that could bring him salvation. But Jesus subtly corrects him with his famous saying, found only in Luke: "Truly I tell you, today you will be with me in paradise" (Luke 23:43). Remarkable words. The man will enter paradise immediately at the point of death. He does not need to wait for some future apocalyptic event, the coming of Christ's kingdom.

Some readers over the years have suggested this saying of Jesus should be punctuated differently, on the understanding that ancient Greek manuscripts did not use any punctuation at all, which is therefore supplied by modern translators. If we move the comma, then Jesus was instead saying: "Truly I tell you today, you will be with me in paradise." In that case, Jesus was *not* telling the man that they will both end up in paradise that very day, as soon as the pain has ended.

On the surface this might make sense, but there are very good arguments against it. On one hand, on the very basic level, this understanding actually does not make any sense. If Jesus is talking to the man and telling him something about paradise, why would he indicate that he was saying it to him on that particular day? What other day would he be saying it? But possibly more important, in Luke's Gospel the word "today" is used some dozen times. In every case it indicates the day on which something significant is happening, often something involving salvation, as is the case here (see also Luke 2:11; 4:21; 13:32–33; 19:9). It never, ever indicates simply the day on which something is *said* to be about to happen. And why would it?

For Luke, the idea that paradise becomes available to the follower of Jesus immediately upon death is confirmed in his second volume in the account of the first Christian martyr, Stephen. Stephen has just antagonized his Jewish opponents by delivering a long, rather hostile sermon (most of Acts 7), at the end of which he looks up to heaven and declares that he sees "the Son of Man standing at the right hand of God" (Acts 7:56). The Jewish leaders are incensed, thinking he has committed blasphemy, and in a mob effort break out the stones to execute him on the spot. Just before he dies, Stephen cries out, "Lord Jesus, receive my spirit" (Acts 7:59). Again, that last word is *pneuma*. Stephen's *pneuma* now will go to heaven to reside with the Lord when his body perishes. This is Greek-influenced theology. Rewards come to the righteous immediately at death. One does not need to wait for the resurrection of the body at the end of time.

Luke's idea of postmortem rewards and punishments—unlike anything found in the words of the historical Jesus himself—is most emphatically and intriguingly conveyed in one of his most famous passages, and possibly the best-known account of the afterlife in the entire New Testament: his story of "Lazarus and the Rich Man."

Glory and Torment After Death in Luke

The story appears in Luke 16:19-31 in the context of a number of parables and other sayings of Jesus. In it, Jesus contrasts two lives. There is an unnamed rich man dressed in fine clothes who enjoys sumptuous meals every day. But at the gate of his home lies a beggar named Lazarus, starving, desperate even to get the scraps off the rich man's table. The scene is pathetic. Dogs come up and lick Lazarus's wounds.

Both men die. Lazarus is carried off by the angels to "Abraham's bosom," a phrase that never occurs in early Jewish literature but probably simply means that Lazarus has been brought to paradise to recline at table beside the great patriarch of Israel. The rich man, on the other hand, is buried and ends up in Hades. It is not a happy place. The man is being tormented in flames. He looks up and sees in the great distance Abraham and Lazarus beside him. He calls out to Abraham for help: Could he send Lazarus just to dip his finger in water and cool his tongue? But Abraham reminds the rich man that he had all good things when living, while Lazarus had nothing. Now their situations are reversed and nothing can be done about it. Between them is an unbridgeable chasm separating paradise from the place of torment: no one can go back and forth.

The rich man then begs Abraham at least to send Lazarus back to earth to his five brothers who are still living and need to be warned of the horrible fate that may be awaiting them. Abraham refuses: his brothers can simply read the Jewish scriptures and they will know what they need to do. But the rich man persists: if someone were to come back from the dead, then they would take notice and repent. Abraham shuts the conversation down by telling the man that "if they do not listen to Moses and the prophets, neither will they be convinced even if someone rises from the dead" (Luke 16:31).

Later Christian readers who come to that last line are shocked into a realization. They know that someone *has been* raised from the dead. And people still don't listen!

This is a moving and memorable story. Its view of the afterlife differs from anything we have found on the lips of the historical Jesus. Here there are definitely rewards and punishments that come immediately at death. The rewards are not given in any detail but can easily be surmised. Lazarus is in a place of great enjoyment, banqueting with the greatest saints of all time. The rich man, by contrast, is being tormented in flames, desperate for simply a drop of water, with no relief in sight.

It is hard to know what to make of the physicality of both descriptions. Abraham has a "bosom," Lazarus has fingers, the rich man has a tongue and obviously a nervous system susceptible to torment by fire. The afterlife here is an embodied existence of some kind, with functioning body parts. Moreover, the respective fates of the two appear to be permanent. There is a vast chasm separating them. Neither will ever leave the place he is in. Lazarus is now—forever, one might suppose—in paradise and the rich man in the fires of Hades.

In trying to unpack the understanding of the afterlife found in the passage, it is important to realize that Luke presents the story as a parable—a simple, imaginative story meant to illustrate a deeper spiritual lesson.[3] It is not a literal description of reality. It is true that Luke does not actually call it a parable, but that's true of most of the parables Jesus tells in this Gospel. This section of Luke's narrative is chock-full of parables—twenty two of them, in close proximity. A number of them begin with the words "a certain man" did such and such. That is the case of two immediately preceding passages: the parable of the prodigal son in Luke 15:11 and of the parable of the dishonest steward in Luke 16:1. And it is true of this very story in Luke 16:19.

Since the account is a parable, an imaginative tale meant to emphasize a point, it would be wrong to press its details for literal descriptions of what awaits people in the afterlife, with bodies in flame, horribly dry tongues, fingers dipped into water, and communications between people in Hades and those in paradise. It is a fictional story meant to convey a lesson. The lesson may be rooted in a certain conception of life after death, but it is designed to teach people how to live in the present. In this case the lesson involves one's relation to wealth.

Some readers have assumed that the parable is not about wealth per se but about being a good or bad person. In that reading, the rewarded Lazarus was righteous and the rich man a sinner. It is striking, however, that the story says nothing about that. What it emphasizes is their wealth and poverty, not their sin and righteousness. Still, some scholars have thought that sin is the ultimate point and have appealed to other stories from the ancient world in support of the idea, other fictional accounts of the reversal of fortunes of the rich and poor in the afterlife. The best known—among historians of religion, at least—is an Egyptian tale of a man named Setne and his adult son Si-Osire.[4]

In the story the two of them are looking out the window of their house and see the coffin of a rich man being carried out to the cemetery with great honors. They then see the corpse of a poor beggar carried out on a mat, with no one attending his funeral. Setne says to his son: "By Ptah, the great god, how much happier is the rich man who is honored with the sound of wailing than the poor man who is carried to the cemetery." Si-Osire surprises his father by telling him that the poor man will be much better off in the afterlife than the rich one. He surprises him even more by proving it.

He takes Setne down to the underworld, where they see how the unrighteous are punished, including some who are in dire hunger and thirst with food and drink just out of reach above their heads. In particular, they see a man lying on the ground before a great hall with a large gate; the hinge of the gate is fixed in the man's eye socket, swiveling as the gate opens and shuts, with the man pleading and crying for help. This, as it turns out, is the rich man they had seen being taken off for burial with great honor. When he arrived in the underworld the judges weighed his misdeeds against his righteous acts, and he was found seriously wanting. The gate in the eye socket is his punishment.

Setne and Si-Osire also see the rewards of the righteous, including a very rich person finely clothed, standing by the god Osiris. This is none other than the poor man they observed unattended at his burial. When his life was judged, he was found to have done far more good deeds than wicked ones, and so was he rewarded with the very garments the rich man wore at his own burial.

Si-Osire sums up the situation: "Take it to your heart, my father Setne: he who is beneficent on earth, to him one is beneficent in the nether-world. And he who is evil, to him one is evil. So it is so decreed and will remain so forever." Far better, that is, to be dirt-poor and righteous than filthy rich and wicked. Eternal life hinges on it.

Possibly that is the teaching of the story of Lazarus and the rich man as well, an implicit lesson about righteous living. But since, unlike the Egyptian tale, this parable says nothing about sin and righteousness, some interpreters have suggested different ways of understanding it. Maybe the problem with the rich man is not that he is generally wicked but that, more specifically, he hasn't used his wealth in order to help those who were poor. That would be suggested by the statement that Lazarus lay right outside the man's gate, starving to death, while the man feasted every day in great luxury. The man had no heart. In support of this view is the fact that the rich man obviously knew all about famished Lazarus. When he is in Hades, he calls him by name.

Moreover, this understanding makes sense of the rest of the story. The rich man is clearly a Jew: he calls Abraham "Father," and it is implied that he, like his brothers, should have paid attention to "Moses and the prophets." The Law of Moses tells people to "love your neighbor as your-self" (Leviticus 19:18). The rich man allowed Lazarus to starve to death when he easily could have done something about it.

Other scholars have argued a more extreme position, maintaining that the problem is not that the rich man did not use his resources to help the poor but that having riches in and of itself is the problem.[5] There are other passages in Luke's Gospel where that does indeed appear to be the case. In Luke's version of the Beatitudes, for example—and only here in the New Testament—Jesus pronounces that those in poverty are blessed (Luke 6:20-25): "Blessed are you poor, because yours is the Kingdom of God." In Matthew, Jesus instead blesses the poor *in spirit* (Matthew 5:3). Not in Luke: he is talking about people who have no money. So too

"Blessed are you who hunger now, for you will be filled." These are not people hungering and thirsting "for righteousness" as in Matthew 5:6; they are people who have nothing to eat or drink.

These blessings for those who suffer now are contrasted by Luke with the fate of the rich, not because they are unrighteous, but simply, apparently, because they are loaded: "Woe to you who are rich, for you have (already) received your consolation. Woe to you who are full now, for you will be hungry" (Luke 6:24–25). This can explain why in Luke's Gospel Jesus explicitly tells his followers to sell everything they have and give the money away. That is how they will have "treasure in heaven" (Luke 12:33). Or, as he says emphatically later, "No one who does not give up all his possessions can be my disciple" (Luke 14:33).

The historical Jesus himself may well have declared that it was impossible to be rich and inherit salvation: "It is easier for a camel to go through the eye of a needle than for a rich person to enter the kingdom of heaven" (Mark 10:25). But Jesus is referring to the kingdom that is soon to come. In Luke he is talking about what will happen to a person immediately after death.

In any event, it should be clear that the historical Jesus himself did not tell the story of Lazarus and the rich man. The ending itself is a dead giveaway. When Abraham tells the rich man that there is no point in sending Lazarus to warn his brothers, because they would not come to believe even if someone *were* raised from the dead, the story is presupposing knowledge of Jesus's fate and the Christian proclamation that his resurrection should lead people to repent. A similar point is stressed time and again throughout the speeches of the apostles in the book of Acts (see Acts 2:22–39 and 3:14–21). Moreover, for Luke, turning to God is not simply a matter of mental assent; the rich need to give their wealth to help the poor.

We have seen that neither Jesus nor Paul appears to have taught anything about eternal punishment for the wicked. The story of Lazarus and the rich man in Luke is the first time we find such a notion suggested anywhere in the Bible. In fact, it is the *only* place we find it. Later I will be arguing that it is not the teaching of the later writings of the New Testament, not even the book of Revelation. But it was to become the standard Christian view. The doctrines of heaven and hell are rooted in this imaginative story attributed to Jesus only in Luke, a story readers later took literally to describe what the afterlife would be like for the righteous and wicked.

Eternal Life in the Here and Now: The Gospel of John

Since the early centuries of Christianity, the Gospel of John has been recognized as significantly different from the other three canonical accounts of Jesus's life. The very beginning of the Gospel presents a far more exalted understanding of Jesus. Here Christ is not simply a Jewish messiah or Son of God who must die for the sins of the world. He is explicitly a divine being who was with God the Father in eternity past and who created the universe before later becoming incarnate as a human being. The earlier Gospels provided significant hints that their authors understood Jesus in some sense to be a divine being; in John there is no ambiguity at all. Jesus is God (see John 1:1–18).[6]

This change is reflected in Jesus's sayings in the Fourth Gospel. In the other three accounts Jesus only rarely says anything about his identity and never explicitly declares himself to be divine. All that is different in John, where Jesus says such things as "I and the Father are one" (John 10:30); "Before Abraham was, I am" (John 8:58); and "If you have seen me you have seen the Father" (John 14:9). These exalted claims, found only in John, are the occasion of serious opposition in the narrative, as Jewish leaders believe Jesus has committed execrable blasphemy by equating himself with God. They repeatedly take up stones to execute him for it (John 8:59; 10:31).

Also different here are Jesus's teachings about the afterlife. As we have seen, John was the last canonical Gospel written, probably sixty to sixty-five years after Jesus's death. At this far remove from Jesus's life, his message has become even more thoroughly de-apocalypticized. In John, Jesus no longer speaks of the coming intervention of God to bring in his glorious kingdom. Instead, he principally talks about heaven above and how people can go there by believing in him.

That is not to say there are absolutely no remnants of the idea that a day of judgment is coming. On several occasions Jesus speaks of "the last day" (e.g., John 6:39; 7:37; 11:24), and at one point he says he "will raise up" the one who believes in him (John 6:40). Most famously, he makes the declaration commonly read at funerals even today:

> In my Father's house there are many rooms [the King James Version translates the word as "mansions"]. Otherwise, would I tell you that I am going to prepare a place for you? And if I go and prepare a place for you, I am coming again and will take you to myself, so that where I am you might be also. (John 14:2–3)

Jesus, then, is portrayed as going to heaven to be with God at his death. He also will bring those who believe in him there. Many readers take this to be a promise of postmortem rewards. If that reading is correct, it would be comparable to what can be found in Luke: paradise at the point of death. But it could also be read as a reference to Jesus's return in glory ("I am coming again"), in which case it would be a remnant of the early Christian apocalyptic idea that at his second coming Jesus will raise his followers from the dead, a notion we have seen in the writings of Paul. If that understanding is correct, this would be one of the few places in John that the older view of the physical return of Jesus can be found.

Far more frequently in John, unlike the other Gospels, we find references to eternal rewards and punishment coming in the here and now, in this life. Followers of Jesus, and those who reject him, do not need to wait until an eschatological Day of Judgment and its resurrection of the dead to be blessed or cursed by God; nor will they be rewarded or punished only at the moment following their deaths. Instead, in this Gospel, anyone who believes in Jesus is said *already* to have experienced the joys of eternity. As he says to his enemies in chapter 5:

> Truly, truly I tell you, the one who hears my word and believes in the one who sent me has eternal life and does not come into judgment, but has passed from death to life. (John 5:24)

Everlasting life is not something that comes later. It is a present reality. Believers in Jesus *have* eternal life. And so he can continue on to say,

> Truly, truly I tell you, an hour is coming and now is, when the dead will hear the voice of the Son of God and those who hear will live. (John 5:25)

As elsewhere in John, the verse seems to contain a remnant of the older apocalyptic view that there will be a future resurrection at Jesus's return, but this view is trumped by the author's explanation that this coming "hour" is already here. It "now is." Those who believe Jesus have already entered into life. They do not need to wait for something future. This is a very serious de-apocalypticization of Jesus's message indeed.

The same applies to judgment. The matter is summed up with fine concision at the end of one of John's most remarkable chapters: "Whoever believes in the Son has eternal life; whoever does not obey the Son will not see life, but the wrath of God remains on him" (John 3:36). The final verb is in the present tense: nonbelievers are already experiencing God's wrath.

John's teaching that eternal life is present right now to anyone who believes in Jesus is brilliantly conveyed in one of the most memorable episodes of the entire Gospel, the story of the raising of Lazarus (John 11). This is obviously a different Lazarus from the one who appears in Jesus's parable in Luke 16, although interpreters have long wondered if John, writing at a later time, had heard a parable connected with someone named Lazarus who could, in principle, return from the dead, and developed the story into an actual narrative where it happened. It is certainly possible, but very hard to prove.

In John's story, Jesus is very good friends with Lazarus, along with his sisters Mary and Martha. We are told at the beginning of the story that Lazarus fell ill, and the sisters came to tell Jesus, presumably so he could come heal him (John 11:1–3). Then comes one of the truly remarkable verses of the entire New Testament, even though most readers have simply never noticed: "Now Jesus loved Martha and her sister and Lazarus. So, when he heard that Lazarus was sick, he stayed in the place he was for two days." That's how much he loved Lazarus! When he heard he was sick, he stayed away.

But John explains why he did this. It was so Jesus could be "glorified" by Lazarus's situation. Jesus wanted Lazarus to die so he could raise him from the dead to prove that he is the Son of God: "I am glad I was not here, so that you may believe" (John 11:15).

What especially matters for our purposes is the conversation that Jesus has with one of the sisters before he performs the miracle. By the time Jesus gets to their town of Bethany, Lazarus has been dead and buried for four days. The author wants to stress that he was really and completely dead. When Martha hears that Jesus has come, she goes to meet with him and gives him a mild reprimand: "Lord, if you had been here my brother would not have died" (John 11:21). But then she hints a miracle is still possible: "I also know that whatever you ask God, he will give you" (John 11:22).

Jesus's reply encapsulates the older view found in the teachings of the historical Jesus himself and in the writings of Paul: "Your brother will arise." Obviously, in that older context, this would have meant that on the last day, when the Son of Man arrives in judgment on the world, the dead will be raised and rewarded. And that's what Martha understands Jesus to mean. "Martha said to him: 'I know that he will rise at the resurrection on the last day'" (John 11:24).

But Jesus corrects her in words that could be found nowhere in the New Testament outside the Gospel of John: "I am the resurrection and the life. The one who believes in me, will live, even if he dies; and everyone who lives and believes in me will never die" (John 11:25–26). He wants to know if Martha believes him, and she tells him that she believes he really is the Christ, the Son of God. Jesus then performs the miracle, raising Lazarus from the dead.

To put this miracle in its literary context, it is important to recognize that throughout John's Gospel Jesus does his miraculous signs precisely to prove that what he says about himself is true. These claims he makes about himself are found only in John. At one point Jesus claims he is "the bread of life," meaning that he can provide the sustenance that leads to eternal life. He proves it by multiplying the loaves for the multitudes (John 5). Later he claims he is "the light of the world" and proves it by restoring sight to a man born blind (John 9). Now here, prior to his final sign, he claims that he himself is the resurrection and the life. He proves it by raising Lazarus from the dead.

For this Gospel, no one needs to wait for a future apocalyptic act of God, an end-of-time resurrection of the dead, to enter eternal life. One does not even need to die first. Those who believe in Christ already have eternal life. Those who do not believe stand under the wrath of God. Eternity is now.

Even though the Gospel of John has long been the favorite account of Jesus's life and words, its view of eternity proved to be a dead end (or at least a cul-de-sac) in the history of Christian theology. Later Christians, as a rule, became far more interested in knowing their fate at the time of death than in thinking they were experiencing the joys of heaven in the present. But John's views did not die an immediate death. Some Christian circles even heightened such de-apocalpyticizing of Jesus's message. A yet more radical view can be found in a later Gospel not included in the New Testament, the Gospel of Thomas. Here Jesus not only speaks words that lack any apocalyptic content; he actually attacks apocalyptic views. Now we are moving into the realm of an anti-apocalyptic movement—allegedly endorsed by Jesus himself.

The Kingdom of God Within You

The Gospel of Thomas is the most famous of the writings discovered in a cache of documents unearthed in 1945 near Nag Hammadi, Egypt: the so-called Gnostic Gospels. The book consists of 114 sayings of Jesus, and only that. About half of these are versions of sayings of Jesus found earlier in Matthew, Mark, and Luke. The other half are the ones that have attracted the most scholarly attention. Taken together, all these sayings are presented as a kind of secret mystical knowledge that, when understood, can provide eternal life. The very first words of the text encapsulate this intention: "These are the hidden sayings that the living Jesus spoke and Didymus Judas Thomas wrote down. And he said, 'Whoever finds the interpretation of these sayings will not taste death.'"[7] Never has there been a greater burden imposed on the interpreter: the (only) way to live forever is to find the correct meaning of the words of the book!

Many of the sayings placed on Jesus's lips here are mysterious indeed and hard to fathom. Then again, if they were simple and clear, just *anyone* could have eternal life. Some of the sayings focus precisely on the need to acquire proper knowledge for salvation. Eternal life comes not by faith but by knowing the secret truths Jesus reveals and by living accordingly. In particular, those who belong to the truth will not be concerned with the needs and demands of the body but, on the contrary, will despise the physical realities of existence and yearn for a return to the heavenly realm whence they have come.

This return will not happen at a future apocalyptic moment when an actual Kingdom of God arrives on earth. Quite the contrary, Jesus here preaches against the idea that the kingdom is a realm outside a person that is to be expected in an eschatological moment to come. The importance of this anti-apocalyptic theme is shown by the fact that at both the beginning of the Gospel (saying 2) and at its end (saying 113) Jesus corrects the older understanding of the coming Kingdom of God—that is, the understanding of the historical Jesus himself.

Thus, at the beginning, Jesus condemns those who preach an actual, physical Kingdom of God either in heaven or on earth:

> Jesus said, "If your leaders say to you, 'Look, the kingdom is in the sky,' then the birds of the sky will precede you. If they say to you, 'It is in the sea,' then the fish will precede you. But the kingdom is within you, and it is outside you." (saying 2)

The kingdom, in other words, is not a place you will see and enter; it is a reality within and around us. The point is reemphasized near the end of the collection of sayings:

> His disciples said to him, "When will the kingdom come?" [Jesus replied:] "It will not come by waiting for it. They will not say, 'Look here it is,' or 'Look, it is there.' Rather the kingdom of the Father is spread out upon the earth, and people do not see it." (saying 113)

God's kingdom is not a place to come later, a place that can be located here or there. It is everywhere and it is now. People should find it in the present, both within themselves and scattered throughout their daily experiences.

And so, in the middle of the Gospel, we have an exchange between Jesus and his disciples:

> His disciples said to him, "When will the repose of the dead take place? And when will the new world come?" He said to them, "What you are looking for has come, but for your part you do not know it." (saying 51)

The resurrection of the dead is not a future event to come with the appearance of a new heaven and earth. It comes now, to those who grasp the hidden sayings of Jesus. Understanding these sayings is how one can "see Jesus" not as one who comes in the future but as one who is here with us now.

In addition, seeing him requires abandoning the passions and desires of this life, moving beyond the demands of the body, and seeking the spiritual truth that is available. And so, in one of the most graphic statements of this view, Jesus likens the concerns and demands of the body to clothing that needs to be stripped off and despised if one wants to understand who Christ really is.

> His disciples said, "When will you appear to us and when shall we see you?" Jesus said, "When you strip naked without being ashamed and take your clothes and place them under your feet like little children and stamp on them, then you will see the Son of the Living One, and you will not be afraid." (saying 37)

Interpreting and Altering the Words of Jesus

And so, in the Gospel of Thomas, the last of the Gospels we will consider, we find words placed on Jesus's lips that differ radically from anything the historical Jesus himself actually said.[8] It would be a mistake, however, to think that in altering Jesus's message the anonymous author of this text was doing something significantly different from what the authors of earlier Gospels had done. From the outset of the Christian movement, those who reported the words of Jesus changed them in light of their own new situations, translating them into idioms that made more sense in their own present, and making them embody and capture views the authors themselves had, even if these were different from those of the historical Jesus. That was true for all of Jesus's teachings, including his apocalyptic notions of the coming Kingdom of God.

The interpretations of Jesus found in the Gospel of Thomas did not widely catch on, however, probably for a variety of reasons. Among other things, these alternative sayings of Jesus were never included in the New Testament. The books that did become canonical Scripture talked about the great eternal rewards that would come to the faithful and the horrible punishment that would come to sinners. These views themselves developed in various directions over time. By the second century very few followers of Jesus held to his views of the afterlife. Instead they subscribed to ideas of heaven and hell that later formed the basis of Christian beliefs that have come down to us today.

CHAPTER ELEVEN

The Afterlife Mysteries of the Book of Revelation

No writing of the New Testament has fascinated and befuddled readers more than the book of Revelation. The book details what will happen at the end of time, when God unleashes his wrath on this world, bringing massive calamity and destruction, including the complete and decisive overthrow of all the forces of evil: the devil, his agents, Hades, and death itself. But the rich and complex symbolism throughout the book creates a near-perfect irony. It is called the "Revelation" but no one can agree on what it reveals. Throughout Christian history down to our own day, confident interpreters have asserted views that stand radically at odds with one another: Does the book give a literal description of what will happen in our future? Could the cosmic upheavals it describes symbolize something other than actual catastrophes on earth? Is an Antichrist soon to appear? Who is the mysterious "Beast" whose number is 666? Is it some wicked tyrant ruling already now—or one who will arise very soon? Can we expect Armageddon in our own day? Maybe in a few weeks?

Throughout history, many, many interpreters of the book of Revelation have argued its predictions were coming true in their own time.

Each and every one of them has been incontrovertibly and demonstrably wrong. That is not because they have applied insufficient effort and ingenuity to their interpretations, but because they have, to a person, thought the book was referring to events that were yet to transpire in human history. I will be arguing in this chapter that this specific approach to interpretation—the one most readers take—is wrong. It was a mistake to think that the number of "the Beast" (= God's ultimate enemy, the so-called Antichrist), 666, referred to Hitler, the pope, or Saddam Hussein, or that the end of history was to come in 1844 or 1988 or in the aftermath of 9/11, not because of simple error in calculation but because of a fundamental flaw in interpretation. This book, like all books of the Bible, was written both in and for its own day, and if we want to understand what its author meant, we have to place his book in its own historical context.

In addition, we have to understand better what *kind* of book it is. I will be arguing that it is not a prediction of what was to happen thousands of years after the author's day. He was describing what he thought would take place in his own time. He did so by using a literary genre common at the time, called the "apocalypse," a genre found in a number of works, especially during the four-hundred-year period between the Maccabean Revolt and the end of the second Christian century. We have already seen three examples: 1 Enoch, Daniel, and 4 Ezra. To understand the book of Revelation in its own context—instead of taking it out of context—we have to begin by recognizing more fully how writings of this literary genre worked, especially in their use of bizarre symbolism.

That matters for our present purposes because the later Christian understandings of heaven and hell depend heavily on the book's depiction of the heavenly Jerusalem, the dwelling place for all eternity of the saints, a city with gates of pearl and streets of gold, as well as its fearful references to the eternal "lake of fire," the destination of sinners. If, as I will try to show, the rest of the book was meant to be understood symbolically, we are faced with a pressing question: Why should we take these descriptions of the eternal fates of saints and sinners literally?[1]

The Apocalypse Genre

The title of the book "Revelation" is simply the Latin form of the Greek word "apocalypse," which, as we have seen, means a revealing or an unveiling. Nearly all other ancient apocalypses—i.e., books in this literary genre—are written pseudonymously, and for reasons we have seen: the heavenly mysteries "revealed" to these divine seers could obviously not come to just anyone. And so the authors claimed to be famous holy men of the past, those especially chosen to receive divine revelations that unveil the mysteries of the universe.

The best-known exception to the "rule" that apocalypses were pseudonymous is the book of Revelation itself. The author tells us who he is, someone named John (Revelation 1:1, 9). He does not tell us *which* "John" he was, which is disappointing, because it was a common name. Later readers assumed he was none other than Jesus's disciple, John the son of Zebedee, whom they identified also as the author of the Fourth Gospel. But scholars have long known, going back to the third Christian century, that these two books must have been written by different people. On one hand, their writing styles are nothing at all alike—a bit like reading a page from a Dickens novel and then another from a sophomore in a creative writing class. Whoever the John was who wrote the book of Revelation, it was not someone highly literate or trained in ancient Greek, its original language. This book, unlike the Gospel of John, is written in an extremely awkward style. The author in fact makes a number of basic grammatical mistakes.

Not only that, but the theological views of the two books are quite distinct, even at odds. Nowhere is this more true than in their understandings of the "end times." The Gospel of John, as we have seen, radically de-apocalypticized the message of Jesus, so that he no longer predicts what will happen at the end of the age. The book of Revelation is all about the end of the age.

Thus these are two different authors with different sets of concerns and contrasting theologies. The irony is that the book of Revelation, which claims to be written by someone named John, is not called John, while the Fourth Gospel, which does not claim to be written by someone named John, is called John. As to who wrote each book, we are almost completely in the dark. Neither author was probably John the son of Zebedee, who, as a lower-class day laborer in a rural part of Galilee almost certainly could not write at all (as explicitly stated in Acts 4:13, where John is literally called "illiterate").[2]

Our main concern with Revelation is not with the identity of the author but with the meaning of the book. Apocalypses—whether 1 Enoch or 4 Ezra, Daniel or Revelation—are prose narratives written in the first person by someone who receives mystical and perplexing revelations from God. Sometimes these revelations are deeply veiled descriptions of the future of earth—as we saw, for example, in the book of Daniel; sometimes they are bizarre visions of the heavenly realm itself, as in 1 Enoch. Both kinds of revelations—of the future or of the world above—are always given in highly symbolic terms. It is very common to find bizarre descriptions of fantastically shaped beasts, angels, and other living creatures; veiled references to divine activities; visions of mind-boggling locations and structures in heaven; and detailed but opaque expositions of future events. These symbolic visions are consistently puzzling not only for the readers but, strikingly, for the narrators themselves. One common feature of these texts (though not consistently found in Revelation itself) is that the visions are typically mediated to the author through an angelic interpreter who explains to him what he is seeing.

In most instances the text provides its own keys to interpreting the symbols, so that a reader who is careful and diligent can make sense of the symbolism. The ultimate point of these books is almost always to show that, despite the vast mysteries of the cosmic realms and the puzzling events that are transpiring on earth, God ultimately is sovereign. Evil may be manifest in unfathomable ways, but in the end there is only one Lord Almighty, and he is in control. When this world comes to a close, when all is said and done, God will reassert his power and triumph over all that is opposed to him. The symbols of the narrative portray this ultimate truth. The point is not to give some kind of literal description of what you would really see if you were yourself transported to the world above the clouds, or what is really going to transpire down here on earth in a way that can be put on a time line. It is instead to use deeply mystical language to portray what cannot be expressed in literal words, to embrace the ultimate reality behind all there is: God himself, the master of the world and everything that happens in it.

The Book of Revelation and Its Symbols

To make sense of the afterlife images found in the book of Revelation, it is important, first, to have a sense of the overall flow of the narrative. The book begins with the author experiencing a highly symbolic vision of Christ, "one like a Son of Man," who tells him to write letters encouraging and exhorting the seven churches of Asia Minor and then to describe all that he is about to be shown: the visions of the heavenly realm that foreshadow what will happen on earth (Revelation 1:12–20).

After John writes the correspondence (Revelation 2–3), the revelations begin in chapter 4, where he is ordered to ascend through a door in the sky to the world above. When he arrives in heaven, he sees God in his brilliance, seated on his throne, with flashes of lightning and peals of thunder, surrounded by twenty-four elders wearing white robes and golden crowns, and four creatures representing all living things, worshiping God forever. John then sees in the hand of the one seated on the throne a scroll sealed with seven seals. The scroll contains a written account of what will transpire on earth. The prophet weeps when he sees that no one is worthy to break the seals so as to unroll the scroll. But one of the elders tells him that there is, in fact, one who is worthy. John then sees next to the throne "a Lamb standing as if it had been slaughtered." The Lamb, of course, is Christ (Revelation 4:1–5:14).

The Lamb takes the scroll from the hand of God and breaks its seals, one at a time (Revelation 6). With the breaking of each seal, a major catastrophe happens on earth: war, famine, economic collapse, and death. When he breaks the sixth seal, cosmic disasters ensue: the sun turns black, the moon red; the stars fall from the sky; and the sky vanishes. You would think that this, now, is the end of all existence, the destruction of the universe. But we are only in chapter 6.

The breaking of the seventh seal leads not to another disaster but to a new sequence of disasters. Seven angels appear, each bearing a trumpet. As each one blows his trumpet, a new disaster hits the earth. Natural disasters on land and sea and in the sky; the appearance of horrible beasts who wreak havoc; massive calamity and unspeakable suffering (Revelation 8–9). The seventh trumpet marks the beginning of the end: the "Beast" (the so-called Antichrist) appears along with his false prophet (Revelation 12–13). But then we are introduced to seven more angels, each bearing a bowl of God's wrath. Each one pours his bowl out upon the earth in turn, leading to yet more calamities, one after the other: epidemics, universal misery, and death (Revelation 15–16).

The end comes with the destruction of the great "whore of Babylon," the city responsible for the persecution of the saints (Revelation 17). The city is overthrown amid great weeping and wailing on earth but much rejoicing in heaven (Revelation 18–19). Then there comes a final cosmic battle between the heavenly Christ, with his heavenly armies, and the

Beast and the forces aligned with him. It is, in fact, no contest: Christ wins quickly and decisively. The enemies of God are completely crushed and the Beast and the false prophet are thrown into "the lake of fire that burns with sulfur" (Revelation 19:21).

An angel then comes from heaven to capture Satan and bind him for a thousand years in a bottomless pit while Christ rules the earth with the many, many martyrs who had been killed for their faith. At the end of this "millennium," Satan is released for a time to wreak temporary havoc on the earth, but then finally he is captured and also thrown into the lake of fire, where with the Beast and prophet he would be "tormented day and night forever and ever" (Revelation 10).

Then there is a final resurrection of the dead. Humans are all raised to face judgment. Those whose names are written in "the book of life" are rewarded; those not found in the book are thrown into the lake of fire. The book concludes with the prophet's vision of a New Jerusalem that descends from heaven to earth, the dwelling place of all saints forever. It is an enormous place, 1,500 miles square, made of gold and with gates of pearl; it has no need of light because God himself and his Lamb enlighten it. This will be an eternal place of joy, with no more fear or darkness, no pain, misery, suffering, or tears. Good will reign forever and the righteous will forever bask in its light (Revelation 21–22). The prophet John ends the book by stressing his vision is true and Christ is "coming soon" (Revelation 22:20).

The Symbols of Revelation

None of this breathtaking vision can be read literally as an indication of what, chronologically, will happen at the end of time. It is impossible to place the events it portrays in a linear time line: as we have seen, the universe has collapsed less than a third of the way into the book. Moreover, the author himself indicates that his account is symbolic and in fact gives keys to the interpretations of his symbols. This can be readily demonstrated from two key passages.

In chapter 17, one of the seven angels who will pour out bowls of God's wrath on the earth takes the prophet to show him a "great whore who is seated on many waters" (Revelation 17:1). He is told that this prostitute has "committed fornication" with the kings of the earth. When he goes into the wilderness he sees a woman sitting on a scarlet-colored beast that has seven heads and ten horns. The woman is luxuriously arrayed in purple and scarlet, wearing gold, jewels, and pearls; she is holding a golden cup filled with abominations and on her head is "written a name, a mystery: 'Babylon the great, mother of whores and of earth's abominations.'" We are told that the woman is "drunk with the blood of the saints and . . . of the witnesses to Jesus" (Revelation 17:6). In the King James Version of the Bible we are confronted at this point by a slight problem with Jacobean English: we are told that the prophet looks upon this great whore "with great admiration." Modern translations rectify the problem. The prophet is deeply amazed. As well he might be.

Who or what in the world is this "Whore of Babylon"? The prophet himself cannot figure it out, but the angel explains to him by assuring him: "This calls for a mind that has wisdom" (Revelation 17:9). He first indicates that the beast on which the woman is seated is destined to ascend from the bottomless pit (Revelation 17:8). Looking ahead, the reader knows that in Revelation 20:2 it is Satan who is bound for this pit; moreover, there he is called the Dragon, the Serpent of old. The woman is supported, then, by the devil himself.

But who is the woman? The angel goes on to explain that the seven heads of the beast are actually seven mountains on which the woman is seated (Revelation 17:9). Anyone living in the ancient world would by now have no trouble figuring out who she is. For those who do not understand the clue, the angel provides the final answer: "The woman you saw is the great city that rules over the kings of the earth" (Revelation 17:18).

Who is the city ruling the world of John's day? Rome, famous even in antiquity for being the city "built on seven hills" (= the beast with seven heads). Why is she called "Babylon"? That was the city that in 586 BCE destroyed Jerusalem and burned the temple under the direction of the Babylonian ruler Nebuchadnezzar. Now, six centuries later, in 70 CE, it is Rome who has destroyed Jerusalem and burned its second temple, under the Roman emperor Vespasian. This is the city ruled ultimately by Satan, the enemy of God, the city responsible both for the economic exploitation of the earth (hence her luxurious attire and many jewels) and for the persecution of Christians (she is drunk with the blood of the martyrs). Thus, for the author of Revelation, the enemy of God is the Roman Empire and its rulers. It is not some wicked woman bound to appear soon in the twenty-first century.

The attentive reader of Revelation will recognize that this beast in chapter 17 has already appeared in chapter 13. There we are told of a Beast "rising out of the sea," again with ten horns and seven heads. Moreover, "the whole earth followed the Beast," worshiping it. The Beast in this earlier chapter is said to be haughty and blasphemous, and to have waged war on the saints. At the end of the chapter comes the most famous cryptic statement of the entire book, as the author reveals the identity of the Beast: "This calls for wisdom: let anyone with understanding calculate the number of the Beast, for it is the number of a person. Its number is six hundred sixty-six" (Revelation 13:18). In some manuscripts of Revelation the number of the Beast is given as 616 rather than 666. How are we to explain all this?

Brilliant and extravagant explanations have appeared over the centuries, with readers of each generation claiming that this Antichrist figure has arisen in their own day with authors in the century past loudly proclaiming their "evidence" that in fact it refers to Mussolini, Henry

Kissinger, or Pope Paul VI. But this author was writing for his own day, not for modern times, and the symbolism he uses makes the best sense for his own context.

If we know from chapter 17 that the Beast is Satan-controlled Rome and its rulers, we can probably assume that's what the author means for chapter 13 too. But how do we make sense of the number 666? The author, in fact, is appealing to an ancient form of literary interpretation known as gematria, which involves determining the numerical value of words and names. In ancient languages such as Greek and Hebrew, the letters of the alphabet served also as numerals, so that, for example, in Greek, 1 was represented by alpha, 2 by beta, and so on. And that means every word had a numerical value, which could be calculated simply by adding up the value of each letter. The author of Revelation is indicating that the Beast is a person whose name has a numerical value of 666 (or 616).

Modern interpreters have long recognized the answer to this puzzle. The ruler of Rome long thought to be the first imperial archenemy of the Christians, because of the violent persecution that he sponsored, leading to horrible, bloody martrydoms, was the emperor Nero (ruled 54–68 CE). It is surely no accident that if you spell "Caesar Neron" in Hebrew letters, they add up to 666. Even more striking, there is an alternative spelling of the name: "Nero" instead of "Neron." Without that final *n*, the name adds up to 616.

When the author of Revelation describes both "the Beast rising out of the sea" and the "whore of Babylon," he is not speaking of a literal beast or a literal prostitute. And he is not referring to a figure about to appear in the twenty-first century. He is using these images symbolically to refer, interchangeably, to the city and empire of Rome and the empire's rulers—the enemies of the Christians in his own day. In short, the key to interpreting the book of Revelation is to recognize its symbols for what they are.

And so we return to my earlier question: If the book is full of symbols and is clearly meant to be interpreted figuratively, why should we think that the horrible, eternal "lake of fire" or the fantastically beautiful "New Jerusalem" are *literal* descriptions of the afterlife? In fact, these too are symbolic descriptions of realities that are beyond words to convey in a straightforward sense. My thesis is that the lake of fire is a symbolic description not of eternal torment awaiting sinners but of their ultimate annihilation for all time, with no hope of life ever after. The New Jerusalem refers to the unimaginable utopian existence the followers of Jesus will receive in the life to come.

The Afterlife of Christian Martyrs

The first reference to the afterlife in Revelation occurs in chapter 6 with the breaking of the fifth seal (Revelation 6:9–11). Nothing happens on earth, but the prophet sees the souls of those who have been "slaughtered for the word of God" and the "witness they gave" under an altar in heaven as they cry out to God: "How long before you judge and avenge our blood on those who dwell on earth?" An altar, of course, is the point of contact between God and humans, so these martyrs for Christ have a special access to the divine presence. They want to be vindicated for their faithfulness. But they are deferred in their wishes: each is given a white robe and told to "rest a little while longer" until all their fellow Christians also destined for martyrdom have met their fates.

These other martyrs are described in chapter 7 after the breaking of the sixth seal. There are two groups: 144,000 Jews, 12,000 from each of the twelve tribes, and "an enormous crowd that no one could number" from among peoples of "every nation" (Revelation 7:4–9). The numbers are staggering and cannot be used to document how many Christians were actually martyred for their faith in John's time. In periods of persecution, it often seems to those who are suffering that their entire population is being decimated. But there were not even 144,000 Christians in the world at the time, and recent studies have convincingly shown that martyrdom was rare rather than regular.[3]

It is striking that for the entire book of Revelation these martyrs appear to be the only souls in heaven. They are at rest and are kindly treated by God, but no other saints are said to be destined for such favorable divine treatment. Dying for the faith brought a special reward. The rest of the righteous will eventually inherit a glorious existence on earth in the New Jerusalem after the final judgment. (So too, presumably, will these martyrs after their temporary residence under the altar in heaven.) But to our possible chagrin the book of Revelation never indicates what, in the author's opinion, is happening to all the other believers who have died before the final judgment. Are they somewhere in the underworld? Are they asleep in the grave? Have they simply ceased to exist for a time? He doesn't say.

What he does indicate is what will happen to sinners leading up to the last day. In chapter 14 an angel appears in heaven crying out that "Babylon the great is fallen" (Revelation 14:8). That is, the prophet foresees the coming destruction of Rome. Another angel appears and announces that all who have thrown in their lot with "the Beast" (= Rome) will "drink the wine of God's wrath that is poured out, undiluted, from the cup of his anger" (Revelation 14:10). This horrible punishment is not described specifically as "the lake of fire," but we are told that these enemies of God "will be tormented in fire and sulfur before the holy angels and the Lamb, and the fire of their torment goes up forever and ever: they will have no rest day and night" (Revelation 14:10–11).

There is an obvious contrast here. The martyrs of Christ reside in glory, clothed by God and given "rest" in heaven (Revelation 6), while their earthly adversaries, the ones who persecuted and killed them, will be given "no rest," burning day and night (Revelation 14). The author cannot literally mean that they will be fried forever, since he later will describe their "final" judgment. They, like the martyrs, are experiencing a temporary fate while waiting for the realities of eternity to begin.

The burning image itself is an obvious symbol, not a literal description of people toasting for eternity. "Their smoke" goes up "forever and ever" because they have no chance of turning back: their punishment is permanent. This figurative turn of phrase occurs commonly in the Bible, and is never meant literally. We find it in Isaiah 34, a description of the doleful fate of the nation of Edom, which will be "turned into pitch, and her soil into sulfur." This land will "become burning pitch; night and day it shall not be quenched, its smoke shall go up forever" (Isaiah 34:10). No one thinks that if you make a trip to the Middle East today you will see Edom still burning, with smoke that has been rising nonstop for millennia. Isaiah means that Edom will be destroyed permanently.

So too the author of Revelation. The supporters of Rome will not be given rest in the world to come. Eventually, in chapter 20, they will be annihilated for all time. We should not be too concerned that in chapter 14 the prophet indicates the torment will last forever, when he actually means it will last six chapters. We have already seen that his account cannot be seen as chronologically literal, nor was it meant to be. Otherwise there would be no Rome to be destroyed anytime after the sixth seal.

The Final Judgment of the Wicked

John's horrifying "lake of fire" makes its first appearance in Revelation 19. Christ, along with his heavenly armies, appears from heaven for the "Last Battle." In a flash their archenemies on earth are soundly defeated and punished. The supernatural opponents of Christ—the Beast and his prophet—are thrown, living, into the "lake of fire that burns with sulfur." Their human allies, on the other hand, are "slain with a sword," and all the birds become "gorged with their flesh" (Revelation 19:20–21). In other words, the dead, for now, are dead.

If the author has already indicated that the Beast is actually the empire of Rome, then obviously it is difficult to imagine how it could be thrown alive into a sulfurous lake. Fire and sulfur are often used in biblical texts to refer to the judgment of God. All the way back in Genesis, God rains fire and sulfur down on the heinous sinners of Sodom and Gomorrah (Genesis 19:24); Ezekiel imagines a similar fate for the mythical kingdom of Gog at the end of time (Ezekiel 38:22); the psalmist speaks of God raining down coals of fire and sulfur on the wicked (Psalm 11:6).

The image no doubt was particularly poignant among those who knew, or at least had heard, that Christians had been put to grisly deaths by fire. For this author, their enemies would face a similar fate. But for them it would not be a pyre that burns out after a time; it would be an entire lake seething with eternal fire whose smoke never stops rising.

In contrast, the martyrs themselves will receive a fantastic reward. While God's enemies are bobbing on waves of eternal flame, those they had earlier killed will come back to life and rule with Christ on earth for a thousand years (Revelation 20:1–6). It is often overlooked by readers of Revelation that this glorious millennium on earth is reserved only for those who had been "beheaded for their testimony to Jesus and on account of the word of God" (Revelation 20:4–5). It is not for all saints—for example, those who died peacefully in their beds. Their own day will come, but it will be only after these thousand years that the martyrs enjoy on earth with Christ.

When that period ends, Satan will return from his bottomless pit and rouse other nations against the saints (Revelation 20:7–9). But he and his allies will soon be defeated. The hostile armies will be destroyed by fire from heaven. The devil has a worst fate. He will be thrown in the lake of fire to join the Beast and his prophet, who have been roasting nonstop for a thousand years already. The three of them will then be "tormented day and night forever and ever" (Revelation 20:10). The first thousand years are scarcely even a beginning.

It is worth noting: there are no humans in this sulfurous lake. The supporters of the Beast have all been slain. They are dead. But then will come the Last Judgment.

The Final End of Sinners

The judgment of the dead—both wicked and righteous—comes in the terse description of Revelation 20:11–15. A "great white throne" is set up and all the dead "great and small" are brought to stand before the one who sits on it. No one is exempt. Books are opened, and then a solitary book. The latter is the book of life. The books record the deeds of everyone who has ever lived, and all "the dead were judged by the things written in the books, according to what they had done" (Revelation 20:12). Any one whose name is not written in the "book of life" is condemned and "thrown into the lake of fire." What is more, Death and Hades themselves are thrown into the lake. The author tells us, "This is the second death, the lake of fire" (Revelation 20:14).

Once again, of course, it makes no sense to imagine that living beings known as "Death" or "Hades" are literally thrown into a lake boiling with fire to be punished forever. This is describing the ultimate destruction of all that is opposed to God. God is the author of life. Death is his enemy, and it, along with the entire realm of the dead, will be destroyed permanently. They will not exist anymore. That is why the lake is called "the second death." It is the final annihilation of all that is dead, including all humans who are dead. For them there is no more life—ever.

We earlier saw that both Jesus and Paul believed that the wicked would be exterminated, never to live again. They did not preach or believe in an eternal torment for sinners. God's ultimate vengeance would be their annihilation, with no hope of seeing the glories that the saints would inherit when they enter into God's eternal kingdom. The book of Revelation shares this view. Even though later Christians transformed the symbolic "lake of fire" into a literal description of the fire pits of hell, where people would burn forever—not just for a few trillion years—with no chance of relief or redemption, John agreed with his Lord Jesus and his forerunner Paul. For sinners, death is the end of the story. Life comes only to those who side with God through thick and thin, even if it means persecution and martyrdom. They would receive a heavenly reward for all time, after their enemies were finally destroyed.

The Glorious Destiny of Saints

John's description of the blessings of the saved are meant to defy the imagination. The world we dwell in now is obviously filled with evil, sin, pain, misery, suffering, and death. It will be destroyed. Everything bad about it will be done away with. The world was originally meant for good. It began as a garden—literally a paradise—for those beloved of God to enjoy for all time. But it became corrupt, fallen, and truly awful. God will start again.

After all his enemies and the world they have inhabited are destroyed, God will bring a "new heaven and a new earth" (Revelation 21:1). A "new Jerusalem," the city of God, will descend from heaven, an enormous place inhabited by the saints who have followed Jesus; they will now live in the presence of God. This will be a utopian existence, forever, with no more pain, trouble, or difficulty: God "will wipe away every tear from their eyes, and there will be no death, mourning, weeping, or pain ever again; for the former things have passed away" (Revelation 21:4). The city itself will radiate like a rare jewel, with twelve gates named for the twelve tribes of Israel and twelve foundations for the apostles—that is, this glorious salvation will be built on the sacred traditions of Israel and the church. The walls of the city will be made of jasper and the city itself of gold, clear as glass. It will radiate with the light of God and nothing unclean will ever enter into it.

Even in this description of fantastic splendor there are some ambiguities, much like the rest of this glorious but mystifying book. Even though God has destroyed all that is evil and everyone who has sided with it, we are told that the fruit raised in the city will bring "healing" to the nations (Revelation 22:2). But what nations would those be, and why would they need to be healed if all that remains is good? Why does the author say that the "kings of the earth" will bring their treasures (literally: "glory") to the city (Revelation 21:24)? What kings are these, and what are their kingdoms? And why would the city need or want any more treasure than it already has? Moreover, why, by contrast, does the prophet say that no one will bring anything "unclean" into the city (Revelation 21:27)? How can there be anything unclean at all? The book of Revelation is nothing if not mysterious.

The Abiding Message of John's Revelation

One might sensibly expect that any fantastic and powerful vision of the alternative reality behind our world would be baffling and difficult to grasp. The universe is a mind-boggling place. In his description of the heavenly realm, John is occasionally straightforward in telling his readers that he is writing deeply symbolic language. The Beast is a city built on seven hills that is dominating the world at the time, which is also portrayed as a whore in the wilderness. A human ruler of that city has a name that adds up to 666. And on and on. This is a vision filled with bizarre symbols whose meanings are occasionally hinted at. Sometimes the hints are none too subtle; other times they are clever; yet other times they are virtually impenetrable. By their very nature, symbols are not literal expressions of propositional truth, and that is why Revelation does not "add up" if what we are looking for is a straightforward exposition of what will happen in the future. If John wanted to give that kind of prosaic explanation, he would not have narrated a cosmic and mystifying vision.

Even if parts of the vision are difficult to unpack and explain and others simply do not cohere, the author's main points are clear. His overarching message is that God is ultimately sovereign over this world, even if it doesn't seem like it. We may live in a cesspool of misery and suffering, and things may be getting progressively worse. But God is in charge, and it is all going according to plan. Before the end, all hell will indeed break loose, but then God will intervene to restore all that has become corrupt, to make right all that is wrong. Good will ultimately prevail.

This is bad news for the wicked rulers of this world and those who side with them. John was thinking specifically of the Roman Empire, which had devastated the countries around the Mediterranean and enforced its policies on them, exploiting them economically, dominating them politically, and ruling them militarily. God will destroy the empire and all who side with it. Its rulers and aristocrats may enjoy luxury now at the expense of others, but they will be taken out of power and destroyed. Everyone who has willingly accepted and participated in their rule will face annihilation when God's judgment arrives.

On the other hand, those who have sided with God during the current reign of evil will be rewarded. They may suffer for doing what is right—they may even die for their faith—but they will not be forgotten or forsaken. The future, in fact, is theirs, an eternal life in the presence of God and all the other saints in a utopian state where there will be no more pain, misery, or suffering—only a golden city with gates of pearl and the glories of heaven, for all eternity. The gold and pearl are, of course, symbols. But for John the possibility of a glorious life after death is real. It will come to those who are faithful, and to them alone.[4]

CHAPTER TWELVE

Eternal Life in the Flesh

The palpable problems with the idea of sentient "souls" in the afterlife were occasionally noted by skeptics in antiquity. If the body is left behind at death, how will anyone recognize or enjoy the company of their deceased loved ones: see them with no eyes, hear them with no ears, touch them with no hands? How will a person feel real, tactile pain or experience great physical pleasure without a nervous system, or think with no brain?

But the Christian doctrine of the resurrection was often considered even worse, subject to considerable ridicule from those outside the faith, who found it difficult to believe that anyone could seriously think eternal life was to be lived in the *body*, of all things. For many ancient people (think Plato) the body is precisely the problem, the source of so much pain and misery. If the point of much philosophy is to escape the body, how can I possibly be forced to live in it forever? Moreover (opponents of the apocalyptic view asked), how can a resurrected body even make sense? How old will I be? Will I still have my bodily inadequacies and defects? Will I be raised with my diseases and injuries? Will the body parts I no longer need—e.g., my entire digestive system—be raised with me? With all the hair and nails I ever had?

Still, many—not all—Christians insisted it was so (as did Jewish apocalypticists before them). As the second-century Christian intellectual and defender of the faith, Justin Martyr, affirmed: Christians "expect that our own bodies, even though they should be dead and buried in the earth, will be revived" (*First Apology* 18). He went on to argue that a bodily resurrection is not at all implausible—any more than bodily birth. Who, he asks, could possibly imagine that a sperm could become a human being? God achieves the miracle of birth with a body, and he will achieve the second miracle of rebirth with a restored body.

Pagan Ridicule of the Resurrection of the Body

Pagan opponents of Christianity, however, considered the idea of a bodily afterlife grotesque and risible. No one expressed this rejection more forcefully and effectively than an otherwise unknown intellectual named Celsus, writing near the end of the second Christian century. Celsus produced a learned attack on Christianity called *The True Word*. It is the first pagan assault against Christianity that we can reconstruct at any length. Unfortunately, it has not survived intact but only as it has been quoted by a later Christian author, the brilliant and prolific Origen of Alexandria, who wrote an extensive counterattack called *Against Celsus* some half century or more after Celsus's work had been placed in circulation.[1]

In this reply Origen quotes Celsus's original work at great length in order to refute it point by point. For that reason we appear to have access to Celsus's own words in his reasoned objections to Christian claims. The notion of a final judgment and a bodily resurrection of the dead seemed especially absurd. And so Celsus's witty attack:

It is foolish [of the Christians] to suppose that, when God applies the fire (like a cook!), all the rest of mankind will be thoroughly roasted and that they alone will survive, not merely those who are alive at the time but those also long dead who will rise from the earth possessing the same bodies as before. This is simply the hope of worms. For what sort of human soul would have any further desire for a body that has rotted? The fact that this doctrine is not shared by some of you [Jews] and by some Christians shows its utter repulsiveness, and that it is both revolting and impossible. (*Against Celsus* 5, 14)

It is interesting to note that Celsus realizes that some Christians, as we too will see, rejected this idea, as even did some Jews. Here he is obviously thinking of the Sadducees. He continues then by detailing his objection:

For what sort of body, after being entirely corrupted, could return to its original nature and that same condition which it had before it was dissolved? . . . For the soul, [God] might be able to provide an everlasting life; but as Heraclitus says, "Corpses ought to be thrown away as worse than dung." As for the flesh, which is full of things it is not even nice to mention, God would neither desire nor be able to make it everlasting contrary to reason. (*Against Celsus* 5, 14)

Christian Defenses of the Resurrection

Christian thinkers felt driven to deal with such pagan objections during the first three centuries of the church. They began doing so long before Celsus's day. Probably our earliest Christian writing from outside the New Testament is a book called 1 Clement. The book was later attributed to an early bishop of Rome, Clement, allegedly a successor to the apostle

Peter. But its actual author chose to remain anonymous. The letter, in fact, is written by the entire "church that is in Rome" to another church, in Corinth, to deal with a problem of ecclesiastical leadership that had arisen there. Scholars typically date the book to 95 CE or so, making it earlier than even some of the books of the New Testament.[2]

Among the many issues covered by this unusually long letter is the feasibility of a future physical resurrection of the dead. The author claims the idea is not at all incredible. Resurrection happens all the time: day follows night every twenty-four hours; dead seeds produce living crops year after year. Why not human bodies, come back to life after death?

For proof he recounts the amazing story of the Phoenix, a bird that dwells, he avers, in the area near Arabia. It lives for five hundred years, and as it nears death, it makes a tomb for itself out of frankincense, myrrh, and other spices. When its time has come, it enters the tomb and dies. But out of its rotting flesh a worm is spontaneously born, which is then nourished by the secretions of its decaying predecessor. Once the newly generated bird has grown wings and becomes strong, it takes the tomb containing the corpse and carries it from Arabia to Egypt, to the city of Heliopolis. There, in the broad daylight, it flies onto the altar of the sun, with observers all around, and deposits the tomb before returning home. When the priests at the temple consult the ancient records, they see that this has happened after five hundred years (1 Clement 25).

And so nature itself provides evidence of life out of death, of living bodies coming into being out of corpses. As the anonymous author of the text breathlessly exclaims: "Do we then think that it is so great and marvelous that the Creator of all things will raise everyone who has served him in a holy way . . . with the confidence of good faith, when he shows us the magnificence of his promise even through a bird?" (1 Clement 26.1).

From about eighty years later comes a more thorough defense of the doctrine of the resurrection from the pen of a Christian philosopher named Athenagoras.[3] If God is just, Athenagoras maintains, he will certainly judge people for their sins. But it would not make sense for God to punish a person's soul and not their body. It is the whole person who does wicked deeds or acts of righteousness—the body and soul together in unity. And so both body and soul must answer to justice. "It is certainly unjust and unworthy of the judgment of God to visit upon the soul alone the transgressions that come from passion and their due chastisement" (*On the Resurrection* 21).[4]

In the course of his work Athenagoras deals with well-known pagan objections to the idea that a person's actual body will be revivified for eternal life. Chief among them is a problem that would probably not occur to most modern people. Suppose someone dies and their body is eaten by fish or other animals. Their dead body, once ingested, would provide nourishment for the animal and would, in the process of digestion and nourishment, become part of the animal's body. Anyone who ate the animal would ingest the parts of the first person's body, which would then become part of their own. At the resurrection, which of the two would get those parts?

Or even worse, what about direct ingestion of one human by another in an act of cannibalism? The cannibal will have parts of the other embedded in his body. So when both are raised, which one of them is allotted the parts?

The complications can easily be multiplied, since later animals and cannibals will eat the bodies with body parts ingested in them, and so on for a very long time. But Athenagoras has a solution to the dilemma. It has to do with his theory of digestion. In his view, the body can digest only food that is appropriate to it. What is not appropriate is eliminated. And so a person's parts can never become another's:

> If what is unnatural never turns into nourishment for the parts and portions that need it, and if again what does not turn into nourishment

cannot be incorporated into bodies which it was never intended by nature to nourish, then human bodies can never be incorporated into other human bodies that use them as unnatural food, even should they by some unhappy fate pass through the bowels of such people. (*On the Resurrection* 8)

Surely neither Paul nor Jesus could have imagined the doctrine of the resurrection would create such a tangle. But objections proliferated over time, eventually to be addressed by the most influential theologian of Christian antiquity, the great Augustine (354–430 CE), who devoted the final three books of his classic *City of God* to discussing the afterlife. In part he sought to answer common conundra related to the Christian doctrine of the resurrection of the body.[5]

If bodies will be raised to a perfect form of physicality, will they all be the same size? If they are different sizes, then one size must be better than another . . . but that would mean not everyone would be the perfect size, right? Augustine replies that everyone will be given the body that is perfectly proportioned as it should be; moreover, it will be the body they did have, or would have had, in their prime. For each person, then, the proportion is perfect for their own potentiality.

But what about women? If they are raised "in the image of Christ," would they not have to be raised as men (since Christ was male), with male features, rather than as women? Augustine responds that "the sex of a woman is not a vice but nature." And so women will be raised as women. After all, Jesus had said that in the resurrection there would be no marriages, but he never said there would be no genders.

And what about parts of the body that grow? If the entire body is to be raised, does it come with all the hair and nails that a person has ever had? Christ said that "not a hair of your head will perish." If so, then won't people necessarily be raised extraordinarily hairy with uncannily long nails? Augustine replies that there will be no deformities in heaven, so that no one will be burdened with such abominations. It is the *number* of hairs a person has that will not perish, not their length.

Christians could fend off every snide comment and answer every objection. There will be a bodily resurrection and people will be perfect.

Resurrection of the Body and Resurrection of the Flesh

Even though the resurrection of the body had become the dominant doctrinal view by the time of Augustine, it should not be thought that every Christian always subscribed to it, especially in the earlier centuries. On the contrary, we have seen clear indications otherwise. The very reason Paul had to argue vehemently for the future resurrection of the dead in 1 Corinthians 15 was precisely that some of his opponents had denied it. These were not pagan antagonists but members of the Christian community who either believed they had in some sense already experienced a spiritual resurrection and so had nothing else to expect in the future or, more likely, agreed with the more widespread and generally accepted view of the immortality of the soul. The body would decay and pass out of existence, but the soul would live on forever.

What these people thought about Jesus's resurrection is a matter of debate. Did they think he was "spiritually" raised from the dead somehow—that his corpse remained in the tomb but his spirit came back to life? That appears to have been the view eventually attacked by Luke's account of the resurrection. Recall that in this version, when Jesus appears to his disciples he strives to show that he is not a "spirit" but has "flesh and bones," which could be seen and touched. And that he was capable of eating.[6] Since Luke is writing for a Christian audience, apparently some of them had to be convinced that resurrection involved the body, not simply the spirit.

Luke does not provide any specifics about the nature of the (future) resurrection of believers. That needs to be inferred from his account. Paul, however, is explicit. On one hand, the resurrection would be incontrovertibly physical. The body will return to life. On the other hand, "flesh and blood cannot inherit the Kingdom of God" (1 Corinthians 15:50). So even though the body will be raised, flesh and blood will not be. How can he have it both ways? As we have seen, it is because of Paul's special and rather nuanced view of what will happen. When Christ returns, his followers, whether dead or alive, will experience a radical, physical transformation. Their bodies will be re-created as immortal, glorified beings, just as Jesus himself was at his resurrection. They will then live eternally in these magnificent, imperishable bodies, impervious to defect, injury, illness, aging, or death.

The nuances of Paul's position were completely lost on later generations of Christian thinkers, who latched onto some of his ideas to the exclusion of others. And so one stream of thought, claiming Paul's support, argued that, since "flesh and blood" were not able to inherit the kingdom, the future resurrection of Christians was *not* to be bodily but purely spiritual. That was just the opposite of what Paul thought. On the other hand there were Christians—the ones who ended up winning this debate—who argued, in response, that since the resurrection had to be bodily, it would entail a resurrection precisely "of the flesh"—a view Paul also opposed.

For Paul, "flesh" was a technical term that referred to the part of the human that was opposed to God. It is fallen, susceptible to the draw of sin, filled with passions and desires alien to what God wants (see Romans 7:6, 14–20). Paul absolutely did not think the sin-filled flesh (Greek: *sarx*) would rise from the dead. But the body (Greek: *sōma*) would, a body transformed so as no longer to be infused with that element ("flesh") that was inherently infused with sin and opposed to God.

Paul thus differentiated between the "body" and the "flesh." But his later advocates did not understand the nuance, and some of them, when they insisted that the body itself—the very human body that dies and is buried—will be raised, used the non-Pauline term "flesh."

In short, both sides of the debates of the second century—those who argued for the resurrection of the spirit and those who argued for the resurrection of the flesh—maintained their views were those propounded by the apostle himself, even though he supported neither one.

A Christian Alternative: A Spiritual Resurrection

We have already seen one early Christian text that supports the idea of a "spiritual" rather than bodily resurrection of the dead: the Coptic Gospel of Thomas, which likens the body to clothing that needs to be discarded and trampled if one is to see the Son of God and have eternal life (Gospel of Thomas 37). The point is to escape the body, not to live on in it.

This view is affirmed in yet other Christian writings, but not many of them survive, since it was an idea later deemed "heretical" and stamped out. The Christian texts that supported it were either destroyed or, more often, simply not copied for posterity. One that has turned up by pure serendipity in modern times is a work called the *Letter to Rheginus* or, sometimes, *The Treatise on the Resurrection*. This is one of the so-called Gnostic Gospels found in a buried jar in a wilderness area outside of the village of Nag Hammadi, Egypt, in 1945.[7]

The original text was almost certainly written in the late second century. The anonymous author of the work is giving a response to questions raised by an otherwise unknown Christian named Rheginus about the resurrection, both of Jesus and, more important, of humans. Will there really be a resurrection? And what will it entail?

The author assures Rheginus that the resurrection is by no means an illusion. It is a certain reality. It would, in fact, be "more appropriate to say that the world is an illusion" than that the resurrection is.[8] The evidence comes in Christ himself. Christ "swallowed death" when he died. He had taken on human flesh, and then at his death he laid the flesh aside to be rid of it. That led to his non-bodily existence in the world above: "When he laid aside the perishable world, he exchanged it for an incorruptible eternal realm."

That is what happens to believers as well. The resurrection does not involve some kind of crass revivification of the material body after death. The body passes away but the spirit ascends to the heavenly realm, drawn up by Jesus himself "like rays by the sun." Nothing is able to hold it down. This is a "resurrection of the spirit" that "swallows [that is, dispenses with] the resurrection of the soul and the resurrection of the flesh." The human body, and the breath/soul that animates it, passes away. The spirit lives forever.

In this author's intriguing and controversial view, humans existed in spirit before they were born in the body: "Although once you did not exist in flesh, you took on flesh when you entered this world." And so life does not require the existence of the flesh, which will be abandoned at death: "Leaving this behind will profit you, for you will not give up the better part when you leave." It will be the true, invisible part that will survive. The "mortal part" will die but the spirit will acquire eternal life—not in some future act of judgment on earth but at the moment of death:

> Some inquire further and want to know whether one will be saved immediately, if the body is left behind. Let there be no doubt about this. Surely the visible parts of the body are dead and will not be saved. Only the living parts that are within will rise.

Such views may seem like an innovation, but scholars have long recognized they could claim roots in the New Testament itself. That is what the author himself claims as he appeals to the writings of Paul for apostolic support for his view: "As the apostle said of him, we suffered with him, we arose with him, we ascended with him." It is striking to note that the letter of Colossians, wrongly attributed to Paul, indicates that believers have already been "raised up with Christ" (Colossians 2:12). But since they are still alive, obviously this "resurrection" could not be bodily; it must be spiritual. Ephesians, also wrongly assigned to Paul, takes it a step further: believers are not only raised with Christ, they are already "seated with him in the heavenly places" (Ephesians 2:5–7).[9] And recall the Gospel of John, where the believer already *has* eternal life: there is no need to wait for salvation in a future resurrection.

Even though these canonical writings embrace the idea of some kind of spiritual resurrection of believers in the present, they also continue to hold on to the idea that at the end of time there will be a "new" event, a resurrection of the body. Not so the *Letter to Rheginus*. There will be no bodily resurrection. Only the living part of the person rises. And that happens immediately at death. Eternal life is in the spirit, not in the body.

One historical irony is that even though this view was roundly denounced by orthodox Christians as absolute heresy, it appears to be the view held widely by Christians today. You die and your spirit goes to heaven. Many Christians, to be sure, confess the creed that affirms the future "resurrection of the dead," but not everyone does. For millions of believers, what matters is what happens at death, when a person goes to heaven or hell. Not so for many of the earliest church fathers, hard-core opponents of such views as found in the *Letter to Rheginus*.

The Other Non-Pauline View: Resurrection of the Flesh

The reasons these church fathers advocated strongly for the resurrection of the actual body are various and complicated. On one level, there were some basic theological considerations. There were other Christians—including those traditionally called "Gnostics"—who thought the true God could not have created this world.[10] Look around: earthquakes, hurricanes, volcanic eruptions, droughts, famines, epidemics, birth defects. This world is a cesspool of misery. Do you really want to blame God for it? It must have been created by some other divinity, either evil by nature or just stunningly careless and ignorant.

The orthodox Christians, however, wanted to insist there is only one God and he is the Creator of all things. This God is good, which means the creation is good. If it is now filled with evil, sin, and suffering, it is not God's fault. Forces of evil in the world, including fallen humans filled with sin, have created this mess. But in the end God will vindicate himself, his good name, and his good creation. He will not abandon this world but redeem it. So too with the human body. Yes, it now is weak and pathetic, susceptible to injury, devastating illness, aging, and death. But God created it and God is going to save it. There will be a resurrection.

There may have been more complicated, sociological reasons for the orthodox insistence on a future resurrection.[11] Orthodox Christians maintained that they alone were the ones willing to die for their faith: the heretics, who did not believe God had created the material world or the human body, were certainly not willing to lay down their bodies for his sake. Or so the orthodox claimed. They themselves, on the other hand, were more than willing to do so, and so they suffered terrible persecutions and martyrdoms for what they believed.[12]

The early Christian accounts of Christian martyrdom are detailed, gory, and moving. Some Christians actually reveled in the idea that they would be torn to shreds by the wild beasts as a witness for their faith—in no small measure because this act of self-sacrifice was an "imitation of Christ," who was himself tortured and crucified for the sake of others. These Christian martyrs were intent on arguing that Jesus had a real physical body that really suffered, bled, and died, and then was vindicated by God. They would be too. Christ's death was not some kind of "appearance" of suffering. It was the real thing, and so was theirs. If they suffered in the body, they would be raised in the body; if it was their flesh that was torn, shredded, and destroyed, it was their flesh that would be raised.[13]

And so, lacking the nuance of Paul's insistence that the body, but not the flesh, would be raised (since, for Paul, the "flesh" is the sinful part of the human that will die), the second- and third-century orthodox authors insisted that there would be a resurrection of the flesh. Anyone who believed otherwise could not be a Christian, whatever they might say. As the philosopher Justin Martyr urged in the middle of the second century:

> If you have ever encountered any so-called Christians who do not admit this doctrine, but dare to blaspheme . . . by asserting that there is no resurrection of the dead, but that their souls are taken up to heaven at the moment of their death, do not consider them to be real Christians. (*Dialogue with Trypho* 80)[14]

One wonders how many twenty-first century Christians would escape this charge. Or, as he next says more explicitly:

> I and every other completely orthodox Christian feel certain that there will be a resurrection of the flesh, followed by a thousand years in the rebuilt, embellished, and enlarged city of Jerusalem . . .

Paul Writing Against Paul

One of the great ironies of the early Christian tradition is that the terminology the apostle Paul himself rejected—that the "flesh" would be raised to enter God's Kingdom—came to be espoused in later writings that were actually forged in his name, produced in order to oppose a view that he also opposed: that there would be no future resurrection. This is a case of Paul fighting against Paul, a fabricated and false Paul vehemently arguing for a view that the apostle himself rejected, in order to oppose a view he also rejected but that had been set forth by those claiming to follow his lead.

Nowhere is this irony more pronounced than in a second-century letter allegedly by Paul to the Christians of Corinth. Even though readers of the Bible know about 1 and 2 Corinthians, few realize there is a 3 Corinthians as well, one that did not make it into the canon of Scripture. It comes to us as a part of a legendary account of Paul's missionary journeys called "The Acts of Paul."[15]

The setup for Paul's letter is a written query he has allegedly received, in an equally forged letter, from the Corinthians, who have been visited by two insidious false teachers named Simon and Cleobius, who "overthrow the faith of some through pernicious words." Among other things, these Christian heretics teach that "there is no resurrection of the body."[16]

Despite the historical Paul's own insistence that "flesh and blood cannot inherit the kingdom," the forged response of 3 Corinthians argues that the resurrection *will* be a raising of "the flesh." In the letter, "Paul" maintains that Christ came into the world for this very reason, "that he might raise us in the flesh from the dead" (v. 6). In fact, "those who say that there is no resurrection of the flesh shall have no resurrection, for they do not believe him who had thus risen" (vv. 24–25). The author supports his claim with various proofs. Just as a seed dies but then comes back to life again in a new plant, so will the human flesh: it dies but then will be raised. And just as Jonah was swallowed by a great fish and later, in a sense, ascended from "deepest hell," with "nothing . . . corrupted, not even a hair or an eyelid," so too will it be with humans. Their bodies will die but then be raised, entire, no part left behind. The very flesh itself will inherit eternal life.

"Paul" then declares that everyone who accepts his gospel message—including this teaching of the resurrection—"shall receive a reward, but whomsoever deviates from this rule, fire shall be for him and for those who preceded him therein." In other words, those who reject the doctrine of the resurrection of the flesh will themselves experience it, in graphic and excruciating ways, for all eternity.

The Resurrection of the Flesh in Tertullian

No church father of the second and third centuries argued for the resurrection of the flesh more forcefully than the prolific and acerbic Tertullian of Carthage (circa 155–after 220 CE). Tertullian wore many hats as a Christian author: theologian, ethicist, apologist (that is, intellectual defender of the faith), and heresiologist (attacker of heresies). Notable for his highly rhetorical style, he worked to eviscerate his enemies with vicious wit and barely disguised glee, whether they were pagans, Jews, or heretical Christians.

In a number of writings Tertullian argued for the future resurrection of the flesh; one extended essay is devoted exclusively to the topic. Contrary to the heretical Christian opinion that the future resurrection would be spiritual, Tertullian insisted it will be of the entire body. He agreed with the apostle Paul that just as Christ was raised from the dead, so would Christians be. Christ himself was killed in the body, buried, and raised. What went into his tomb is what came out of it. So too with Christians. The actual fleshly being will be raised.

As others before him, Tertullian reverts to the analogy of seeds (*Treatise on the Resurrection* 52).[17] A wheat seed does not sprout a plant of barley. So it is with the human as well: the resurrected body will be essentially the same in essence, only more full and perfect, even though it has a different form or appearance.

Tertullian knew full well that Paul had insisted: "Flesh and blood cannot inherit the Kingdom of God." Tertullian points out, in fact, that this is the favorite verse of heretics who insist on a spiritual rather than a fleshly resurrection. But in an extended refutation, he claims they completely misconstrue Paul's meaning (*Treatise on the Resurrection* 48–50). When Paul says that "flesh" will not inherit the kingdom, Tertullian contends, he is referring to people who "live according to the flesh"—that is, those who focus on "fleshly" rather than spiritual things, those who live for the passions of their bodies, not bearing the "fruit of the Spirit" (see Galatians 5:17–26). Those who pursue fleshly desires and pleasures are not living according to the Spirit. But to have eternal life, one needs the Spirit within, and anyone who has the Spirit will live according to the Spirit, not according to the flesh.

Therefore those who live by following the passions and desires of the flesh will be refused the kingdom. That does not mean, however, that the flesh—the actual earthly body—will remain dead forever. God will raise the flesh from the dead for eternal rewards and punishments. These will be exquisitely tactile experiences and therefore require flesh. Indeed, Tertullian looks forward to the spectacle of his enemies' fleshly torments with giddy expectation:

> What sight shall wake my wonder, what my laughter, my joy and exultation? As I see all those kings, those great kings . . . groaning in the depths of darkness! And the magistrates who persecuted the name of Jesus, liquefying in fiercer flames than they kindled in their rage against the Christians! Those sages, too, the philosophers blushing before their disciples as they blaze together, the disciples whom they taught that God was concerned with nothing, that men have no souls at all, or that what souls they have never return to their former bodies.

His Schadenfreude extends to other professions as well:

And then there will be the tragic actors to be heard, more vocal in their tragedy; and the players to be seen lither of limb by far in the fire; and then the charioteers to watch, red all over in the wheel of flame; and next, the athletes to be gazed upon, not in their gymnasiums but hurled in the fire.[18]

It is hard to know whether to be amused or disturbed by such reflections: possibly both. But it is also important to remember that Christians in Tertullian's day were an embattled minority. Oppressed outliers often think with joy on the justice to be inflicted on their enemies. This may not be consistent with the Sermon on the Mount, but it certainly has a venerable history elsewhere in the Christian tradition.

The Interim Existence

For all these Christian authors who imagine a future resurrection of the flesh, there is always the question about what will happen in the meantime, starting, as we have seen, with Paul. Now, a century and a half later, the imminent return of Jesus that Paul expected had proved to be not so imminent after all, and Tertullian looks on Paul as ancient history. It is thus no surprise that Tertullian works out a scenario of what will transpire at death.

He explains his view most fully in a work called the *Treatise on the Soul*.[19] In Tertullian's view, at death the soul separates from the body, and different souls go to different places. Only the souls of Christian martyrs, killed for their faith, go immediately and directly to paradise. All other souls, whether good or wicked, go to Hades, an actual space, enormous, located inside the earth. Hades has two divisions, one for the righteous souls who receive temporary rewards and the other for the wicked who are punished, all in anticipation of the permanent destinies to come at the resurrection of the dead.

These tactile experiences of rewards and punishment, Tertullian maintains, are possible because souls can experience pain and joy apart from the body. Just as, when we engage in activities in this life, the mental decision precedes the physical act, so, he argues, it is appropriate that punishments are first experienced by the soul in Hades, and only later by the body at the resurrection.

And the resurrection will certainly happen. The soul will be reunited with the flesh for eternal rewards or punishments. All people will return to the same body they had in life, and in fact in the same state and the same age as when they died. Those who are righteous then will be raised body and soul to the level of perfection of the "peerless angels." The wicked will roast forever.

The Resultant View of the Afterlife

Such views of the afterlife came to be refined and accepted as orthodox by writers of the third and fourth Christian centuries, even though they differed from anything found in the teachings of Jesus, Paul, or Revelation. The soul, like the body, could experience both pleasure and pain, and in fact would experience one or the other immediately after death: ecstatic joy in the presence of God for the righteous, who were defined, typically, as the true followers of Jesus, and horrendous torment in his absence for the wicked, usually defined as everyone else. This teaching of postmortem rewards and punishments, to be followed eventually with a resurrection, came to be the standard view of the Christian church by the third century, just as it is still for many Christians today.

Some observers might consider the views to be a kind of natural development of what the "founders of Christianity" thought, or even as inevitable. But they were not inevitable. Other Christians had different views, and there was no historical, cultural, or religious necessity that the earlier views of ultimate annihilation for sinners had to lead to the notion of never-ending conscious torment. Yet that is what happened.

CHAPTER THIRTEEN

Tactile Ecstasy and Torment in the Christian Hereafter

It is not difficult to see why humans started imagining a glorious and peaceful afterlife. Surely things aren't meant to be the way they are now. Even apart from the ravages of poverty, starvation, disease, debilitating injury, and unfathomable loss, there are the mundane miseries we all have to put up with. Can't we do better than that? One could only imagine what real happiness would be. In antiquity it often came in the form of a fantastically plush and pleasant garden—a "paradise"— with gorgeous and abundant fruit-bearing trees, gentle breezes, and warm sunshine, to be enjoyed in the company of loved ones forevermore. As far back as we have literature, we find recorded imaginations of such a place—the immortal existence of Ut-napishtim in the Gilgamesh epic, or Menelaus's Elysian Fields in Homer's *Odyssey*—at least for the lucky few.

It is also not hard to grasp why heaven's antipode, a place of everlasting punishment, arose. People have always wanted justice, and if it is not to be found in the present world, possibly it will come in the life beyond. Those who have sinned against the gods or abused their fellow humans must surely have to pay a price.

Even so, it is interesting that punishment after death is not a part of the ancient Jewish Scriptures, the Christian Old Testament. There are, however, hints of it in Homer, as we have seen, and it becomes a mainstay of the classical Greek tradition as far back as Aristophanes and Plato. After their days, Hellenistic (that is, "Greek") culture spread throughout the Mediterranean with the conquests of Alexander the Great, and many peoples—including Jews—adopted their conquerors' views on many things, including views of the afterlife. These influenced developments later within Christianity. In many respects, Christian hell is Hellenistic.

Once the ideas of both heaven and hell found fertile soil in the Christian tradition, they took on a life of their own. Heaven became a place of eternal adoration of the one true God who had created all things and brought life into being so that the living could worship him forever. Hell became a place of eternal torment for those who rejected God: instead of submitting to his will, they chose to assert their own wills by harming others.

A particular image of God endowed such afterlife expectations with enduring power. God was imagined as a great king. Or rather *the* Great King, Sovereign over the entire world. Kings must be obeyed. A good king treats his obedient subjects justly. But those who threaten him receive no mercy. So too with the Sovereign God. His subjects either submit to his rule and enjoy his bounty, or they resist and are sent to the dungeons. One wonders what would have happened to views of the afterlife if Christians had chiefly imagined God not as the all-powerful Monarch but as, say, the all-doting Mother.

Among the factors that contributed to the developing Christian views of the afterlife were horrible experiences some of them had as Christians in the present life.[1] I do not want to maintain that Christianity was constantly persecuted by Roman officials at all times and in all places. Modern scholarship has argued this is a myth.[2] But there were times and places where Christians did face considerable antagonism, and there have been Christian martyrs for just about as long as there have been Christians. For the faithful, true religion began with a martyred messiah, and his devoted followers sometimes experienced the same fate.

The experiences of the martyrs—and possibly even more important, the tales told of their gory deaths—had a profound effect on Christian understandings of the afterlife. Public torture and gory executions of those faithful to God would surely be avenged. The martyrs themselves—those who gave their all for the All-mighty—would be avenged postmortem in particularly glorious ways; and those responsible for their deaths would experience divine retribution through intensely tactile torture. Thus the idea of torment after death developed largely in response to the experience of torment in this life. What you give is what you get.

Torn to Shreds for Eternal Life: Ignatius of Antioch

A most remarkable collection of Christian writings comes to us in letters written around 110 CE by the first named martyr of the second century, Ignatius, bishop of Antioch, Syria. We do not know the circumstances of Ignatius's arrest, although it was clearly because of Christian activities. Rather than being punished at the site of his "crime," he was sent, again for unknown reasons, to Rome itself, to be thrown to the wild beasts in the arena. En route to his martyrdom, Ignatius wrote a number of letters, seven of which still survive.[3] Most of them are written to churches that had sent representatives to provide moral support on his journey. One other was written to the Christian community in the Roman capital itself. In many respects this is the most astounding of his letters. Ignatius instructs the Christians there not to intervene in the proceedings against him. He wants to be torn to shreds as a martyr to Christ.

I am willingly dying for God, unless you hinder me. I urge you, do not become an untimely kindness to me. Allow me to be bread for the wild beasts; through them I am able to attain to God. . . . Rather, coax the wild beasts, that they may become a tomb for me and leave no part of my body behind . . . Then I will truly be a disciple of Jesus Christ, when the world does not see even my body. (*Ignatius to the Romans* 4:1–2)

This passion for violent death may seem more than a little pathological to modern readers, but there is a theological logic to it. Ignatius worships a Lord who was tortured to death. He wants to imitate him. That is how he will earn an eternal reward. To that end, the gorier the better.

May I have the full pleasure of the wild beasts prepared for me . . . I will coax them to devour me quickly—not as happens with some, whom they are afraid to touch. And even if they do not wish to do so willingly, I will force them to it . . . May nothing visible or invisible show any envy toward me, that I may attain to Jesus Christ. Fire and cross and packs of wild beasts, cuttings and being torn apart, the scattering of bones, the mangling of limbs, the grinding of the whole body, the evil torments of the devil—let them come upon me, only that I may attain to Jesus Christ. (*Ignatius to the Romans* 5:2–3)

Ignatius never claims that everyone needs to be martyred for eternal life. But it is his own passionate wish: he wants no half measures. If he is ripped to shreds by the beasts, he will then "attain" salvation. It is striking that this salvation will not come at the end of time on the Day of Judgment. It will come at his bloody demise. We do not have a reliable record of what actually happened to Ignatius when he arrived in Rome, only a later legendary account. But it is usually assumed he got his wish.

Ignatius never says anything about the fiery torments awaiting his pagan opponents, but that becomes a key issue in a later work describing another early martyr to the Christian cause, Polycarp of Smyrna. As it turns out, Polycarp is one of the persons Ignatius wrote on his way to Rome. Polycarp also wrote a letter, which we still have. But of greater interest is the account from many years later of his own arrest, trial, and execution.[4]

This *Martyrdom of Polycarp* claims to be by an eyewitness, and if true, it would be the earliest firsthand record we have of a Christian martyrdom, from around 155 ĊE. But recent scholars have argued it was actually produced later, possibly in the early third century by someone using the literary ploy of a first-person observer to provide credence to the report.[5] In any event, the author's views of the afterlife are clear in the graphic account. He begins by referring to martyrdoms that had occurred even before Polycarp's, speaking of the astounding endurance of those tortured for their faith, "when their skin was ripped to shreds by whips, revealing the very anatomy of their flesh, down to the inner veins and arteries," while those looking on wailed in pity. But these martyrs:

> displayed such nobility that none of them either grumbled or moaned, clearly showing us all that in that hour, while under torture, the martyrs of Christ had journeyed far away from the flesh, or rather that the Lord was standing by speaking to them. (*Martyrdom of Polycarp* 2.2)

A miracle indeed. Mercilessly flogged without so much as uttering a groan. But these martyrs saw an eternity of joy opening before them because of their bloody demise:

> They despised the torments of the world, in one hour purchasing for themselves eternal life. And the fire of their inhuman torturers was cold to them, because they kept their eyes on the goal of escaping the fire that is eternal and never extinguished. And with the eyes of their hearts they looked above to the good things preserved for those who endure . . .

which the Lord revealed to them, who were no longer humans but already angels. (*Martrydom of Polycarp* 2.3)

A brief torment now—just an hour—provides an escape route from eternal anguish, the divine fire that never ends. Even more, a bloody death brings a glorious afterlife. Those who survive to eternity are not merely raised in their shredded human bodies, nor do they need to wait to be vindicated in a future Day of Judgment leading to a Kingdom of God here on earth. They become angels immediately at death, divinized in the heavenly realm in exchange for a brief if admittedly horrifying torture in the earthly one.[6]

So it is with Polycarp himself. The bulk of the *Martyrdom* describes how he was sought out, arrested, tried, burned at the stake, and stabbed to death, all for his faith in Christ. This faithful death allowed him to acquire "the crown of immortality": "And now he rejoices together with the apostles and all those who are upright, and he glorifies God the Father and blesses our Lord Jesus Christ" (*Martyrdom of Polycarp* 19.2). It will be an eternity of endless joy and worship in the presence of the Almighty.

But the corollary is important for this text as well. The torment imposed by the wicked authorities will be revisited upon them not merely in due measure but much, much worse. As Polycarp tells his proconsular judge, "You threaten with a fire that burns for an hour and after a short while is extinguished; for you do not know about the fire of the coming judgment and eternal torment, reserved for the ungodly" (*Martyrdom of Polycarp* 11:2). It is not completely clear if Polycarp still retains the idea of a future Day of Judgment or if he is imagining that his persecutors will be punished immediately at death. But whenever the torture starts, it will never end.

This attitude of willing submission to torture and death was not only the talk of Christians encouraging one another in the face of persecution; it was apparently known to outsiders as well. As we have seen, the emperor Marcus Aurelius mentions it in his autobiographical reflections, *The Meditations*, in a brief remark that mocks the Christians for being willing to die out of sheer obstinacy. It is also found on the lips of a pagan named Caecilius in the defense of Christianity by the second-century North African apologist Minucius Felix. In attacking the astounding Christian "stupidity," Caecilius cites the views of afterlife held by foolish Christians when threatened with death: "Tortures of the present they scoff at, but they live in dread of the uncertain tortures of the future; they are afraid to die after they are dead, but meantime they have no fear of death"; on the contrary, they are driven "by the comforting expectation of renewal of life hereafter."[7]

Gaining life by welcoming death; avoiding death by giving up life. The Christians' paradoxical view of life and death stood very much at odds with their pagan opponents, who seem to have been perennially mystified by it.

Tactile Torments and Ecstasies

By the mid–third century we find even more graphic expostulations on the fate of the damned and the glories of the saved, to come immediately at the point of death. Again, these appear principally in the context of Christian persecution and martyrdom. One of the most famous martyrs of the period was Cyprian, bishop of Carthage in North Africa (circa 200–258 CE).

Cyprian was a highly educated and talented rhetorician who had been raised pagan. He converted to Christianity in 246 CE and quickly rose through the Christian ranks, becoming bishop of his large and influential city only two years later. We have numerous letters and essays from his hand, and in them the violent opposition to the Christian faith figures prominently. Not long after his elevation to ecclesiastical office, the persecution instigated under the emperor Decius (reigned 249–51 CE) swept through North Africa. Cyprian himself was eventually martyred during the persecution initiated by Decius's later successor, Valerian, in 258 CE.

Throughout his writings Cyprian shows the intimate connection between the brutal realities believers faced in an antagonistic world and their understandings of divine compensation in the world to come. As he explains in a letter to the Roman proconsul of Asia, Demetrius:

> Our certainty of a vengeance to follow makes us patient . . . The harmless acquiesce in punishments and tortures, sure and confident that whatsoever we suffer will not remain unavenged, and that in proportion to the greatness of the injustice of our persecution so will be the justice and the severity of the vengeance exacted for those persecutions. (*Letter to Demetrius* 17)[8]

As important as it was to the faithful, the persecution of Christians was not the real headline news for the empire at large at the time. This letter, and Cyprian's entire bishopric, came in the middle of that awful period of Roman history scholars call the "Crisis of the Third Century." It was a time of civil war, barbarian invasions, famine, and epidemic. The proconsul Demetrius had charged that the massive upheaval and suffering had come from the pagan gods as an empire-wide punishment for allowing Christians to exist in its midst. Cyprian had other ideas. He informed Demetrius that, on the contrary, the crisis had been brought by the Christian God to a pagan empire for not turning to the truth. This punishment affected not only life in the present, however. It would also come to unbelievers in the horrifying conditions of the world to come: "There remains after all the eternal dungeon, and the continual fire, and the everlasting punishment, nor shall the groaning of the suppliants be heard there." This would not entail eternal annihilation, but conscious torment:

An ever-burning Gehenna will burn up the condemned, and punishment devouring with living flames; nor will there be any source whence at any time they may have either respite or end to their torments. Souls with their bodies will be reserved in infinite tortures for suffering. (*Letter to Demetrius* 24)

The highly educated Cyprian concludes with a rhetorical flourish: "Too late they will believe in eternal punishment who would not believe in eternal life."

In yet other contexts Cyprian revels in his fantasies of the pits of hell: "A horrible place . . . with an awful murmuring and groaning of souls bewailing, and with flames belching forth through the horrid darkness of thick night . . . always breathing out the raging fires of a smoking furnace" (*On the Glories of Martyrdom* 20).[9] But equally prolix are his descriptions of the delights that await the Christian faithful destined for paradise. That is where

grace is found, where in the verdant fields the luxuriant earth clothes itself with tender grass, and is pastured with the scent of flowers; where the groves are carried up to the lofty hill-top, and where the tree clothes with a thicker foliage whatever spot the canopy, expanded by its curving branches, may have shaded. (*On the Glories of Martyrdom* 21)

Christian martyrs and all the righteous can expect to enjoy eternal bliss. It will never be too hot or cold there; the weather will always be perfect; there will be no need for seasons; it will always be light. And it is worth sacrificing everything for:

What a pleasure there is in the heavenly kingdom, without fear of death; and how lofty and perpetual a happiness with eternity of living! There the glorious company of the apostles—there the host of the rejoicing prophets—there the innumerable multitude of martyrs, crowned for the victory of their struggle and passion—there the triumphant virgins, who subdued the lust of the flesh and of the body by the strength of their continency. . . . To these, beloved, let us hasten with an eager desire; let us crave quickly to be with them. (*On Morality*, 26)

Visiting the Realms of the Blessed and the Damned

An interesting development in the understanding of the afterlife occurred after the church had grown, expanded, and become a major force within the Roman world. With a massive influx of converts, there also came large numbers of less-than-devoted souls. And the blessings and punishments of eternity almost inevitably came to be modified as a result. By the end of the fourth century, when Christianity was well on the road to becoming the dominant religion of the empire, some Christian writers started to maintain that heaven was not the destination of all members of the church, or hell the fate reserved only for those outside of it. On the contrary, Christian sinners too could be subject to the eternal wrath of God. Especially to be wary were Christian leaders who did not practice what they preached.[10]

The most popular and influential portrayal of the realms of the blessed and the damned comes to us in a book called the *Apocalypse of Paul*, a fictional narrative of a personal tour granted to the apostle. The book was widely read in the Middle Ages and influenced the great Dante himself. It probably comes from the end of the fourth century or beginning of the fifth.[11] One of its obvious sources was the second-century *Apocalypse of Peter*, which we considered in chapter 1, but this later vision goes into more detail in describing both the glories of heaven and the torments of hell. Like its predecessor, this apocalypse is firmly rooted in its own day and time: now, being written after Christianity was a religion endorsed by the Roman imperial authorities, there is no longer a place in hell especially reserved for pagan persecutors and idolaters (who are no longer a threat). Instead we read of the horrific punishments reserved for slack Christians, unruly officers of the church, and heretics.

When Paul first arrives in the heavenly realm he sees the angelic tormentors of the damned: they are pitiless, with no compassion, with faces filled with wrath, teeth projecting from their mouths, and sparks of fire flashing from their heads. On the other hand, the faces of the blessed angels of the saved shine like the sun; these beneficent beings are dressed in golden girdles and have palms in their hands; they are filled with gentleness and pity, and on their raiment is written the name of the Son of God (*Apocalypse of Paul* 11–12).

The tour begins with the "places of the just" located in the third heaven (*Apocalypse of Paul* 19). Christ will spend a thousand years with his saints in the "land of promise" (*Apocalypse of Paul* 21) with a river flowing with milk and honey, around which are planted fruit trees, each of which bears twelve kinds of fruit each year. The grape vines each have ten thousand bunches with one thousand grapes in each bunch. We can imagine the quality was fantastic. Paradise for drinkers of fine wine.

Paul asks his angelic companion if dwelling in such climes will be the best possible afterlife for the saints. No, he is told, this is merely the place reserved for those who have kept themselves pure from sexual relations outside of marriage. But those who have remained virgins their entire lives, who have hungered and thirsted only for righteousness and have "afflicted themselves for the sake of the name of God," will receive blessings seven times greater (*Apocalypse of Paul* 22).

Paul is then taken to a place called the "City of Christ," the dwelling for those who have fully repented of their sins. The city is made of gold and is surrounded by twelve concentric walls, each as distant from the next as the earth is from heaven. It is a big place. Surrounding the city are rivers of honey, milk, wine, and oil (*Apocalypse of Paul* 23). Outside its gates Paul observes people mourning who are not allowed to enter. He learns from the angel that these are Christians who were highly zealous in their faith, fasting day and night, but who were proud at heart and praised themselves for the good deeds they did. God has mercy on them by permitting them to be close to the city of Christ but they cannot enter because of pride. Still, at the end of time, when Christ enters the city, they will finally be allowed in, even if they will not be on the same level of ecstasy as the other denizens of the place (*Apocalypse of Paul* 24).

Paul goes into the city and sees that each of the interior walls is higher than the one before it, separating one part of the city off from the next. The farther saints are destined to go to spend eternity—based on their level of righteousness—the greater the reward. As fantastic as the outer realms of the city are, the inner beggar description.

Paul is then taken to the other side of things, outside the city, to see the torments of "the souls of the godless and sinners" (*Apocalypse of Paul* 31). What is most striking is that many of the worst punishments are not for wicked sinners from outside the church but for the ecclesiastical transgressors within. He first sees groups of believers punished in a river of boiling fire. Some stand in the torrent up to their knees; these are the ones who came out of church to engage in idle disputes. Others are up to their navels: they are those who committed sexual immorality even after receiving communion. Yet others are up to their lips: the slanderers of other Christians. Still others are up to their eyeballs: believers who agreed together to harm their neighbors.

Sinful leaders of the church are treated with special severity. A presbyter who offered communion after committing fornication finds himself in a river of fire, tortured by angels vigorously piercing his intestines with a three-pronged iron instrument—for all time. A church officer responsible for liturgical reading but who didn't himself follow God's laws has his lips and tongue lacerated with a red-hot razor forever, while standing up to his knees in a river of fire. Monks, both men and women, who seemed to renounce the world but "did not maintain" a single Eucharistic meal (it's not clear what that means), who did not pity widows and orphans, welcome strangers and pilgrims, or show mercy to their neighbors, are clothed in rags filled with burning pitch and fiery sulfur; dragons coil around their necks and bodies, and angels with fiery horns beat and suffocate them (*Apocalypse of Paul* 34–40).

To be sure, more common sins and punishments are on full display as well, with appropriate torments assigned to magicians, adulterers, the wealthy who loaned out money on interest, and girls who lost their virginity outside of marriage. But, interestingly enough, the worst punishment of all, "seven times greater" than all the others, comes to bad theologians, who are enclosed in a deep well with a completely unbearable stench. These are sinners who "do not confess that Christ has come in the flesh and that the Virgin Mary brought him forth, and those who say that the bread and cup of the Eucharist of blessing are not the body and blood of Christ" (*Apocalypse of Paul* 41). One might at first think these are non-Christians, but, no, they are actually heretics within the church who embrace the false view that Christ was so fully God incarnate that he was not a full flesh-and-blood human being. You'd be better off pagan.

Unlike the earlier *Apocalypse of Peter*, which vividly stressed the need to lead a morally upright life to avoid the tortures of hell, now, years later, when Christianity had grown into a massive movement populated by all sorts of people, some of them of dubious ethics and theology, the stress is on what it means to be a true Christian. Faith in Christ is not enough. A Christian had better not fall short in any way. God's demands on committed Christians and especially Christian leaders are exacting. Many are called, but few are chosen.

A Reasoned Portrayal of Eternity:
Augustine's City of God

After the tenuous early centuries of the church had passed, highly trained Christian thinkers could engage in reasoned and intellectual reflections on the fate of souls after death, and none did so more influentially than Augustine (354–430 CE), whom we have seen as the greatest theologian of Christian antiquity. Augustine chose to conclude his great work, *The City of God*, with three books describing how the reality of God manifest in this world would reveal itself in the world to come.[12] The basic premise of the chapters stands in continuity with much that had been long believed in Christian circles: there will be eternal punishment, with real pain, for the wicked, matched by the real, tactile joy of the saved. Unlike some of his predecessors, however, Augustine does not fill his account simply with detailed descriptions of the gore and the glory; he was a thinker, and he reflects deeply on what it might mean to be damned or saved.

In Book 21 Augustine deals with the punishments of hell. Always the philosopher, he is especially interested, at the outset, with the conceptual problems involved. Is "eternal pain" even possible? Wouldn't it lead to death, the cessation of perception? How could a body that is subject to flames not perish? Augustine argues emphatically that everlasting torment is both possible and real, maintaining that all manner of seemingly impossible things happen all the time. He points, for example, to the "fact" that when a peacock dies, its flesh never rots (*City of God* 21.4).

But even just thinking of flames: salamanders live in fire without dying, and mountains erupt in flame without being consumed. If other parts of God's creation can burn but not expire, why not people? "For death will not be abolished but will be eternal . . . The first death drives the soul from the body against her will: the second death holds the soul in the body against her will" (*City of God* 21.3). When God created the human Adam, his body—before he sinned—was made never to die; after humans committed sin, their bodies have to die; and after death they will never die (*City of God* 21.8).

But what about the matter of justice? How can God possibly be just in inflicting an eternal punishment on sins that were committed only for a brief time? Shouldn't a sinful life of, say, twenty years suffer a penalty of twenty years? Why eternity? As sensible as the question seems, Augustine considers it absurd: "As if any law ever regulated the duration of the punishment by the duration of the offence punished" (*City of God* 22.11). Is a robbery or a murder punished only for the length of time that it took to commit it? Eternal punishment comes for sins against an eternal God.

Even so, just as punishments differ on earth depending on the enormity of the crime, so too in the world to come. Punishment will be everlasting, but it will be of varied degrees:

> We must not, however, deny the eternal fire will be proportioned to the deserts of the wicked, so that to some it will be more, and to others less painful, whether this result be accomplished by a variation in the temperature of the fire itself, graduated according to everyone's merit, or whether it be that the heat remains the same, but that all do not feel it with equal intensity of torment. (*City of God* 21.16)

That is to say, all will burn, but it will hurt some more than others. Small comfort, once might suppose, but it does serve Augustine's purpose of showing that God is ultimately just and not completely unreasonable.

Augustine spends all of Book 22 expostulating on the glories of heaven for the blessed. As might be imagined, there are few specifics of what they will actually experience, other than that they will spend eternity gazing on and adoring God. This, for Augustine, will entail a joy that "passes all understanding." As a result, logically speaking, it cannot be understood, let alone communicated. But it can be believed, and Augustine firmly believes it.

He does not know whether the saints enjoying their eternal beatific vision of the Most Holy One will actually see God with their eyes. Probably, in heaven, they will be able to see the glory of God even with their eyes shut, since their vision will be perfect in their spiritual bodies. Spiritual eyes will have "a vastly superior power" and will actually have the "power of seeing things incorporeal" (*City of God* 22.29).

The most important point is that, for Augustine, eternal felicity will come through praising God through all the ages. There will be no evil in this heavenly realm, only true peace. The end of all desires will be God himself, for everyone graciously bestowed with eternal salvation. They will want nothing else.

As in hell, there will, for Augustine, be varying levels of ecstatic forevers: "degrees of honor and glory . . . awarded to the various degrees of merit." But on the upside, since everyone will exist in an overpoweringly glorious state, no one with inferior blessings will envy the superior, "because no one will wish to be what he has not received" (*City of God* 22.30). All the saved will be perfectly and magnificently contented, forever.

Eternal Life in the Meantime

Even though Augustine believed that the final state of things—either eternal torment for the damned or eternal ecstasy for the saved—would come only at the end of the world with the final judgment of God, he, like so many of his predecessors, believed that a foretaste of eternity would come at the time of death. As he says in a book called *The*

Enchiridion, which provides a succinct summary of his key theological views, between a person's death and the final resurrection "souls are kept in hidden places of rest or of punishment depending on what each soul deserves because of the lot they won for themselves while they lived in the flesh" (*Enchiridion* 109).

This, then, is a theme that had started with the apostle Paul himself. There will be a climax of all human history with the Day of Judgment and the resurrection of the dead. But in the meantime there will be interim rewards or punishments. Unlike Paul, however, now by the fifth century Augustine has both spelled out what the eternal blessings would entail, in the everlasting beatific vision of God himself, and developed a view of punishment contrary to that embraced by the apostle and by Jesus before him. Now the wicked would not be annihilated for all time. They would be subject to eternal, conscious torment.

Even if Augustine represented a kind of culmination of thought on the afterlife, he is not the stopping point. There continued to be issues that he himself never resolved and others that continued to be debated after his day. Among these were the question of whether some of the people destined to be saved might first have to experience torments to purge them of their sins. In later centuries this was to become the doctrine of Purgatory.

CHAPTER FOURTEEN

Who Will Inherit the Blessings?
Purgatory, Reincarnation,
and Salvation for All

By the end of the second century, the culmination of human history that Jesus predicted would come in the lifetimes of his disciples still hadn't arrived, and the "sudden destruction" Paul anticipated no longer seemed so sudden. Time had dragged on and showed no signs of abating. The reality of ongoing history could not help shaping how people understood eternity. Early on—even toward the end of Paul's life—followers of Jesus realized that death might come before the Kingdom of God "arrived in power." But what would happen to the dead in the meantime? Would they just enjoy a deep, sound sleep until awakened by the last trumpet? Paul, at least, thought not. At death he would come into the immediate presence of Christ to enjoy a blessed interim state until the (still imminent) Day of Judgment arrived.

When it never did come, questions continued to arise, including one that proved especially salient in later centuries. If immediately after death the righteous believers are "saved" but the wicked are "damned," are those the only two choices? Either ecstatic glories forever or unimaginable torments? What about people who are neither especially saintly nor particularly sinful? Isn't there a middle ground? And are those who are truly righteous, who live fantastically godly lives and die, say, as martyrs to the faith—are these to be rewarded no more than simple but still rather sloppy or inattentive believers, whose basic faith would ultimately bring the inheritance of heaven? Don't the sinners among the faithful have to pay *at all* for their sins? But how do they pay for their sins if they go immediately to paradise? And if it's true that sinners in the church receive the same reward as the truly righteous, what is the incentive not to sin once a person is baptized into the faith? Doesn't the simple binary of heaven and hell lead, necessarily, to lax morals?

To address these questions, there eventually arose another opinion: before entering paradise, some people, possibly most, would have to pay for their sins or, in a different conception, be painfully purged of them. Many centuries later this idea would be crystallized into the medieval doctrine of Purgatory, a place literally located between heaven and hell, where sins of the less-than-perfect would be purged through harsh but temporary suffering. That would apply to most of those who were heavenbound. The intensity of purgatorial suffering, and its duration, would be determined by just how sinful the not-so-saintly saved really were.

The term "Purgatory" itself was not coined until the twelfth century and the idea was not institutionalized as an official part of church teaching until the Second Council of Lyons in 1274.[1] But the basic idea behind it, that some of those who would ultimately be saved would first experience postmortem suffering, goes far back. We find its beginnings in the early centuries of the church.

We have already seen, in fact, a very similar idea in much older sources from pagan realms. In the afterlife myth preserved in the *Phaedo*, Plato speaks of those who lived a "neutral" life—not terribly wicked sinners but also not surpassingly holy—sent to a place of purification to be punished until absolved (*Phaedo* 113d–114e). So too Virgil speaks of souls in the afterlife who were "drilled in punishments" in order to "pay for their old offenses" before being sent to "Elysium's broad expanse" (*Aeneid*, Book 6, lines 854–60). Justice cannot allow everyone to be treated exactly alike. Sinners need to pay for their shortcomings if they hope to enter the glorious happily ever after with those who are truly righteous.

The first Christian source to suggest explicitly that some of those ultimately saved will first suffer horribly is the *Apocalypse of Peter*, which we have already examined. In one of our oldest Greek fragments of the work, we are told that some of the saints in heaven will on occasion pray for those who are experiencing torment in hell. Christ replies that he will "give to my called and my chosen whomsoever they shall ask for, out of torment, and will give them a fair baptism to salvation . . . even a portion of righteousness with my holy ones" (*Apocalypse of Peter* 14.1). This is clearly not a teaching of purgatory per se: there is no "place" reserved for the temporary torments of sinners bound for heaven. But there can be salvation for some of those who suffer first, if the saints in heaven intercede for them.

Princeton historian Peter Brown has shown that this became a common idea—that prayers of others could help those who are suffering in the afterlife. Eventually it came to be thought that the living needed to pray for the dead, to mention them when taking the Eucharist, and especially to give alms on their behalf.[2] It is interesting to see that in our earliest sources this idea that the righteous could help the suffering dead appears particularly in narratives that focus on women and the power of their prayers. The earliest such account, from the second century, involves one of Paul's most famous legendary converts, an upper-class young woman named Thecla.

The Prayer of the Righteous in the Acts of Thecla

The *Acts of Thecla* was once one of the most popular pieces of Christian writing from outside the New Testament.[3] It begins in the pagan Thecla's hometown, Iconium. Paul has arrived in town and begins preaching his gospel in the home of a believer while an attentive and intrigued Thecla listens from an upstairs window next door. Paul's message is all about the saintly lifestyle that can bring eternal salvation. In particular, those who abstain from the joys of sex—even within marriage—will receive a heavenly reward.

This is a compelling message for the young Thecla, who, as it turns out, is soon to be married to a prominent figure in town. She immediately breaks off her engagement, earning the rage of both her estranged fiancé and her mother, who now has suffered a social and, probably, economic setback. Together they turn her over to the local authorities for punishment. The narrative details Thecla's devotion to Paul and her narrow escapes from violent martyrdom, entailing, in one particularly peculiar episode, a vat of flesh-eating seals.

In the course of the narrative the unmarried and vulnerable Thecla is given over to the protection of a onetime queen named Antonia Tryphaena, whose daughter, Falconilla, has recently died. Knowledge of Thecla's great sanctity has apparently reached even into the realm of the dead, where it is known among the departed that Thecla can be of some help. Falconilla appears to her mother in a dream and asks her: "Mother, receive this stranger, the forsaken Thecla, in my place, that she may pray for me and I may come to the place of the just" (*Acts of Thecla* 28). Tryphaena does as she is asked, Thecla makes her prayer, and then the narrative moves on to other matters. But this brief snippet is intriguing on its own terms.

Falconilla is obviously not experiencing a heavenly reward in paradise, and how could she be? She had been a pagan who had never heard of Paul, Christ, or of the Christian religion at all before she died. She is not in the place of the just. But she appears to know that she could be transferred, and the assumption of the text (though not stated) is that Thecla's prayer could and did work the miracle. This is only a glimpse of postmortem possibilities, but it clearly appears to be a case of someone who, though not immediately saved, came to enter a restful place after originally being excluded.

From Torment to Blessedness: Perpetua and Dinocrates

A second tale of the efficacious prayer of a saintly Christian woman comes in the stories of Vibia Perpetua, whom we encountered already in chapter 1 as an imprisoned new convert awaiting her martyrdom in North Africa.[4] We are not told much about Perpetua's background, but since she was a highly educated, literate Roman matron, she must have received some training in the classical literary tradition, and we can assume she was familiar with mythological scenes of the afterlife such as are presented by the well-known Virgil. In any event, she understands that it is possible for a person who is suffering in the afterlife to move to a place of joy. That much is clear from the first pair of dreams she has.[5]

In the portion of the text that is allegedly her diary (*Passion of Perpetua* 7–8), Perpetua indicates that one day while in prayer, for no obvious reason and to her own surprise, she said out loud, "Dinocrates." That was the name of her brother who had died of skin cancer on his face at the tender age of seven. Perpetua realizes she is to pray for him. She does so and sees him in a vision. It is not a happy sight. She is separated from him by an impassable great abyss (as in the story of Lazarus and the rich man in Luke 16). Across from her, Dinocrates is in a foul place, coming out of a dark hole. Others with him are all "very hot and thirsty, pale and dirty." On his face is still a gaping lesion from the cancer. Worst of all, he stands by a pool filled with water, but its rim is too high for him to reach. He is miserably thirsty. Perpetua wakes up, deeply upset, "realizing that my brother was suffering." But she is confident that "I could help him in his trouble; and I prayed for him every day . . . with tears and sighs that this favor might be granted me."

Then comes a second dream. Perpetua sees Dinocrates in the same place, but he is now "all clean, well dressed, and refreshed." The cancer is gone from his face; there is only a scar. And, most happily, the pool of water is now lower, to the level of his waist. Above the rim of the pool hangs a golden bowl full of water. Dinocrates drinks from it, and however much he drinks, the bowl remains full. When he has enough, he goes off "to play as children do." Perpetua concludes her narration of the dream by saying, "Then I awoke, and I realized that he had been delivered from his suffering."

It is a fascinating tale of the saving power of prayer extending to the afterlife. One can only regret it is so brief, as it raises so many questions. Why is Dinocrates, an innocent child, being punished? Was his punishment meant to be temporary from the outset, or was it eternal? What is the place he is actually in? Who are the others with him?

It should be clear that he is not in a kind of "purgatory," at least as later defined: it is not a place in which suffering will purge him of his sins, enabling him to enter the heavenly realm. He actually stays in the same place after he is moved from misery to happiness. And the text says nothing about his suffering having any function at all, let alone of purgation leading to salvation. Instead, it is Perpetua's prayer that saves him. In an interesting way Perpetua's vision stands in stark contrast with the biblical account of Lazarus in Luke 16 (with which she may have been familiar), where the torment experienced by the damned "Rich Man" cannot be ameliorated, not even by the great patriarch Abraham himself. By contrast, Dinocrates is a hopelessly miserable soul granted relief and ending up with a happy existence, going off to play like the deceased child he is. This may not be "purgatory" but it is a place of temporary suffering prior to eternal joy, a clear forerunner of the doctrines that were to develop later in the thinking of the church.

Sinful Saints Suffering for Sin

Soon after these narratives were written, we increasingly begin to see heaven-bound sinners suffer for their sins. Sometimes this suffering was considered punitive: crimes must be punished! At other times, though, it was believed suffering could cleanse the soul from sin, a kind of violent hard scrub to remove the taints of impurity. In this latter case, postmortem misery was not retribution but divine purgation. Our earliest sources do not make this kind of clean distinction; it took some time for the logic of temporary suffering to be worked out.

Among our earliest theologians to discuss the issue was the third-century Tertullian, soon after Perpetua and also in North Africa. In one brief passage Tertullian indicates that after the thousand-year reign of Christ on earth would come a resurrection of the saints, who would not all rise at once but in waves, "sooner or later according to their deserts" (*Against Marcion* 3.24).[6] The greater the sin, the longer the wait for eternal joy.

In another place Tertullian goes into greater length while explaining an intriguing saying of Jesus preserved in the Sermon on the Mount. The passage originally had nothing at all to do with the afterlife, let alone purgatory. Jesus tells his hearers that if they are at the temple worshiping God, preparing to give a gift at the altar, but suddenly remember they have wronged someone, they should first be reconciled before offering the gift. Otherwise, if they don't make terms with their accuser, "he will hand you over to the judge; the judge will hand you over to the guard; and the guard will throw you in prison. Truly I tell you, you will not come out of there until you pay the last penny" (Matthew 5:26; the King James Version renders the last term, famously, "the last farthing").

In Tertullian's exposition, Jesus's words are symbolic of deeper spiritual realities. The accuser Jesus speaks of is actually the devil. A person who seeks to be reconciled with the devil must renounce him and all his ways. Anyone who fails to do so will be delivered over to God, the judge, who in turn will hand him over to his avenging angel: "And he will commit you to the prison of hell, out of which there will be no dismissal until the smallest even of your delinquencies be paid off in the period before the resurrection" (*On the Soul* 35.3). In other words, even those sinners bound for heavenly glory need to pay for their transgressions before being raised from the dead.

This is an idea also discussed a century and a half later by the great theologian Augustine, sometimes wrongly called "the father of purgatory."[7] Augustine was never completely convinced of the need of postmortem purgation of sins, but in some places he allows it, conceding with reluctance: "This I do not contradict, because possibly it's true" (*City of God* 21.26).[8] And so, he admits it is possible that "some shall in the last judgment suffer some kind of purgatorial punishments" (*City of God* 20.25). Later he concedes: "Of those who suffer temporary punishments after death, all are not doomed to those everlasting pains which are to follow that judgment; for to some . . . what is not remitted in this world is remitted in the next, that is, they are not punished with the eternal punishment of the world to come" (*City of God* 21.26). There may be real suffering after death for those destined to be saved, but it is temporary, not the eternal stuff reserved for the wicked unbelievers.

The idea of Christians suffering for sin after death fulfilled several functions in the growing church of the third, fourth, and fifth centuries, as it became increasingly filled with "saints" at all levels of saintliness. On one hand, it allowed for a more nuanced understanding of divine justice, in contrast to a rather harsh binary of undifferentiated glorious ecstasies for all who were saved and unending fires for all the damned. There are grades of reward and punishment. Moreover, it provided greater incentive for a saint to behave like one. You may have heaven as your ultimate destination, but if you slip up in the meanwhile, there will be purgatory to pay.

At the same time, this very idea that after death people could atone for their sins by intense but temporary suffering—or be painfully purged of their sinful character—brought forth another pressing question. If that was true for some sinners, why not all of them? If suffering can resolve the problem of sin, why cannot prolonged suffering take care of even the greatest of sinners? In that connection, why not think that if God is truly just, all people will eventually have that chance to earn their salvation? And if God is absolutely sovereign, why not think that eventually God will establish his rule over everything in his creation—so that all people, even the worst sinners, will eventually turn to him, and adore him, and, even if it takes countless ages, come to earn the right to stand in his presence? Why not think that ultimately, through intense suffering, salvation will come to all?

Will Everyone Be Saved?

Not everyone entertained these questions. Traditional views of the afterlife were emphatic and obdurate, and these had insisted that the damned were damned forever. Many Christian leaders claimed this was true of everyone who did not believe in Christ, no matter how virtuous. Others even maintained that those who converted to the faith but died before baptism were lost forever to unending torment. As the great Christian preacher of Constantinople, John Chrysostom (347–407 CE), declared:

> If it should come to pass (which God forbid!) that through the sudden arrival of death we depart hence unbaptized, though we have ten thousand virtues, our portion will be no other than hell, and the venomous worm, and fire unquenchable, and bonds indissoluble. (*Homily on John* 5.25)[9]

Others somewhat more generously thought there was wiggle room and took hope in comments made already by the apostle Paul in the Christian Scriptures themselves. In his great letter to the Romans, for example, Paul contrasted the judgment that came to be inflicted on the entire human race because of the sin of the first man, Adam, with the salvation to come with equal universal force through the righteous act of redemption of the second Adam, Christ: "And so, as condemnation came to all people through the transgression of one person, so too the righteousness that leads to life comes to all people through the righteous act of one person" (Romans 5:18). Here righteousness and life come not to some but to all. He also later indicates that God imprisoned all people in lives of disobedience "so that he might show mercy to all" (Romans 11:32). Once again "all": as many as are disobedient are saved.

Or, as Paul says in the book of Philippians, when Christ was exalted at his resurrection, God gave him the divine name that is above every name, so that at the name of Jesus, in the end, "every knee will bow, of those in heaven, and on the earth, and under the earth" (Philippians 2:10). Not some knees, but every knee. Indeed, as Paul says in 1 Corinthians 15, at the end of time, "all things" will be subject to the Lordship of Christ, who will then subject all things to God himself, "so that God may be all in all" (1 Corinthians 15:28). Everything, then, will return to submission to God. Surely that means all living creatures, including sinners, no?

That was certainly the view of the greatest theologian of the Christian church of the first three centuries, Origen of Alexandria (circa 185–circa 254 CE). Origen was massively learned and extraordinarily prolific, a one-man publishing industry who produced a fantastic number of treatises, commentaries, and homilies. Because the theology of the church had not been tackled yet by serious intellectuals, the philosophically trained and theologically adept Origen took on the task, going down paths others had not yet trod, cognizant that even though most church leaders agreed on many of the basics of the faith, they were surrounded by numerous gray areas. In the end, Origen fleshed out the rudiments of the faith in ways that would be abundantly fruitful for decades and even centuries to come—even if some of the theological paths he took did lead to dead ends.

The most systematic expression of his thought comes in a work called *On First Principles*. Origen wrote the book relatively early in his career, in 229 CE. But his views never changed significantly. Much to the regret of scholars interested in the history of Christian theology, we do not have a complete copy of the book in its original Greek language. Most of it is preserved only in a later Latin translation produced at the end of the fourth century by a scholar named Tyrannius Rufinus, who frankly admits to having changed what Origen wrote in places in order to make his views fall into line with later orthodox theology. Even so, it is possible to get a relatively clear understanding of Origen's thought, and one of his thoughts was that, in the end, everyone will submit to God's sovereignty and be saved. That includes the most wicked of humans. And the demons. Even the devil. God will literally be "all in all."[10]

The backdrop for Origen's view of the end comes in in his understanding of the beginning. In the first book of *On First Principles*, Origen explains how all sentient beings originally came into existence. In eternity past, before the world began, God created an enormous number of souls, whose purpose was to contemplate and adore him forever. True adoration, of course, requires freedom of the will: beings need to *choose* to adore God if their worship is a true honor. That means all souls must also have had the capacity to choose *not* to worship God—that is, to do evil. None of these created souls were inherently evil, however, and none—not even the soul that was to become the devil—"was incapable of good" (*On First Principles* 1.8.1–3).

As it happened, virtually all the souls failed in their task. There was only one, in fact, who remained in constant adoration of God through an unceasing, ages-long adoration. So attuned was this soul to the glories of

God that it became fused with him, assuming all his characteristics, just as an iron placed in a fire eventually takes on all the fire's very characteristics and, in a sense, becomes "one" with the fire. This one faithful soul became Christ, the Son of God.

All other souls fell away from the contemplation of God. Some fell in a very big way—none more than the devil. Others fell somewhat less and became demons. Others fell into human bodies. Yet others became brute animals or even plants. This very bad situation played itself out over the course of many ages in the history of the world. Ultimately, though, Origen maintained that since God is sovereign over all, his sovereignty will be recognized by all. Otherwise he is not really the Lord God Almighty but only *relatively* mighty and *partially* sovereign.

The goal of human life is to return to the original intention of existence, the contemplation of God. For that to happen, people need to be purged of their sin, which interferes with their adoration of the One above all things. Those who do not learn to do so in this life—the vast majority of the human race, of course—must learn to do so after death, and that is why there is postmortem suffering. Suffering is meant to purge souls of their sin so they can return to their eternal destiny of contemplative adoration of the one who made them. Some people—the more sinful, obviously—have to suffer more than others. But after many, many ages, all will eventually return to God of their own free will, purged completely of their sins. As Origen says in one place: "We believe that the goodness of God through Christ will restore his entire creation to one end, even his enemies being conquered and subdued" (*On First Principles* 1.6.1). In support of his view, Origen quotes the words of Paul: that at the end God will place all of Christ's enemies under his feet in "subjection to him" (1 Corinthians 15:25). In Origen's understanding, "the word 'subjection' when used of our subjection to Christ, implies the salvation . . . of those who are subject" (*On First Principles* 1.6.1).

This will be true of "all those beings who started from one beginning but were drawn in various directions by their own individual impulses." Even those who ended up becoming demons or dandelions. They will progress up the chain of being until they return to their original state. This transformation, however, will not "happen all of a sudden, but gradually and by degrees, during the lapse of infinite and immeasurable ages." But eventually all things will come to "that end, namely, blessedness, to which we are told that even God's enemies themselves are to be subjected, the end in which God is said to be 'all' and 'in all'" (*On First Principles* 1.6.4).

This teaching of the "restoration of all things"—known among scholars as the *apocatastasis*—proved to be Origen's most controversial teaching, since it affirmed both the preexistence of souls and the salvation for all that live, even the most wicked. But Origen understood that torture has a way of changing people's minds. They may have to be induced, but eventually everyone yields. "And so, for all wicked men, and for demons too, punishment has an end, and both wicked men and demons shall be restored to their former rank" (*On First Principles* 2.10.3). When that happens, all rational souls—which means everything that lives—will be transformed into spiritual bodies, and in that state, they will live forever. They will be "joined to God and made one spirit with him" (*On First Principles* 3.6.6).

This, then, is not a doctrine of "purgatory" as it was later to develop, a place between heaven and hell for those who are destined for eternal glory but need to suffer first. On the contrary, it is suffering for all beings apart from Christ who must be purged of the sin that taints them. The suffering is not retributive, a "punishment" per se. It is purgative, cleansing away the impurity of sin.

But given the logic of the system, if suffering can purge one person from sin, it can purge another. It can purge even the worst of sinners. Even the devil. Even if it has to take place over "immeasurable ages." That, however, leads to another controversial side of this bit of theological musing. Origen suggested that during these immeasurable ages people who have been punished will be given further chances in life by being brought back from death. At one stage of his career, Origen believed in reincarnation.

Reincarnation in the Christian Tradition

The idea of reincarnation had been floated for centuries before Origen. In ancient Greece the great philosopher Pythagoras was widely believed to have been the first to perpetrate, or at least to popularize, the idea. Later it was allegedly held by such figures as Parmenides and Empedocles, the latter of whom is reported to have said, "Before now I was a boy, and a maid, a bush and a bird, and a dumb fish leaping out of the sea."[11]

We also find it in the Roman tradition, as when Virgil's Aeneas visits the underworld and sees innumerable souls gathered around the river Lethe (Forgetfulness) before being sent back to earth in a "second body." He doesn't understand why anyone would want to leave paradise for the miseries of life, but he is told that "the wretches are not completely purged of all the taints, nor are they wholly freed of all the body's plagues" and so they need to be "drilled in punishments" in order to "pay for their old offenses." Only then can they "revisit the overarching world once more" by returning to bodies, to try again (*Aeneid*, Book 6, lines 865–96).

It is sometimes said today that reincarnation was a widespread teaching in early Christianity as well. In fact, the evidence for it is sparse. To be sure, later interpreters have detected possible traces of the idea already in the New Testament. When Jesus asks his disciples, "Who do people say that I am," they tell him that some say he is John the Baptist come back from the dead, or Elijah, or one of the prophets (Mark 8:27–28). This may not indicate that everyone has had a previous life, but it certainly shows that some people thought Jesus did. Also in the Gospel of John the puzzled Jewish leaders ask John the Baptist: "Are you Elijah?" (John 1:21). He denies it, but it's interesting that they thought it was possible. And even more interesting, if less obvious, later in the same Gospel, Jesus passes by a man who was born blind, and his disciples ask him, "Rabbi, who sinned, this person or his parents, that he should be born blind?" (John 9:2). It's a revealing question: if the man was born blind because of his own sin, obviously he had to have committed the sin before his birth. Voila. Reincarnation.

Possibly our most intriguing instance of reincarnation belief in the early church occurred among a group of so-called Gnostic Christians attacked by the heresy hunter Irenaeus in his five-volume work *Against the Heresies* (about 180 CE). Among the nefarious false-teachers Irenaeus maligns was a group called the Carpocratians, said to practice magic and engage in outrageously licentious activities in pursuit of their peculiar religious ideas. Without having our modern vocabulary, Irenaeus accuses the Carpocratians of having postmodern ethics: for them, there was no good or evil per se; it was all a matter of personal, subjective judgment. In one context or another, everything was good, and for that reason everything was permitted. In fact, for the Carpocratians, Irenaeus avers, everything was required. Anyone who had not had the full human experience—in every way—had to come back and try it again until every possible experience had been undergone. In context, Irenaeus is clearly thinking of sex acts.

> They maintain that things are evil or good, simply in virtue of human opinion. They deem it necessary, therefore, that by means of transmigration from body to body, souls should have experience of every kind of life as well as ever kind of action, unless, indeed, by a single incarnation, one may be able to prevent the need for others . . . doing all those things which we dare not either speak or hear of, nay, which we must not even conceive of in our thoughts, nor think credible. (*Against the Heresies* 1.25.4)[12]

As one might imagine, this must have led to some rather interesting worship experiences. Or at least Irenaeus imagined it did. Those who did not enjoy the full run of all the options "must pass from body to body, until he has experienced every kind of action which can be practiced in this world, and when nothing is longer wanting to him, then his liberated soul should soar upwards to that God who is above the angels, the makers of the world. In this way also all souls are saved." Long story short: you're going to have to do it sooner or later, so you may as well enjoy it now.

Origen was about as far removed from this kind of reasoning as one could be. He stressed, instead, traditional morality and an ascetic lifestyle. For him, reincarnation was a way of moving up the chain of being, by becoming increasingly sanctified until one could enter back into the heavenly realm to engage in the eternal contemplation of God. Not exactly a rollicking good time by Carpocratian standards, but for Origen and those like him, this was an eternity to long for. Before it happens, though, there are numerous incarnations in a variety of forms:

> By some inclination towards evil these [heavenly] souls lose their wings and come into bodies, first of humans; then through their association with the irrational passions, after the allotted span of human life they are changed into beasts; from which they sink to the level of insensate nature. (*Against the Heresies* 1.8.4)

This descent from human to "irrational animal" to "the insensate life of a plant" is then reversed: "From this condition it rises again through the same stages and is restored to its heavenly place." The "fall" into lower life forms occurs because of the temptations of the flesh. If you can't restrain yourself now, you'll become a toadstool later. It is through purgative suffering that eventually the soul rises back again, gradually, to the heavenly realm. Origen is not absolutely convinced that it happens this way: "For our part, we beg leave to mention these things not as fixed doctrines, but as opinions to be discussed and then rejected" (*Against the Heresies* 1.8.4). But later he was condemned for holding such views. Long after he entered eternity, his entire system of the preexistence of souls and reincarnation came to be condemned by theologians of another day.

In some circles, however, the idea of universal salvation lived on.

Ultimate Salvation for All

Among scholars from the later church, the most famous theologian to countenance universal salvation was a self-confessed advocate of Origen, the late fourth-century Gregory of Nyssa (circa 335–circa 394 CE). In a dialogue called *On the Soul and the Resurrection*, held with his own sister and fellow theologian Macrina the Younger, Gregory insists that suffering after death is not meant to be a punishment for sin but as a way of driving evil out of the soul.[13] His sister agrees, at some length. Moreover, she claims that when evil is finally driven out, it will disappear, since evil cannot exist outside of the will of a person. And when that happens, Macrina maintains, there will be a "complete annihilation of evil." Then God will be all and "in all." That is, all will be saved.

In many ways the most intriguing suggestions of eternal salvation come in one of the great narrative Gospels put in circulation sometime in the late fourth century, even though it may well have been based on traditions of earlier times.[14] It is variously called the Acts of Pilate (since Pontius Pilate figures prominently in its opening account of Jesus's trial) or the Gospel of Nicodemus (since it is allegedly written by this figure known otherwise from the Gospel of John). The narrative contains a highly legendary record of Jesus's last hours, which does not, however, end with his crucifixion. On the contrary, it goes on to describe what happened next, prior to the resurrection. This is our first surviving account of the story that later came to be known as the "Harrowing of Hell," in which, after his death, Jesus went down to Hades in order to free its prisoners. The basic idea behind the story is that salvation could not come to the world—not even to the saints—before Jesus had died for sins. But once he died, the redemption he achieved was made available to those who had come before. He himself went down to Hades to put it on offer. The question is: Would anyone, given the choice, really say no?

In the Gospel of Nicodemus we hear the story from two people who actually experienced it, two sons of Saint Simeon, the holy man who recognized Jesus as an infant in Luke 2:25–35. They themselves were in Hades and saw Jesus there before being raised by him from the dead. Now, returned to life, they are telling the whole tale to the dubious Jewish leaders who are investigating the question.[15]

They indicate that they were down in deep, dark Hades with everyone else who had ever lived, when suddenly, out of nowhere, a light appeared, bright as the sun. John the Baptist, one of the deceased, came forward to announce that the Son of God had now come, giving people a chance to repent from worshiping idols. If they refused to do so now, there would be no second chance. Obviously John was not addressing only the saints among the Jews: this salvation of Christ was available to all, including pagans.

Then the account gets very weird. Hades is portrayed as an actual sentient being who had swallowed all the dead, who are living inside of him. This personified Hades expressed his fear to Satan that if Christ raised people from the dead during his life, there would be nothing to stop him now from raising "all the others." And if that happened, "None of the dead will be left to me" (Gospel of Nicodemus 20:3). Hades was not thinking he might suffer a moderate loss. He was afraid his winnings would be totally obliterated. No one would be left. This would be salvation for all.

In fact, it happened. Christ crashed through the gates of hell and smashed the bars of iron restraining its inhabitants, and "all the dead who were bound were released from their bonds" (Gospel of Nicodemus 21:3). Hades then complained to the devil, "O Beelzeboul . . . Turn and see: none of the dead is left in me" (Gospel of Nicodemus 23:1). While they were talking, Christ took the first man, Adam, and raised him up and then turned to all the dead, saying: "Come with me all you who experienced death through the tree that this one touched; for now see, I am raising all of you up through the tree of the cross" (Gospel of Nicodemus 24:1).

The text may leave some slight wavering on the question of whether absolutely everyone was saved from Hades. It next indicates that it is the prophets of Israel and all the saints who emerged, praising Christ, as he made the sign of the cross on the foreheads of "the patriarchs, prophets, martyrs, and ancestors; then taking them he sprang up from Hades" (Gospel of Nicodemus 24:1). So are they the only ones brought forth? It may seem so, since Christ then handed "all the righteous" to the archangel Michael to be inducted into heaven (Gospel of Nicodemus 25:1). But it appears more likely that he has made *everyone* righteous by his act of righteousness on the cross. Hades himself at least had no doubts about what had happened. He had been completely emptied out. No one remained.

Ending in Paradise

And so we end our study on a happy note. Everyone is saved. That view did not become the dominant opinion in the Christian tradition, of course. Hell continued on and Purgatory later came into existence. For most Christian theologians, salvation could not be as easy as the Gospel of Nicodemus would have it, a matter of everyone simply being led from Hades by the victorious Christ. It would be hard, and eventually it would get even harder, not guaranteed even to those who converted to faith in Christ. For one thing, they had to be baptized. And to live a moral life— an unbelievably moral life. Anything short, and it could be the flames of hell.

Not everyone took this hard line. There have always been Christians who have insisted that even though God is just, he is even more merciful. As the New Testament itself attests, "Mercy triumphs over judgment" (James 2:13). In this view, the love of God knows no bounds and cannot be overcome, either by evil, powers of darkness, human suffering, or wicked free will. In fact, it cannot be overcome by the other qualities and characteristics of God, even his seemingly inveterate and obstinate insistence on justice. In the words of one modern Christian author, once himself a committed evangelical with a passion for the biblical witness, in the end "Love Wins."[16]

There is indeed a movement within the widespread Christian communities of our day—even conservative evangelicalism—to emphasize the ultimate sovereignty of the loving God that will make itself known on this world, even on the stubborn and ignorant people that inhabit it. Harkening back to Origen, and Paul before him, these committed believers maintain that in the end no one will be able to resist the love of God. Good will triumph over evil. All that is wrong will be made right. And somehow, in some way, and at some time, everyone will be saved.[17]

Afterword

How do we decide if something we were taught from infancy is in fact true or not? Most people have never worried about the matter. Our beliefs and ideas simply make "deep sense" to us, no matter how bizarre they may seem to those raised on other views. Nowhere is that more evident than in the world of religion. It just seems naturally "true" to most Muslims that the mortal Mohammed ascended for a tour of the seven heavens, or to Mormons that Joseph Smith translated the golden plates, or to Southern Baptists that Jesus literally walked on the water. Such beliefs are not "matters of faith": they are simply what happened, as people have always known. To outsiders, though, such "common sense" is often seen as "non-sense."

For those of us who want to consider the truth of our own deeply held beliefs, the only choice is to consider our options thoughtfully. I pride myself on taking a rational view of life, even if I tend to go overboard. In college my friends called me "Mr. Spock": all thought, no emotion. And so, when someone tells me they are terrified of flying, I'm one of those obnoxious people tempted to cite the statistical evidence that they are more likely to be killed during the drive to the airport. But it is impossible to be completely rational all of the time unless you do nothing but linear algebra. And so I too instinctively jump in terror when I see a harmless garter snake in my yard—whatever my mind is trying to tell me. At the same time, that doesn't mean my unfettered emotions have to dictate my rational understanding. I don't have to think that the garter snake is going to eat me just because I have a visceral reaction to it.

It is important for us to have a reasoned understanding not only of the world around us—airplanes and snakes—but also of "things unseen." In particular, as a scholar of religion I think we should be rational about what we believe. I'm not saying that faith is purely a matter of rationality—that we can logically figure out the claims of faith. I don't think that at all. There are many billions of things that we cannot figure out about our world and our place in it, and life is far more than rational thought processes. Even so, surely we should examine religious claims about what happened in the past rationally: Did Moses part the Red Sea? Was Jesus born of a virgin? Did Mohammed perform amazing miracles? We should also reflect carefully on what is going to happen in the future, including our possible existence after this life. It is better to have a thoughtful view of such things than a thoughtless one.

Many people in our modern context have indeed been raised with certain beliefs about the afterlife—for example, the glories of heaven and the fires of hell—to such an extent that these places of reward and punishment simply seem *natural* to them. They have always "known" these places exist for as long as they can remember thinking about them. These beliefs are reinforced by their emotions, especially the remarkably powerful emotions of hope and fear. Some of the most rational people I know hope for a satisfying, fulfilling, even joyful afterlife, and cringe in fear of an eternity of hellish torment. Others find such views primitive and nonsensical.

It is interesting that these views—dominant especially in Christianity and Islam—cannot be found in the Old Testament or in the teachings of the historical Jesus. They are later developments. But it is also interesting to ask why such views have remained dominant for some nineteen hundred years of Western culture. My guess is that the idea that we will be personally rewarded or punished for the quality of our lives, or for our personal faith commitments, meets very deep human needs and aspirations. As moral beings, we simply think, need to think, and aspire to think that the world makes sense, that in the end there is justice, and that good will ultimately triumph over evil. That obviously doesn't happen in this life, in a world filled with innocent victims of human cruelty and natural disaster. Can that be right? Is it fair? The notion of heaven and hell assures us that it will all be reversed later. In the end, justice will be done, good will triumph, and God will prevail. When we die, we will be rewarded or punished.

It is hard to know how long these ideas will continue to dominate Western thinking about the afterlife. At least in Western Europe and parts of the Americas, more and more people are becoming convinced—either reluctantly or with relief—that, despite widespread hopes, longings, and "common sense," we really are here because of a series of freak chances of nature, starting with a big bang and ending no one knows how or when. Whether that view will continue to grow and eventually dominate is anyone's guess.

In any event, here is how I myself line up, at this stage, on the age-old question of heaven and hell. Even though I have an instinctual fear of torment after death—as the view drilled into me from the time I could think about such things—I simply don't believe it. Is it truly rational to think, as in the age-old Christian doctrine, that there is a divine being who created this world, loves all who are in it, and wants the very best for them, yet who has designed reality in such a way that if people make mistakes in life or do not believe the right things, they will die and be subjected to indescribable torments, not for the length of the time they committed their "offenses," but for trillions of years—and that only as the beginning? Are we really to think that God is some kind of transcendent sadist intent on torturing people (or at least willing to allow them to be tortured) for all eternity, a divine being infinitely more vengeful than the worst monster who has ever existed? I just don't believe it. Even if I instinctually fear it, I don't believe it.

Is there some other kind of afterlife existence? I have no way of knowing. And neither does anyone else. To be sure, we all know the "evidence": anecdotes of friends, near-death experiences, proof texts from the Bible, and the like. And I am certain I will be receiving emails very soon from people who want to assure me that they do "know." But alas, none of us do.

Still, is life after death at least plausible? In particular, what about the other half of the afterlife equation? Is it reasonable to think that there will be a decent or even a glorious life after death? Hope can be as strong an emotion as fear, and this view too has been driven into me from my childhood.

I certainly don't think the notion of a happy afterlife is as irrational as the fires of hell; at least it does not contradict the notion of a benevolent creative force behind the universe. So I'm completely open to the idea and deep down even hopeful about it. But I have to say that at the end of the day I really don't believe it either. My sense is that this life is all there is.

Many people simply have trouble imagining nonexistence. Ever since they have been able to think, they have recognized—at an instinctual level, to begin with—that they existed. *Cogito, ergo sum.* It is very difficult for most of us to think about not existing. But I have fewer problems with nonexistence than I used to, in part because I have listened to some of the great philosophers of the past, such as Epicurus and Lucretius.

As these Greek thinkers pointed out, none of us existed for the entire history of this universe before we were born, and none of us was upset or bothered about it at the time. By modern calculations, that was 13.8 billion years. And so it shouldn't be hard to believe we also won't exist for the billions of years yet to come. If I didn't exist before I was born, why should I exist after I die?

I don't know that this will happen, but it's what I suspect. Is that a fearful prospect? For me, not so much. The best analogy I can think of is a general anesthetic. I had a medical procedure a few years ago and was put under. One second I was there and the very next thing I remembered, an hour later, I woke up out of it. What was I thinking during the time I was "away"? I wasn't thinking anything. Was I anxious, disturbed, troubled, eager to get out of there? Not in the least. My consciousness simply wasn't functioning. I think death will be like that. We won't exist.

Rather than creating any real anxiety for me, this just makes me very sad. I love this existence. I love my incredible wife, my fantastic kids and grandkids, and my simple pleasures: good friends who believe in lively and intelligent conversation; good novels, good music, meaningful research and writing; quality food and fine wine; casual walks through the woods, serious hikes through the mountains, trips to foreign lands; watching sports, working out, taking steam baths—all the joys of life. I won't miss them when I'm gone, since I won't have any consciousness. Still, for now, while alive and reasonably alert, I'm sad that I will have to see them go.

But I believe I will. Everyone who has ever lived has had to die. Then other people have had their chance. I hope it will go on like that for a very long time.

While it does for me, I will continue to reflect on life, death, and whether there is a hereafter. After reading many hundreds of authors dealing with these issues over the years, at the end of the day I continue to throw in my lot with the great Socrates, who said it best. In his view death was one of two things. Either it was a deep, dreamless sleep, far deeper than anything we experience normally. None of us is afraid of getting a fantastic night's sleep and none of us regrets it. Death would be even better, even if there is no activity or even consciousness—a restful cessation of existence. There is nothing to fear in it. In modern terms, this is my general anesthetic.

The alternative for Socrates: after death would come a great reunion, where he would be able to meet and converse with all those who went before. For the Athenian philosopher, that meant having a chance to speak with the greats of his Greek culture: Orpheus, Hesiod, and Homer. For me I suppose it would be speaking with those of mine: Dickens, Shakespeare, and Jesus.

Even though it is debated, in my mind it is relatively clear which of these two choices Socrates, or rather, his ventriloquist, Plato, actually thought. He believed death was the end of the story. But this was not a source of anxiety for him, and it doesn't need to be for us either. It is instead a motivation to love this life as much as we can for as long as we can, to enjoy it to its utmost as far as possible, and to help others do the same. If all of us do that, we will live on after death—not in a personal consciousness once our brains have died, but in the lives of those we have touched.

Notes

Preface

http://www.pewresearch.org/fact-tank/2015/11/10/most-americans
-believe-in-heaven-and-hell/

Chapter One: Guided Tours of Heaven and Hell

1 It is mentioned already by Clement of Alexandria at the end of the second century; see Eusebius, *History of the Church* 6.14; Eusebius himself, writing in the early fourth century, suggests that some Christians considered it to be canonical Scripture (*History of the Church* 3.25). Scholars have determined that the sixty-six-page book that contains the Greek text was produced some time in the sixth century; see Peter van Minnen, "The Greek *Apocalypse of Peter*," in Jan Bremmer and István Czachesz, eds., *The Apocalypse of Peter* (Leuven, Belgium: Peeters, 2003), pp. 15–39.

2 I'll be following the older, Ethiopic version of the text in my summary. For side-by-side English translations of both the Greek and Ethiopic texts, see J. K. Elliott, *The Apocryphal New Testament* (Oxford, UK: Clarendon Press, 1993), pp. 593–612. Quotations are from this edition.

3 For later exceptions in the Christian tradition, see chapter 14.

4 One recent study has argued that this is one of the major functions of various descriptions of hell in early Christianity. See Meghan Henning, *Educating Early Christians through the Rhetoric of Hell: "Weeping and Gnashing of Teeth" as Paideia in Matthew and the Early Church* (Tübingen, Germany: Mohr Siebeck, 2014).

5 For a recent full-length study, see Eliezer Gonzalez, *The Fate of the Dead in Early Third-Century North African Christianity: The Passion of Perpetua and Felicitas and Tertullian*. STAC 83 (Tübingen, Germany: Mohr Siebeck,

2014). For a new edition and translation of the text, with commentary, see Thomas J. Heffernan, *The Passion of Perpetua and Felicity* (New York: Oxford University Press, 2012).

6　As argued, for example, Ross Kraemer and Shira Lander, "Perpetua and Felicitas," in *The Early Christian World*, vol. 2, ed. Philip Esler (London: Taylor & Francis, 2000); pp. 1048–65. For an alternative view, see Jeffrey A. Trumbower, *Rescue for the Dead: The Posthumous Salvation of Non-Christians in Early Christianity* (New York: Oxford University Press, 2001).

7　For an English translation, see Herbert Musurillo, *The Acts of the Christian Martyrs* (Oxford, UK: Clarendon Press, 1972), pp. 106–31; translations will be taken from this edition.

8　Translation of G. M. A. Grube, cited in his edition of Marcus Aurelius Antoninus, *The Meditations* (Indianapolis: Hackett, 1983), p. 111.

9　For an English translation, see Elliott, *Apocryphal New Testament*, pp. 439–511. Quotations are taken from this edition.

Chapter Two: The Fear of Death

1　Translation of Stephanie Dalley, from *Myths from Mesopotamia: Creation, The Flood, Gilgamesh, and Others* (New York: Oxford University Press, 1989).

2　I take the phrase from Stephen Mitchell's version, *Gilgamesh: A New English Version* (New York: Free Press, 2004).

3　Even though Socrates, Plato, and all their Greek contemporaries were polytheists, Socrates speaks of his "God" in the singular.

4　Translation of Hugh Tredennick, in *The Collected Dialogues of Plato*, ed. Edith Hamilton and Huntington Cairns (Princeton, NJ: Princeton University Press, 1961).

Chapter Three: Life After Death Before There Was Life After Death

1　Erwin Rohde: *Psyche: The Cult of Souls and Belief in Immortality among the Greeks*. 8th ed., trans. W. B. Hillis (Eugene, OR: Wipf and Stock, 2006; German original of 8th ed. 1925), p. 4. In this context Rohde was referring specifically to the view found in Homer.

2　I am using the translation of Robert Fagles, *The Iliad* (New York: Penguin, 1990). The line numbers are those in this edition.

3　Rohde, *Psyche*, p. 9.

4　This point is made with even greater poignancy in the *Iliad*, Book 23, when the ghost of Achilles's best friend Patroclus appears to him, begging him to bury him immediately and relieve him of his anguish. Other kinds of people are also not allowed full entrance into Hades, including, for example, those who have been killed before their appointed time.

5   Homer never mentions their particular crimes; these are known only from other myths about them.

6   There are some suggestions in the Homeric epics that yet others may face torment in Hades—in particular, on a couple of occasions the gods are said to punish those who violate their sworn oaths; but Homer provides us with no details. See, for example, *Iliad* 19.259.

7   "On Funerals," 2; translation of A. M. Harmon, "Lucian," IV, Loeb Classical Library, 162 (Cambridge, MA: Harvard University Press, 1969).

8   Translation of Robert Fagles, *The Aeneid* (New York: Viking, 2006); line numbers are from this edition.

9   For those who have descended Hades and returned alive, Virgil is thinking of myths connected with Hercules and Orpheus.

Chapter Four: Will Justice Be Done? The Rise of Postmortem Rewards and Punishments

1   *Process and Reality*, 2nd ed. (New York: Free Press, 1979), p. 39.

2   See, for example, Dale Martin, *Inventing Superstition* (Cambridge, MA: Harvard University Press, 2004). This older view continues to be held today, of course, to the extent that people sometimes claim they have seen the "ghost" or "soul" of their loved one after death. (You can't "see" what is invisible!) It is a bit hard to describe the views of the materiality of the soul held by many ancients (not all of them; some Platonists may have been exceptions). When I say that the soul was a kind of "matter," I do not mean that Greeks would use the typical word for "matter" (*hylē*) to describe it. *Hylē* (= wood, or "material stuff") stands in contrast with "soul" (= *psychē*) for most Greeks. But conceptually *psychē* is still is made up of a kind of "stuff." It is non-hylic stuff that has bodily characteristics: it can be contained, for example, within physical boundaries (the human body) and can course through the veins, and so on—all of which requires it to have a non-hylic kind of materiality, a more refined kind of stuff from what we normally think of as physical stuff.

3   Translation of Hugh Tredennick, in *The Collected Dialogues of Plato*, ed. Edith Hamilton and Huntington Cairns (Princeton, NJ: Princeton University Press, 1961).

4   See, for example, the study of Radcliffe G. Edmonds, *Myths of the Underworld*

Journey: Plato, Aristophanes, and the "Orphic" Gold Tablets (New York: Cambridge University Press, 2004).

5   Translation of Hugh Tredennick, in *The Collected Dialogues of Plato*, ed. Edith Hamilton and Huntington Cairns (Princeton, NJ: Princeton University Press, 1961).

6   Translation of Paul Shorey, in *The Collected Dialogues of Plato*, ed. Edith Hamilton and Huntington Cairns (Princeton, NJ: Princeton University Press, 1961).

7   Translation of David Barrett, *The Wasps, The Poet and the Women, The Frogs* (New York: Penguin, 1964).

8   Translation of Lionel Casson, *Selected Satires of Lucian* (New York: Norton, 1962).

9   Translation of Brad Inwood and L. P. Gerson, *The Epicurus Reader: Selected Writings and Testimonia* (Indianapolis: Hackett, 1994). Almost all of Epicurus's writings are lost. Cited here are letters and quotations from lost works given by his later biographer, Diogenes Laertius, *Lives of Eminent Philosophers.*

10   This translation is by R. D. Hicks, *Diogenes Laertius: Lives of Eminent Philosophers*, Loeb Classical Library 125 (Cambridge, MA: Harvard University Press, 1925).

11   The preceding two translations are from Inwood and Gerson, *Epicurean Reader.*

12   Translation of R. E. Latham, *Lucretius: On the Nature of the Universe* (New York: Viking Penguin, 1951). All quotations come from Book 3; some have been slightly modified.

13   *Tusculan Disputations* 1. 36, 38. Translation of J. E. King, *Cicero: Tusculan Disputations*, Loeb Classical Library 141 (Cambridge MA: Harvard University Press, 1927).

14   The classic study is William Harris, *Ancient Literacy* (Cambridge, MA: Harvard University Press, 1991).

15   See, for example, Robert Garland, *The Greek Way of Death*, 2nd ed. (Ithaca, NY: Cornell University Press, 2001).

16   See, for example, the moving epilogue by Lucy Kalanithi to her husband Paul Kalanithi's dying memoir, *When Breath Becomes Air* (New York: Random House, 2016), pp. 222–23.

17   The classic study is Richmond Lattimore, *Themes in Greek and Latin Epitaphs* (Urbana, IL: University of Illinois Press, 1962). I have taken my examples from his collection.

18   Both the preceding (CIL 9.1837 and CIL 6.26003) are quoted in Keith

Hopkins, *Death and Renewal* (Cambridge, UK: Cambridge University Press, 1983), p. 230.

19 Lattimore, *Themes in Greek and Latin Epitaphs*, p. 75.

Chapter Five: Death After Death in the Hebrew Bible

1 Some readers may wonder why I am not contrasting this view of Job with the famous passage of Job 19:25–26, made most famous by Handel's "Messiah." In the King James Version, the verses read: "For I know that my redeemer liveth, and that he shall stand at the latter day upon the earth: And though after my skin worms destroy this body, yet in my flesh shall I see God . . ." Scholars have long recognized the massive problems attendant to these verses. The Hebrew text was jumbled over the course of its transmission, so that it is impossible to know how to translate the text or determine exactly what it means. That is to say, even though it makes good sense in most English translations, the Hebrew is a mess. As scholar of Judaism Alan Segal has said, in his thorough analysis of ancient views of the afterlife: "The text has been garbled and we cannot tell exactly what Job intended to say." Segal goes on to give his best explanation of the text, which shows that Job is almost certainly not talking about seeing God in the afterlife but is instead hoping to argue a case for his innocence before God himself, with the help of a court attorney (his "redeemer"). See Alan F. Segal, *Life After Death: A History of the Afterlife in the Religions of the West* (New York: Doubleday, 2004), pp. 150–52.

2 There are indeed some passages of the Hebrew Bible that may be read this way, where Sheol is imagined as an actual place of residence. See, for example, Isaiah 14:9–11 and Ezekiel 31:15–17; 32:21. I owe this insight to my colleague Joseph Lam, who has, despite my resistance, convinced me. But these passages are all highly symbolic and metaphorical—not descriptions of what the authors thought was a literal reality.

3 See the preceding note. It should not be objected that, since the Patriarchs were buried in *caves*, they did not actually go *down*. We often use directional terms metaphorically, such as when we say we are going downtown. "Going down" was itself simply a metaphor based on the normal procedures for burial.

4 Jon D. Levenson, *Resurrection and the Restoration of Israel: The Ultimate Victory of the God of Life* (New Haven, CT: Yale University Press, 2006), p. 80. Levenson takes this point on to a different direction from me, however, and draws a conclusion that I think is untenable—namely, that Sheol as a horrible place was reserved only for particularly bad sinners, not for all.

5 Alan F. Segal, *Life After Death: A History of the Afterlife in the Religions of the West* (New York: Doubleday, 2004), p. 135.

6 For a good basic introduction to Amos and its later editor, see John J. Collins, *Introduction to the Hebrew Bible* (Minneapolis: Fortress Press, 2004), pp. 286–95.

7 For the different writings that now make up Isaiah, and their dates and contexts, see Collins, *Introduction to the Hebrew Bible*, pp. 307–21; 379–400.

Chapter Six: Dead Bodies That Return to Life: The Resurrection in Ancient Israel

1 For useful recent discussions, embodying the scholarly back and forth on the question, see C. D. Elledge, *Resurrection of the Dead in Early Judaism 200 BCE–CE 200* (New York: Oxford University Press, 2017); Anders Hulgard, "Persian Apocalypticism," chapter 2 of John J. Collins, ed., *The Encyclopedia of Apocalypticism*, Vol. 1: *The Origins of Apocalypticism in Judaism and Christianity* (New York: Continuum, 1998); and Jan N. Bremmer, *The Rise and Fall of the Afterlife* (New York: Routledge, 2002), especially chapter 4, "The Resurrection from Zoroaster to Late Antiquity."

2 For example, the anxieties raised throughout the Mediterranean by the conquests of Alexander the Great and the subsequent spread of Hellenistic culture in the fourth to third centuries BCE; or the terrible events of the Maccabean Revolt in the second century BCE. See the overview of the early apocalyptic texts in John Collins, "The Afterlife in Apocalyptic Literature," in Alan J. Avery-Peck and Jacob Neusner, eds. *Death, Life-After-Death, Resurrection and the World-to-Come in the Judaisms of Antiquity*, vol. 4 of *Judaism in Late Antiquity* (Leiden, Netherlands: Brill, 2001), chapter 5.

3 My fullest reflections on the biblical responses to the problem of suffering can be found in *God's Problem: How the Bible Fails to Answer Our Most Important Question—Why We Suffer* (San Francisco: HarperOne, 2009).

4 Thus Elledge, *Resurrection of the Dead*, and, most persuasively, Levenson, *Resurrection*.

5 For a full discussion see the authoritative account of John Collins, *The Scepter and the Star: Jewish Messianism in Light of the Dead Sea Scrolls* (Grand Rapids, MI: Eerdmans 2010).

6 For the factors that led Christians to think Jesus was the messiah, see my book *How Jesus Became God: The Exaltation of a Jewish Preacher from Galilee* (San Francisco: HarperOne, 2015).

7 See the discussion of Isaiah in Collins, *Introduction to the Hebrew Bible*, pp. 307–21; 379–400.

8   For an English translation with an introduction to the book describing its divisions, see Michael Knibb, *The Ethiopic Book of Enoch: A New Edition in the Light of the Aramaic Dead Sea Fragments*, 2 vols. (New York: Oxford University Press, 1979); my quotations are taken from this edition.

9   Especially in the portion known as the Similitudes; see 1 Enoch 38–39, 48, and 51 for example.

10 One of the best discussions of the historical context of the book and exposition of its text is the commentary by John Collins, *Daniel: A Commentary on the Book of Daniel (Hermeneia: A Critical and Historical Commentary on the Bible)* (Minneapolis: Fortress Press, 1994).

11 The situation is recorded in the book of 1 Maccabees, part of the Apocrypha of the Old Testament. For a modern discussion of the period, see Shaye Cohen, *From the Maccabees to the Mishnah*, 3rd ed. (Louisville, KY: Westminster John Knox, 2014).

12 For a collection of ancient Jewish apocalypses, see James Charlesworth, ed., *Old Testament Pseudepigrapha* (Garden City, NY: Doubleday, 1983), vol. 1.

13 See the discussion in Collins, *Daniel*, for these verses.

14 See my discussion in *How Jesus Became God*, p. 60.

15 The classic statement is in Oscar Cullmann, *Immortality of the Soul? Or Resurrection of the Dead?* (New York: Macmillan, 1964).

16 See pp. 43–44.

Chapter Seven: Why Wait for the Resurrection?
Life After Death Right After Death

1   Translations are available in any edition of the Old Testament Apocrypha (e.g., in the New Revised Standard Version, which I follow here).

2   Also available in the NRSV translation of the Old Testament Apocrypha.

3   The classic analysis is Martin Hengel, *Judaism and Hellenism: Studies in their Encounter in Palestine during the Hellenistic Period*, 2 vols. (Philadelphia: Fortress Press, 1981).

4   Another good example appears in the apocryphal text *The Wisdom of Solomon*.

5   See the introduction and translation of Bruce M. Metzger, in James Charlesworth, ed., *Old Testament Pseudepigrapha*, vol. 1 (Garden City, NY: Doubleday, 1983) pp. 517–59. For a more thorough analysis, see Michael Stone, *4 Ezra (Hermeneia: A Critical and Historical Commentary on the Bible)* (Minneapolis: Fortress, 1990).

6   There are two versions of the text; neither is the copy of the other; both

probably descend from the same original account. I'll be following the one called Recension A. For a translation, see E. P. Sanders, "The Testament of Abraham," in Charlesworth, ed., *Old Testament Pseudepigrapha*, vol. 1, pp. 871–902.

7 See, for example, Elizabeth Bloch-Smith, *Judahite Burial Practices and Beliefs About the Dead* (Sheffield, UK: Sheffield Academic Press, 1992); Rachel S. Hallote, *Death, Burial, and Afterlife in the Biblical World: How the Israelites and Their Neighbors Treated the Dead* (Chicago: Ivan R. Dee, 2001); and Byron R. McCane, *Roll Back the Stone: Death and Burial in the World of Jesus* (Harrisburg, PA: Trinity Press International, 2003).

8 P. W. van der Horst, *Ancient Jewish Epitaphs: An Introductory Survey of a Millennium of Jewish Funerary Epigraphy* (300 BCE–700 CE) (Kampen, Netherlands: Kok Pharos, 1991).

9 Ibid., p. 114.

10 Ibid., p. 137

11 See Josephus, *Antiquities*, 18.14, 16, and 18; and *Jewish Wars*, 2.8.11 and 14. The latter is the description I am following here. For a good summary of Josephus's life and writings, see Steven Mason, *Josephus and the New Testament* (Peabody, MA: Hendrickson, 2003), especially chapters 1–3.

12 For all these groups and their beliefs, see Cohen, *From the Maccabees to the Mishnah* (Louisville, KY: Westminster John Knox, 2014) and E. P. Sanders, *Judaism: Practice and Belief, 63 BCE–66 CE* (Minneapolis: Fortress Press, 2016).

Chapter Eight: Jesus and the Afterlife

1 For a full account of the story, see Bruce M. Metzger, "Literary Forgeries and Canonical Pseudepigrapha," *Journal of Biblical Literature* 91 (1972), p. 4, as well as Metzger's autobiography, *Reminiscences of an Octogenarian* (Peabody, MA: Hendrickson, 1997), pp. 136–39.

2 We do not know why early Christians chose not to copy the work and keep it in circulation. One theory—probably the dominant one—is that later orthodox Christians did not approve of Papias and his views. The later church father Eusebius says about him that he was "a man of very little intelligence" (Eusebius, *Church History* 3.39). For a translation of the surviving remnant of Papias's works, see Bart D. Ehrman, *The Apostolic Fathers*, Loeb Classical Library (Cambridge, MA: Harvard University Press, 2004), vol. 2.

3 See my discussion in *Forged*, pp. 223–28.

4 For more extended discussion, see the chapters on the Gospels in my book *The New Testament: A Historical Introduction to the Early Christian Writings*, 7th edition (New York: Oxford University Press, 2019).

5   I give the full evidence of this in my book *Jesus Before the Gospels* (San Francisco: HarperOne, 2016).

6   See my book *Jesus Interrupted: Revealing the Hidden Contradictions of the Bible (And Why We Don't Know About Them)* (San Francisco: HarperOne, 2009).

7   When it comes to the Gospels of the New Testament, scholars have long known that Matthew and Luke both used Mark—so when all three of them report a saying of Jesus, they are not three independent sources; ultimately such a saying goes back just to Mark (Matthew and Luke having borrowed it). So Matthew and Luke also have a number of sayings that are exactly or almost exactly alike; scholars have long argued that these two authors had access to a now-lost collection of Jesus's sayings called "Q" (for the German word *Quelle*, which means source). Matthew and Luke also had their own unique sources of information: Matthew's is called "M"; Luke's is "L." Mark, Q, M, and L are all independent of each other, and John is independent of all of them. And so if the same *kind* of saying is found in all of them—for example, some comment about the coming Kingdom of God—which is not actually the very *same* saying, then this would be evidence that Jesus said some such thing, since it is independently reported. See the discussion in my book *The New Testament: A Historical Introduction*, chapters 8 and 14.

8   I marshal the evidence in my book *Jesus: Apocalyptic Prophet of the New Millennium* (New York: Oxford University Press, 1999). For a classic statement, see Albert Schweitzer, *Quest of the Historical Jesus* (Minneapolis: Fortress Press, 2001; German original 1906).

9   See Lloyd R. Bailey, "Gehenna: The Topography of Hell," *Biblical Archaeologist* 49 (1986), 187–91.

10   It is not clear if that is because it was originally made for the immortal beings of the devil and the demons (who, since they cannot die, will indeed burn forever) or if Jesus is speaking metaphorically, as in other passages of the Bible involving "eternal fire."

Chapter Nine: The Afterlife After Jesus's Life: Paul the Apostle

1   See the discussion of Paul in my book *The Triumph of Christianity: How a Forbidden Religion Swept the World* (New York: Simon & Schuster, 2018), chapter 2.

2   For a fuller discussion of this issue, see my book *Forged: Writing in the Name of God; Why the Bible's Authors Are Not Who We Think They Are* (San Francisco: HarperOne, 2012). I give a more extensive and scholarly discussion in my academic book *Forgery and Counterforgery: The Use of Literary Deceit in Early Christian Polemics* (New York: Oxford University Press, 2012).

3 Romans, 1 and 2 Corinthians, Galatians, Philippians, 1 Thessalonians, and Philemon.

4 See the discussion in my book *Peter, Paul, and Mary Magdalene* (New York: Oxford University Press, 2008), chapters 7–12.

5 For the two major positions, see David Wenham, *Paul and Jesus: The True Story* (Grand Rapids, MI: Eerdmans, 2002) and Victor Paul Furnish, *Jesus According to Paul* (Cambridge, UK: Cambridge University Press, 1993).

6 For a fuller discussion of the letter, see chapter 21 in my book *The New Testament: A Historical Introduction*.

7 It is often pointed out that this would be a familiar image to city dwellers in a Roman province, who, when a high-ranking Roman official came to visit on official business, would go out to meet him with great ceremony to escort him into the city.

8 As with all things Jewish, there are of course isolated exceptions, as seen, for example, in the book of Jubilees (23:30–31), as my friend and perennial corrector Joel Marcus has pointed out to me. Again, I am not saying that all Jews held to the view of bodily resurrection, or that all pagans believed in the immortality of the soul.

Chapter Ten: Altering the Views of Jesus: The Later Gospels

1 For overviews of both books, see chapters 10 and 19 in my book *The New Testament: A Historical Introduction*.

2 See my discussion in chapter 7 of *The New Testament: A Historical Introduction*.

3 For recent book-length studies of just this parable, see Outi Lehtipuu, *The Afterlife Imagery in Luke's Story of the Rich Man and Lazarus* (Leiden, Netherlands: Brill, 2007) and Matthew Ryan Hauge, *The Biblical Tour of Hell* (London: Bloomsbury T&T Clark, 2013).

4 For the translation see Miriam Lichtheim, *Ancient Egyptian Literature: The Late Period*, vol. 3 (Berkeley: University of California Press, 2006). In places the manuscript she is translating has small gaps; I have taken over her reconstructions without enclosing them in parentheses here.

5 Thus, for example, Richard Bauckham, *The Fate of the Dead: Studies on the Jewish and Christian Apocalypses* (Leiden, Netherlands: Brill, 1998), chapter 4, on "The Rich Man and Lazarus."

6 See my book *How Jesus Became God: The Exaltation of a Jewish Preacher from Galilee* (San Francisco: HarperOne, 2014), pp. 269–79.

7 Translation of Zlatko Pleše in Bart Ehrman and Zlatko Pleše, *The Apocryphal Gospels: Texts and Translations* (New York: Oxford University Press, 2011).

8 I am not saying that all the sayings of the Gospel of Thomas are "later" and different from Jesus's actual words. Some of the sayings may indeed represent things he said—especially the ones that are like those found in our earlier Gospels. But the ones that deal with apocalyptic eschatology all represent later modifications of Jesus's own teachings. See my discussion in *The New Testament: A Historical Introduction*, pp. 218–23.

Chapter Eleven: The Afterlife Mysteries of the Book of Revelation

1 For a simple overview of the book of Revelation written for a broad reading audience, see Bruce M. Metzger, *Breaking the Code* (Nashville: Abingdon, 2006). There are a number of excellent commentaries on Revelation written from a historical perspective; see, for example, Craig Koester, *Revelation: A New Translation with Introduction and Commentary* (New Haven, CT: Yale University Press, 2014).

2 See the discussion of Peter in my book *Forged: Writing in the Name of God; Why the Bible's Authors Are Not Who We Think They Are* (San Francisco: HarperOne, 2011), pp. 70–73. The same comments apply to his companion and fellow fisherman John.

3 On the relative infrequency of Christian martyrdom, see Candida Moss, *The Myth of Persecution* (San Francisco: HarperOne, 2014). On the numbers of Christians in the ancient world at various points in the early centuries, see my book *The Triumph of Christianity* (San Francisco: HarperOne, 2017), p. 294.

4 One might wonder if this utopian salvation for the saints is itself part of John's symbolism. If the entire book is filled with symbols, is eternal life itself a symbol, not to be taken literally? One could certainly make that case, since we have other writers from antiquity who used tales of the afterlife not as literal descriptions of what would happen but as "morality tales" to guide life in the present. Plato would certainly fit in that camp. But possibly not John: he uses a lake of fire and a new Jerusalem as symbols of other realities—annihilation and eternal life. Nothing suggests that the ideas *conveyed* by his symbols are themselves symbolic.

Chapter Twelve: Eternal Life in the Flesh

1 For an English translation, see Henry Chadwick, *Contra Celsum*, reprint edition (Cambridge: Cambridge University Press, 1980). Quotations are from this edition.

2   For an introduction and translation, see Bart Ehrman, *The Apostolic Fathers*, vol. 1, Loeb Classical Library (Cambridge MA: Harvard University Press, 2004). Quotations come from this edition.

3   Some scholars think that this treatise is not actually by Athenagoras, but the name of the author does not much matter for the point I'm trying to make. Whoever wrote it, it was almost certainly at the end of the second century.

4   Quotations are taken from the translation of Joseph H. Crehan, *Athenagoras: Embassy for the Christians; The Resurrection of the Dead* (New York: Newman Press, 1955).

5   All these come from *City of God*, Book 22, chapter 12. For a convenient English translation, see Marcus Dods, *City of God,* reprint edition (Peabody, MA: Hendrickson, 2009).

6   See p. 195.

7   See p. 208.

8   Translation of Marvin Meyer, *The Nag Hammadi Scriptures* (San Francisco: HarperOne, 2009), pp. 52–55.

9   For the non-Pauline authorship of Colossians and Ephesians, see my book *Forged*, pp. 108–14.

10 Gnosticism is an inordinately complex set of religions. For a recent attempt to unpack Gnostic views and practices, see David Brakke, *The Gnostics* (Cambridge, MA: Harvard University Press, 2012).

11 One of the first to address this sociological issue was Elaine Pagels, in her book *Gnostic Gospels*, reissued edition (New York: Vintage, 1989), chapter 4.

12 On the actual extent of early persecutions, see Moss, *The Myth of Persecution*.

13 See the quotations from the martyr Ignatius on pp. 255–56.

14 Translation of Thomas B. Falls, *The Writings of Justin Martyr* (Washington, DC: Catholic University of America, 1948).

15 For a translation, see J. K. Elliott, *Apocryphal New Testament*, pp. 380–81.

16 Quotations are taken from the translation in J. K. Elliott, *Apocryphal New Testament*, pp. 380–82.

17 For an English translation of the treatise, see Ernest Evans, ed., *Tertullian's Treatise on the Resurrection* (London: S.P.C.K., 1960).

18 Both quotations come from "On the Spectacles," 30; translation of T. R. Glover, *Tertullian: Apology, De Spectaculis*, Loeb Classical Library (Cambridge, MA: Harvard University Press, 1931).

19 For a translation, see *The Ante-Nicene Fathers*, ed. Alexander Roberts and James Donaldson; rev. ed. A. Cleveland Coxe; 10 vols. (Boston: Hendrickson Publishers, 1994; Reprint of New York: Christian Literature Publishing Company, 1885), vol. 3.

Chapter Thirteen: Tactile Ecstasy and
Torment in the Christian Hereafter

1 This is analogous to the situation with Jews during periods of persecution, leading to new views of the afterlife, as we saw in chapter 7.

2 See, especially, Moss, *Myth of Persecution*.

3 More than seven letters allegedly by Ignatius were circulated down through the Middle Ages and are still known today, but scholars unanimously consider the others to be later forgeries. See my discussion in *The Apostolic Fathers*, vol. 1, Loeb Classical Library (Cambridge, MA: Harvard University Press, 2004), pp. 203–17. Quotations come from this edition.

4 For both the Letter and the Martyrdom of Polycarp, see Ehrman, *Apostolic Fathers*; quotations are taken from this edition.

5 See the discussion and bibliography in my book *Forgery and Counterforgery*, pp. 497–502.

6 Recall the views of Daniel 12:1–3 that at the resurrection, bodies of the righteous brought out of the dust will shine as the stars of heaven—that is, taken on angelic form. See pp. 121–23.

7 Minucius Felix, *Octavius* 8.5; quotation is taken from G. W. Clarke, *The Octavius of Minucius Felix* (New York: Paulist Press, 1974).

8 Translation of Ernest Wallis in *Ante-Nicene Fathers*, vol. 5.

9 Scholars debate whether this Treatise on "The Glories of Martyrdom" actually comes from Cyprian's pen or from another, but for our purposes the question does not much matter. It expresses views held by some Christians at the time.

10 In the notes for chapter 14 I will discuss the origins of the idea of "Purgatory."

11 The date is debated among scholars. It is widely thought, though, that our surviving edition was based on a version first circulated in the early third century. See the discussion in J. K. Elliott, *Apocryphal New Testament*, pp. 616–44. I have taken my quotations from this edition.

12 I will be using the edition of Marcus Dods, *The City of God* (New York: Random House, 1950).

Chapter Fourteen: Who Will Inherit the Blessings?
Purgatory, Reincarnation, and Salvation for All

1 The classic study is Jacques Le Goff, *The Birth of Purgatory*, trans. Arthur Goldhammer (Chicago: University of Chicago Press, 1984; French original 1981). One of Le Goff's main theses is that the medieval doctrine of

NOTES

purgatory developed in relation to the social world out of which it emerged. Just as in European society, with the development of the middle class, a third place was being devised between the elite and the poor, so too the afterlife: there was an in-between place between the "haves" (the saved) and the "have-nots" (the damned).

2 Peter Brown, *Ransom for the Soul: Afterlife and Wealth in Early Western Christianity* (Cambridge, MA: Harvard University Press, 2015).

3 For an introduction and translation, see J. K. Elliott, *Apocryphal New Testament*, pp. 364–72. I have taken my quotations from this edition.

4 See pp. 5–8.

5 I will be citing the translation of Musurillo, *Acts of the Christian Martyrs*, pp. 106–31.

6 Quotations are from the translation in *Ante-Nicene Fathers*, vol. 3.

7 The best discussion of the "history" of purgatory *before* Augustine—calling into question whether he is the "father" of the idea—is, unfortunately, only in German. But for those skilled in foreign tongues, I cite it here: Andreas Merkt, *Das Fegefeuer: Entstehung und Funktion einer Idee* (Darmstadt, Germany: Wissenschaftliche Buchgesellschaft, 2005).

8 I am using, again, the translation of Marcus Dods. See note 12, chapter 13.

9 Translation in *The Nicene and Post-Nicene Fathers*, First Series, vol. 14; American edition edited by Philip Schaff (Peabody, MA: Hendrickson Publishers, 1999; reprint of 1889 original).

10 A useful edition, with English translations of both the surviving (partial) Greek and the (complete) Latin side by side is in W. W. Butterworth, *Origen: On First Principles* (Gloucester, MA: Peter Smith, 1973). Quotations come from this edition. See also now John Behr, *Origen: First Principles*. Oxford Early Christian Texts. (Oxford, UK: Oxford University Press, 2018).

11 Quoted in Diogenes Laertius, *Lives of Eminent Philosophers* 8.77; translation of R. D. Hicks, *Diogenes Laertius*, vol. 2, Loeb Classical Library (Cambridge, MA: Harvard University Press, 1925).

12 Translation in *Ante Nicene Fathers*, vol. 1.

13 Translation in *Nicene and Post-Nicene Fathers*, series 2, vol. 5, pp. 430–68.

14 See the introduction to the text in Bart D. Ehrman and Zlatko Pleše, *The Apocryphal Gospels: Texts and Translations* (New York: Oxford University Press, 2011), p. 419–23.

15 My summary and quotations here come from the version of the story known as Gospel of Nicodemus B; see my translation in Ehrman and Pleše, *Apocryphal Gospels*, pp. 469–89.

16 See Rob Bell. *Love Wins: A Book About Heaven, Hell, and the Fate of Every Person Who Ever Lived* (San Francisco: HarperOne, 2011).

17 See the discussion of options even among Bible-believing conservative evangelical Christians as set forth, for example, in Danny Burk, John Stackhouse, Robin Parry, and Jerry Walls, *Four Views on Hell*, 2nd ed. (Grand Rapids, MI: Zondervan, 2016).

Index

INDEX

animals, 63, 109, 113, 159, 286
anti-apocalyptic movement, 208, 209
Antichrist, 213, 214, 218
Anticleia, 41, 44
Antiochus Epiphanes, 118–19, 120–21,
    122, 128–30, 133, 134
antiquity, 35, 71, 76, 100–101
    Christian, 149
    Greek and Roman, 65, 66, 75, 77
Antonia Tryphaena, 274
Anunnaki, 23
Apocalypse of John, *see* Revelation, Book of
Apocalypse of Paul, 262–65
Apocalypse of Peter, 2–5, 9, 69, 116, 262, 273
"apocalypticism," 107–8, 109, 166–67
apocalyptic literature, 119–20, 214, 215
apocalyptic thinking, 106–8, 109, 114–20,
    126, 129, 134–35, 161, 166–67,
    192–93
Apollo, 48
Apology (Plato), 27–30
Arabia, 236
Arabic language, 148, 236
Aramaic language, 151
archaeology, 1, 2, 19, 76, 143, 158
Aristophanes, 65–67
Armageddon, 213
Asclepius, 33–34
Assyria, 19, 94–95, 106
Athenagoras, 237
Athens, 27, 28, 65
Augustine, Bishop of Hippo, 238, 266–69,
    278

Babylon, 119, 221
Babylonians, 97, 98, 100, 104, 112
baptism, 6, 174, 178–79, 273
"Beast," 213, 214, 218, 219, 221, 222, 224,
    225–27, 229
Beatitudes, 201
Beelzebul, 107
Bethany, 206
Bible, 16, 18, 19, 46
    culturally conditioned views in, xvi, xvii
    as inspired word of God, xvi
    King James version of, 204, 220, 277, 301
    see also specific books

birds, 21, 159
birth defects, 106
blasphemy, 3, 197, 203–4, 221
blessings, 66, 69
    of God, 106, 122
blindness, 180, 207
bodies:
    burial of, 44, 45, 49, 85, 142, 156, 206,
        234
    death of, 74, 82–83, 159–60, 197
    deterioration of, 180
    distinction between souls and, 58–60,
        135–36
    immortal, 125, 182, 185
    parts of, 233–34, 237–39
    pleasures of, 67, 70, 71
    relationship of minds and, 74
    resurrection of, 103–26, 134, 146, 180,
        234, 239–41
    separation of souls and, 32, 39, 42,
        59–60, 62, 71–72, 74, 78, 124–26,
        139, 179
    spiritual, 183, 195
    torment of, 104
    transformation of, 184–87, 195
    unification of souls and, 126
Book of Watchers, 119, 121
    battle between good and evil in, 116
    five sections of, 115
    resurrection in, 114–18
breathing, 125, 160
    cessation of, 82–83
    of God, 99
Brown, Peter, 273
"bull of heaven," 20

Caecilius, 259
cancer, 275–76
cannibalism, 237
Carpocratians, 285–86
catechumens, 6
Cebes, 32–33
Celsus, 234–35
Cerberus, 50, 66, 78
charity, 13–14
Charon, 78
chastity, 11, 13

INDEX

justice, xx, xxi, 18, 29, 253
   divine, 66, 132, 133
   postmortem, 57–79, 137, 139–40
   swift, 127
   see also God, justice of
Justin Martyr, 234, 245

Kimhi, David, 158
Kings, Book of, 109
Kissinger, Henry, 221–22

Lamb of God, 218, 219, 224
Latin language, 5, 8, 47, 79, 215
Law of Moses, 89, 90, 94, 128, 136, 137,
   145, 161, 173, 201
Laws (Plato), 59–60
Lethe River, 54
Leto, 46
Letter to Demetrius, 261
Letter to Rheginus, 241–42, 243
Levenson, Jon, 88
Leviticus, Book of, 89, 201
"lex talionis," 3
life, 13
   appreciation of, xxiii
   breath of, 125
   diminution of, 86
   divine origin of, 109
   end of, 18, 35, 47, 82
   enjoyment of good things in, 86
   eternal, 7, 21–24, 109, 125–26, 132,
     135, 162, 165, 166, 173, 182, 189,
     192, 203–8, 230–31, 255–59, 268–69
   form vs. substance of, 37
   goal of, 31
   happiness in, 50, 70, 71, 106
   in the here and now of, 11, 15–16, 33,
     203–8
   immediately after death, 127–46
   long and full, 87
   losing out on the pleasures of, 35
   plant of, 24
   prolonging of, 24–25
   after resurrection, 161–62
   righteous, 122
   shortness of, 19, 25
   trials and tribulations of, 7

literacy, 75
Lives of Eminent Philosophers (Diogenes
   Laertius), 72
loneliness, 17
Lord, 91, 96
   obedience to, 85
   spirit of, 98
   suffering servant of, 109–14
love, 4, 5, 29, 70
   fraternal, 15
   of God, 86, 290
Lucian of Samosata, 8–9, 46–47, 68–70
Lucretius, 73–75, 79, 294
Luke, Gospel of, xix, 150, 152, 193–203,
   206, 239–40, 275
   glory and torment after death in, 197–203
   story of Lazarus and the Rich Man in,
     166, 197–201, 202–3
Luxor, 1
lying, 68

Maccabees, 119
   revolt of, 118, 122, 128, 136, 214, 302
Maccabees, Books of, 128–33, 135–36, 303
   martyrdom of seven brothers and their
     mother in, 129–33
Macedonia, 175
Mammitum, 23
Marcus Aurelius, Emperor of Rome, 8, 259
Mark, Gospel of, 2, 150, 151, 152, 153,
   154, 157, 161, 166–67, 192, 194,
   196, 202
Marlowe, Christopher, 36
marriage, 161–62
martyrdom, 101, 135, 222, 274
   afterlife and, 223–25
   of Jews, 128, 129–33
   literary descriptions of, 9
   see also Christians, martyrdom of
Martyrdom of Polycarp, 257–58
Matthew, Gospel of, 2, 150, 152, 154–57,
   160, 163–66, 192, 201–2, 277, 305
   "Parable of the Faithful and Unfaithful
     Servant" in, 148, 165
   "Parable of the Weeds" in, 156
Measure for Measure (Shakespeare), 17
Meditations, The (Marcus Aurelius), 8, 259

INDEX

INDEX

INDEX

About the Author

Bart D. Ehrman is the author or editor of more than thirty books, including the *New York Times* bestsellers *Misquoting Jesus*, *How Jesus Became God*, and *The Triumph of Christianity*. Ehrman is a professor of religious studies at the University of North Carolina, Chapel Hill, and a leading authority on the New Testament and the history of early Christianity. He has been featured in *Time*, the *New Yorker*, and the *Washington Post*, and has appeared on NBC, CNN, the *Daily Show* with Jon Stewart, the History channel, the National Geographic channel, BBC, major NPR shows, and other top print and broadcast media outlets.